# Bella's CHOICE

## BY

## LYNELLE CLARK

This is a Revised Edition
Previously published as Lawyer's Dessert

# Author's Note

I have read a few books on ménage, and swinging; finding it interesting and fascinating at times. It definitely has its place on the genre shelves. Many couples live this lifestyle as an everyday occurrence. If this is your choice and you are happy with it, I say enjoy. But, I am also curious and often ask questions like:

What about the children?

Do they know?

What effect does this have on them?

Bella's Choice was born from these questions and originally written as an erotic story. However, I thought it best to change it and look at it from a different perspective. In South Africa, there are a great number of people who follow this lifestyle, although hidden in the folds of society. The reason it is hidden is because it's not acceptable to the normal way of life, and is condemned by the average person. I spent some time on one of the sites available and learned that the people who have chosen this way of life are normal, everyday people with a love for the outdoors and their children, and would do nothing to harm them. Unlike the parents in this book. This is the extreme and has been entirely concocted in my mind. They went overboard, became addicted to the lifestyle, and almost destroyed their children in the process.

Everyone I've met within the swinging community are caring parents, always careful about whom they meet with and where, never allowing their children to come to any harm. I have met beautiful couples with a love for the adventurous side of lovemaking when they want more than just the average married life. I must admit that I was surprised to see the huge number of followers in my country, even in my region. Not long ago, this lifestyle made headlines claiming this fact.

Trust is a major point within this group; you have to be comfortable with each other in order to connect with the right couple or couples; meeting on common ground to test the waters, before plunging in and indulging in sex. If this mutual connection does not exist, it will not happen—ever.

It's a long, sifting process where courting is very important. Not the old fashioned way, of course, but rather by talking and discovering who these people are. Sharing photographs also helps in the connection part of such relationships. Both husband and wife must be comfortable with the idea of sharing, or it will not advance to the next step.

These are groups of people who like to explore all possibilities but not lose themselves in the process, or cause those around them any harm.

In my story, trust is also a major issue for Anabella—the main character—who suffers from images she's witnessed at home, which inevitably try to pull her into this lifestyle. She finds herself in situations where she has to defend not only herself, but the choices she makes. It is an individual choice, one that should never be forced on anyone, as is the case with Anabella and her parents.

No matter how carefree and wonderful it all sounds, the consequences can be devastating to those around us. We are not alone in this world; our actions do have reactions that can create much pain and suffering to a certain individual.

This is also a story of forgiveness and moving forward, where the choice is to step away and choose something different, something Anabella would be comfortable with.

Please read with an open mind. If you are easily offended, please do not purchase a copy.

# Table of Contents

Copyright © 2014 Lynelle Clark

ISBN number: 978-0-620-58843-0

# DEDICATION AND ACKNOWLEDGEMENTS

To all the people who believed in me.

I have to say thank you to Paul for all his assistance, and financial support during the writing of this book. There were times I wanted to throw in the towel, but he encouraged me to continue.

To my children: there were times I just couldn't be there for you, but yet you never complained.

And lastly, to Sandra Valente. You, dear lady, made the impossible, possible. Words can never express how I feel about your support, help and guidance throughout the last stages of the book. You are a godsend.

The fabulous cover for Kindle was done by Sandra Valente.

The stunning book cover for paperback was done by Manuela Cardiga

# Chapter One

Anabella emerged from the swimming pool—the rippling water a clear aqua right to the tiled floor—wiping water from her eyes with a brush of her hands, and making sure her hair was neat. She had just swum twenty laps as part of her training program for her upcoming championship and felt good, energized, excited, and ready to compete. She had put in long hours, focused every effort to accomplish this one gold medal; her dream for many years. It would open doors for her future plans and was in reach—she could feel it. Anabella knew she was ready.

"How do you feel, Anabella?" asked Mr. Rhodes, her coach.

"Excellent! I'm not even tired. This was a good workout," she answered.

"Are your parents bringing you to the venue, or should I pick you up?"

"They are out of town, so I would really appreciate it if you could pick me up." Although she could easily drive herself to the championship, she preferred to go with someone. The tension and stiffness of sore muscles after a hard race brought numbness to her limbs, which made driving almost impossible.

"Then it is settled. I will pick you up at 7am, sharp. Don't be late," her coach said sternly.

"I won't be, Mr. Rhodes."

"Go and rest, relax this afternoon, and make sure you are in bed early. Don't worry about anything; all will be fine. You have worked hard these past few months."

"Yes, sir." She knew she had worked hard. The sore muscles were evidence, as well as the fact that she had not spent much time with family or friends. She had enough confidence in her abilities not to be worried at all and loved the competitive side of the sport; racing against a good competitor, and the excitement of winning after giving it her all.

There was solitude once you dove into the water, only you and it, and the lane stretching ahead. Sounds of the crowd did not bother her. At moments like these, she could allow the water to enclose her and swim through the currents created by other swimmers. An unsurpassed sense of freedom and accomplishment ran through her veins, and the adrenaline rushed through her core, making her feel alive. Here, she felt whole, forgetting everything else. Here, she was in control of her surroundings and her own life. Here, she set the pace, overcoming all fears.

It was her home, the place she felt safe. Over the years, the swimming pool had been the only place she'd considered a safe haven in her otherwise dysfunctional life. How she had longed for a healthy family life, to wrap her arms around a loving father and a caring mother, to tell them about her day, to include them in her life. She sighed as she turned away from the pool, burying the negative thoughts wanting to rob her from her jovial mood.

Confidence radiated from her whole posture and she felt good, really good. She never let on what was taking place within her mind. She never allowed outsiders into her life. She was always the outsider, never part of the family concept. Her only confidence came from who she was, as well as her accomplishments in either sports or academics.

However, it neither made her arrogant or self-absorbed.

While Mr. Rhodes was talking, she managed to dry herself and put her sweatpants and top on, ready to go to her house.

"Bye, sir. See you tomorrow at 7am, and thanks." She respected her coach for his time and devotion where she was concerned. He had put in just as much time as she had the last couple of months during training. She had learned to trust him for all the advice and his continued motivation, and would miss him when she went off to varsity the following year. He had influenced her to study to be a physiotherapist as her passion was to work with people.

"Bye, Anabella. See you in the morning."

"Goodbye, Mr. Rhodes."

Once home, she went straight to the shower. The warm water was soothing to her sore muscles and she fully relaxed under the spray. She was all alone—for a change there weren't a lot of people in the house. Her parents had gone to a business seminar for the weekend, and would only be back on Sunday evening.

Her two older brothers, Roy and Derek, were not back from work yet, not that she expected them because they would usually go straight to the pub, or a friend's house. It was Friday night after all, and their parents weren't there to arrange their weekend. How she wished they could be a real family. She loved her brothers, but living at home kept them apart and they did not spend time together.

It was not unfamiliar to Anabella to be on her own on a weekend. If her parents were there, they didn't speak to her anyway, because they would be busy entertaining their friends. She wrinkled her nose in disgust.

A long time ago, Anabella had decided not to be part of their lifestyle and because of this, there was no relationship between them. She had learned to distance herself, choosing to rather throw her time and energy into her sport. At first, it was a way out of the house. Now it had become her life; a life she appreciated and cherished.

She had the shower all to herself for as long as she wanted.

Once in her room, she got dressed, brushing her hair until it shone. Music played softly from the radio and she sang along with the well-known song.

Suddenly her cell phone rang, disturbing the stillness, but she smiled. The Caller ID showed it was her best friend, Monica. Of all her friends, she was closest to her, and was the heart of the group with her sparkling personality; always busy arranging parties or schemes, especially where boys were concerned.

Anabella trusted her as she was the only one who knew what was really going on at her house. Not that she ever allowed her to come over. For that, she was too ashamed, but she knew enough and was always close. When things got really bad, she could always turn to her. Although Monica was a cheerful person and looked like a 'dumb blond', she had shown maturity in a lot of things over the years, something that was not well known in their group.

"Hi, Moni."

"Hi, Bell! You in the mood for a party at my house tonight?"

She could hear Monica was excited—almost out of breath because of it—and she could see her, as if she was standing right in front of her. However,

Anabella did need to rest. Her muscles were still stiff after the practice.

"Not tonight, Moni, I really need to rest. Tomorrow is a big day and I must be in top form," she said with a sigh, smiling because of her friend's anxiousness.

"Please, Bell, do come, please, even if it is only for an hour or so." Monica sounded very eager, almost desperate.

*What was she up to again?* "Moni, I can't come, please understand."

"Bell, pretty please, a hunk of a guy is here, a friend of my brother's, and I want you to meet him. Please come."

In the background, Anabella could hear a shout, as if someone was screaming at her.

"Please, Bell!" It was Monica's brother, Tim. He was twelve years older than they were and a lawyer, working for a well-known law firm in the city. Again he shouted in a deep voice, laughing, "Please, Bell, come!"

Anabella smiled at this and then said, "All right, Moni, but only for an hour. I do need to have a good night's rest." Reluctantly, she gave in. She knew her friend would not stop until she said yes. Her friend's family was like a real family to her. Over the years, she had learned what it was like to have parents, and many times she would find herself crying afterward, longing for parents like theirs.

"Great. I expect you at seven, and you can leave at nine. Will that be early enough?" There was relief in her voice.

"Yes, that'll be fine. Thanks for the invite. See you later."

With an hour to spare, she stood in front of her closet. She took out a light, cream-colored winter dress with three-quarter-length sleeves. It fell to just above her knees. There was still a chill in the air this late in September and she didn't want to be cold. Long, dark-brown boots completed her outfit. Her long, straight, dark-brown hair hung loose over her shoulders. Even after the winter, she'd kept her tan, which was noticeable on her face, knees and forearms.

She left the house at ten to seven as Monica only lived fifteen blocks from her. It was already dark outside, and stars dotted the sky. A light breeze ruffled through her hair but it wasn't freezing, which she was glad about. It had been a long time since she had seen her friends, and maybe it would be good to see them all again. She got into her silver Renault Clio, a gift from her parents on her eighteenth birthday. To say she had been stunned to find the car parked in the driveway the morning of her birthday would have been putting it mildly. She had not seen either of them for almost a week, so Roy and Derek handed her the keys.

She'd spent a great morning with them, driving them to the nearest Mugg and Bean, enjoying breakfast together. Like ordinary young people, they laughed about silly stuff. No one mentioned the always absent parents. They had spent the previous night with friends and didn't return home until two days later. It was good to hear her brothers laugh and be the young handsome men they were. Normality was not a word which described them, but on that day they had come very close to it. They even took a few photos together, which had been framed and now hung in her room. They reminded her that if they tried hard enough, they could be a regular, happy family, the one thing she craved the most.

She had an air of confidence about her, but at the same time she was very humble and shy. Through life's trials, she had learned not to boast in her own abilities but to stay in the background and do her own thing. She had been forced to learn to stand on her own two feet, and not depend on her parents. They never cared, or were interested in her life. Although they took great care of her material needs, they emotionally distanced themselves, which bordered on abuse. Their own life and lifestyle was all that mattered to them. Her brothers would protect her at times but only to some degree, before they would leave her alone to fight or fend for herself. She loved her brothers, and she knew there were a lot of sacrifices they had to make to adjust to their parents' way of life, but she could never pay that price.

Her innocence was precious to her. It was a significant issue, or rather an embarrassment to them, especially her mother. They thought she was uptight. She was always proud of the fact that she could still be a lady, watching Mrs. Richter, who played a huge role in her life. Her example of grace and humbleness was the measure of a woman, which made Anabella determined to be similar. She wanted to be graceful, elegant and have respect for herself, with a husband who would adore her. From teachers and classmates she only received respect and admiration.

In less than two months, she would complete her schooling. She looked forward to the following year as she would be attending the University of Cape Town where she would study physiotherapy, with her main focus in sports. She had always loved sports; there wasn't one she had not tried at one time or another. She liked the commitment, the discipline it brought into her life, and the joy of competing. When competing in a team sport or as an individual, she felt that she was accepted for who she was as a person. In the beginning, it was a way to escape her home life, but now it had become her lifestyle.

Aldrich was standing at the big living room window looking out at the parking area when the silver Renault Clio pulled up and stopped. At first, he only saw long, booted legs appearing out of the car, and then the girl climbed out and stood up. She was a beauty from where he stood. She walked to the house until she reached the door and knocked. Illuminated by the light of the porch, he could see she was definitely a beauty, a tall beautiful girl with long, straight hair. This had to be Anabella. He had heard so much about Monica's swimmer friend.

Tim had also mentioned her often, especially over the last month, to the point of nagging. At first, Aldrich hadn't wanted to go but Tim kept on, convincing him. Tim had said he wanted to introduce him to someone special, a friend of Monica's. He had met Monica a few times over the years, and knew she was much younger. That would make her friend the same age and he was not in the mood for babysitting. However, if this was the same girl, she was not only very young, but a very pretty young girl.

*Perhaps I will stay a while and check things out. If nothing comes of it, I can always leave.*

She was graceful in movement and strength, not typical of a girl her age, so it caught his attention. *She is definitely young, maybe eighteen,* he thought. Maybe too young, but Tim had insisted he must meet this girl.

"She's really special," he said.

From Tim's stories, she'd been practically raised by his parents.

People gathered around, coming closer to the door to greet her, as Monica called out, "Anabella is here!" excited that her friend made it, making a big announcement of it. Apparently, everyone was glad about this news.

Aldrich watched her carefully, his eyes curiously fixed on the young girl.

"Come in, Anabella!" Monica greeted her with a big smile. "I am so glad you came." She pulled her by the hand. "You look beautiful."

Monica welcomed her into the house, glad to see her friend. For the past few weeks, they had both been busy with studies and outdoor activities. Both were also on the Prefect list with their own assigned duties. Not much time was left for visits or chatting.

Monica was also very attractive, but smaller build; slender. She was very blond. At first you would think it came from a bottle, but on closer inspection, she was all natural with big, blue eyes and a broad smile that reached her eyes.

"Hi, my friend." She hugged Anabella fiercely, joyful as she talked.

"It's lovely to see you again, thanks for the invite."

A beautiful smile adorned her face, two identical dimples appeared in her cheeks, and Aldrich believed that it was the most beautiful smile he had ever seen. His interest was growing rapidly.

"Hi, Mr. and Mrs. Richter, how are you?" She looked at Monica's parents, reaching for their hands.

"Very well," replied Mr. Richter. "Tomorrow is the big day, hey?" Mr. Richter continued, squeezing her hand. "I know it will go well for you. The gold medal is practically yours as I see it. It is only a formality. You have put in the time and effort. We will be watching it on TV tomorrow."

"Thanks, Mr. Richter, I appreciate the confidence you have in me. I hope to make you all proud." A light blush appeared on her cheeks, enhancing the young, oval face.

Monica plucked at Anabella's sleeve. "Come, Anabella, I want you to meet Tim's friend, Aldrich."

Anabella turned to face him. Her mouth became dry, and her heart stopped for a second. *This must be the hunk,* she contemplated her friend's words as she continued chattering away.

"They work together at the same firm in the city."

She looked at the most gorgeous man she had ever seen. She had to look up at him, and although she was five-foot-ten, he was still taller. Short, dark, golden-blond hair cut in the latest fashion crowned his head. He had big, sea-blue eyes. He was not a typical pretty boy, but a man with a firm jawline and rugged face. The shadow of day-old stubble made its appearance in a sexy manner. Charming character was written all over him, as well as experience in life; his lifelines a giveaway. Yet, he had a softness about him that made her want to step into his embrace and hug him, like a big teddy bear. Everything about him looked inviting to her.

*I would love to be hugged by him,* she thought, and almost giggled but covered it just in time. He had broad, straight shoulders that said *lean on me.* He was solid all right, and she bet that his clothes disguised muscles all over.

Sea-blue and emerald eyes met, and Anabella felt weak at the knees at the interested look he gave her. Throughout her young life, she had seen many men walk through the door of her parents' house. Pretty and handsome ones, her mother's favorite kind, but empty shells all the same; things in men that turned her off completely. But this man looked at her as if he saw her—past her outward appearance and at the real person—and that was a welcome first.

She knew she was beautiful. Many people had told her so, but somehow, under his gaze, she felt stunning and a warm feeling nestled in her belly.

*A bit old for me, but very attractive*, she thought and smiled at him, not the dimpled-smile previously given to her friends, but enough for Aldrich to have a good look at.

And as soon as he'd seen that look, he'd immediately been in the mood for strawberries and cream, his favorite dessert. The rich velvet texture of the cream mixed with the sweet, pink fruit had always appealed to him. She reminded him of that, all velvety sweetness, and he smacked his lips. A soft smile appeared on his very lush lips.

This was the first time Anabella had felt this way about any man. She had never experienced weak knees, or a racing heart for the opposite sex. In fact, because of her parents' lifestyle she saw men as self-absorbed and horny, only interested in one thing. With this man, it was different. She felt safe, not wanting to run as far as possible. Yet, she hadn't even spoken to him and already she felt a certain way about him. In fact, she wanted to get even closer.

Her innocence and shyness caused her to look away when she caught the smile on his face. In turn, he was feeling a bit out of place, but he returned her gaze. He could tell she was aware of his gaze by the constant blush on her cheeks. He did not reveal anything but a good dose of curiosity, and a beautiful smile.

With a deep, strong voice he greeted her, taking her hand in his. "Hello, sweetheart," he said. The endearing word fell naturally from his lips.

She nodded and greeted him as if it was the most natural thing to do. "Aldrich, pleased to meet you."

"The pleasure is all mine, sweetheart."

She looked up at him and saw a spark of approval in his eyes. His hands were muscular and calloused, not the hands of an office jock.

He was self-assured, and confidence oozed out of him. As he spoke, his voice resembled the sound of a summer rain rumbling. It made her tingle all over and those eyes... she could disappear into them. She let go of his hand as she smiled, not too sure what to reply, and looked around the room for her friend who had left her right after the introduction.

Before long, she returned her gaze to him. His closeness affected her heart rate greatly, his presence sent out rays of calmness that filtered through her, and she felt at ease next to him.

Mr. Richter came in with drinks and a glass of orange juice on a tray, offering it to Anabella and Aldrich. They turned as he spoke from behind them, forcing them to break the gaze they had been sharing for a few minutes, though they were still very much aware of each other.

"Something to drink, Aldrich? Here is your orange juice, Anabella."

Both reached out, Anabella taking the orange juice, and Aldrich the drink offered to him.

"Thanks, sir. Can I help with the tray?" Aldrich offered.

"It's fine," he replied, placing the tray in the hands of his son who had just joined them.

"This is a girl to watch on TV tomorrow, Aldrich," Mr. Richter said proudly.

Anabella couldn't help but blush; she was never one for much attention.

"Tomorrow, she will bring a gold medal or two back for swimming. As a community, we are very proud of her accomplishments." Admiration was evident on Mr. Richter's face when he looked at her.

For a moment, Anabella thought about her parents, who didn't care or ever speak to her in the same manner as Mr. Richter. They never gave her any attention. As parents, they missed it completely. For a fleeting moment, a sad look appeared in her eyes, a look that Aldrich didn't miss before the sparkle returned.

Aldrich wondered what could have upset this vibrant girl. The air around her was filled with energy and excitement; so why then the brief sadness? He knew very little about her, but he wanted to be the one who could wipe that sadness away. He wanted to know more.

"Thanks, Mr. Richter, you are very kind. Now I know I have to bring back the gold medal," Anabella replied softly, the blush still on her cheeks. She could feel Aldrich's gaze and looked away, hoping to find Monica somewhere in the room. However, she was nowhere to be seen.

"I only say it because it is true, Anabella. You have worked hard."

"Thank you, sir." She accepted the praise, taking a sip of her orange juice in an attempt to swallow past the lump in her throat.

"It is a lovely evening, spring is in the air; I can smell it. Let's go outdoors, tables and chairs have already been put outside. Make yourselves comfortable and enjoy the evening," Mr. Richter said to the group.

"I know I will enjoy the evening," said Aldrich, and he looked down at Anabella.

A pleased look appeared in those big, blue eyes as she spoke to Mr. Richter. "Thanks again, sir."

Anabella looked up to find Aldrich's gaze on her. A delighted chill ran down her spine. His words had sounded like a promise of enjoyment—only meant for her.

Mr. Richter chuckled, adding playfully, "Enjoy, you two."

Aldrich grinned with delight, taking a sip of his drink.

The blush on her face said it all.

# Chapter Two

Everyone turned and made their way out to the patio. Aldrich and Anabella found themselves at the back of the group, waiting patiently for them to go through the patio doors. He moved forward, pressing against her. His body heat surrounded her and Anabella could pick up his cologne; spicy with a hint of sea breeze. She inhaled with pleasure, fully aware of the man directly behind her.

Aldrich himself found it hard to think of anything else for some reason. He was attracted to the young girl. It was just not his style to be interested in a mere child, but she intrigued him. Her innocence was a thing of beauty. There was also something else, a sadness she carefully hid from everyone, but it drew him to her.

He wanted to shield her, his hands almost reaching to touch her and hold her safe. The last time he felt this kind of protectiveness was when he'd been married all those years ago. Since then, he hadn't felt it with any other woman. She was a young girl trapped in a woman's body, with no idea of where she belonged.

Instead of giving in to the need to touch her, he bent over and asked in a low voice, "How old are you?"

"Eighteen." She was self-assured but careful. She turned and saw his lips up close and wondered how they would taste. As he talked, a mere thought flashed through her mind, images of other lips throwing kisses her way invaded her head. She closed her eyes, willing the visions to disappear.

When she looked up, his eyes held a question, and she knew that she was staring. A blush formed over her cheeks with the shame and guilt she felt over the thoughts she was conjuring about him. *He is not like my parents,* she reminded herself impatiently.

He gave her a broad smile, but asked her ordinary questions. Her age was not an issue at that moment. She relaxed. She hadn't realized how nervous she was, and it helped that his questions were calming, deflecting her knotted nerves.

"In what events will you compete?"

"The two-hundred meter backstroke, butterfly, and relay."

"I will definitely make some time to watch, sweetheart," he said softly, touching her arm as they moved forward.

"Thank you." She liked the endearment and smiled, turning back to step outside.

*Yes, I will definitely make some time.* He watched as she walked in front of him with a gentle sway to her hips, appreciating her slender body.

Once outside, he led her to an unoccupied chair where she sat down, bending shapely legs under her. He sat directly in front of her, his eyes never wavering, even though it seemed she was not aware of him.

Anabella was aware; the butterflies in her tummy told her he was watching her every move. Even when Mr. Richter and Tim spoke to him, she could still feel his gaze on her, sipping away at his drink. His posture was relaxed and at ease. He knew the family well she realized as she watched him listen to Mr. Richter with keen interest.

Sometimes, she turned to Monica and her other friends to talk to them, only to look back at him. Each time she found his eyes on her and a smile playing on his lips. She wasn't uncomfortable under his stare; she rather enjoyed his blunt way of looking at her.

Anabella wished she was a bit more outgoing in order to speak to him, but she didn't know what to say. She knew he was a lawyer at a successful firm, but other than that she knew nothing about him. This was something she wanted to change, but her shyness prevented her from speaking freely, and then there was the age difference.

He was out of her league; no way would he find her fascinating. She couldn't understand why she felt so uneasy about it. There were many couples whose age difference wasn't a problem. Her parents were an example. Her mother and father differed in age by fifteen years and they had a 'happy' marriage. If you could call what they had a marriage—it worked for them.

So far, he was keeping his distance. On the one hand, she appreciated it but on the other, she loved the idea of getting to know him better.

*What could I offer a man like him?* Her attention was drawn to him regularly, distracting her from her own conversation. He looked intelligent, sharp, missed nothing and was almost intimidating as she watched him casually. He was surely a worthy opponent in the court room. His confidence held great appeal to her. There was something about him that captivated her curiosity.

Aldrich was also lost in his own thoughts. He was thinking of their age difference and the obstacles it presented. Eighteen was still very young. At thirty, he was ready to settle down. He watched her chatting with her friends. They had nothing in common, and her entire life was still in front of her. Yet he found himself intrigued, especially by the sad look he'd seen for a fleeting moment. Then, of course, there was the whole innocence factor. She was untouched by a man. The way she blushed at his remarks, her loss for words; if he wanted to know her better it had to come from him. The question was: did he need that in his life?

When he looked at her once again, his eyes taking in the full splendor of the young woman, the decision was very clear to him. He would make the effort. There was something about her that kept his interest.

However, he would have to be patient. Although her innocence was appealing to him, it could create problems. She was not like the typical girls her age. Her eyes gave away a sense of maturity he didn't expect from a girl this young. She had a look that said she had seen it all before and it made him curious.

Her actions said she was new to love from a man. Maybe it was his lawyer instinct, but he could pick up that all was not well with her.

Monica made sure everyone had a good time. She was always the heart of any party, and as a good host her timing was impeccable.

She turned to Tim and motioned for him to put some music on. Almost immediately, *Butterfly Kisses* filled the night sky from the speakers in the corner. Monica made her way to Aldrich, and asked him for a dance. She knew him well and really liked him as a friend. It was why she'd known she just had to arrange a party for her two friends to meet. When she mentioned it to Tim, he agreed that it would be a splendid idea, but he also offered a warning. She would need to tread carefully and not push anything. Allow them to find themselves without any pressure from her. Reluctantly she had agreed, and so far it was working out wonderfully.

He smiled when she stood in front of him asking for a dance. He stood up, accepting her invitation. She led him to the floor and he followed, taking her in his arms—not too close—but with a comfortable space between them, simply enjoying the song. At one point, when they were next to Anabella's chair, Monica reached out to grab her friend's hand.

Startled at the sudden touch, Anabella looked at her, then at him.

Monica pulled her up, placing her hand in Aldrich's and smiled.

Aldrich immediately picked up on what Monica was doing and took over with a grin. He really didn't need help from an eighteen-year-old in this department, but appreciated the gesture. He pulled Anabella closer to him, one hand lightly touching her lower back, the other engulfing her right hand as they danced away.

They were both good dancers and their feet moved in synchronization with the music, melting together. At first, she was surprised but didn't mind the closeness. Willingly, she drew closer as they danced, her lips close to his neck where she could see his pulse beat in the hollow of his neck. He smelled so good.

She wondered how it would feel to kiss him there. Heat rushed through her whole body. As if he could hear her musings, he pulled her in closer. She fitted perfectly in his arms. Her hand on his shoulder held him gently.

As the second song continued, they didn't part. If someone had asked them what the song was called, they would not have been able to recall it. Anabella tried hard not to think too much; simply enjoying the closeness and the feeling of safety he created. His heat was intoxicating, and she couldn't help but brush the part of his skin just above the collar of his shirt with her fingers.

He looked down at her, her emerald eyes were glowing. He leaned in, their cheeks touching, and she sighed softly, laying her head on his shoulder. It was amazing how comfortable they felt with each other, no words necessary to break the silence.

His hands were warm and gentle, the one on her lower back caressing her softly; the same soft, gentle touch she bestowed on him was evidently being returned. During the last song, he encircled her with both his arms, surrounding her.

Through hazy eyes, she looked at her arm around his neck, noticing the time on her watch. It was already nine-fifteen. She had to leave, but her body was sending out different messages than what her mind told her. Finally, she whispered in his ear to let her go as she needed to leave.

"I must go," she said softly. He turned and looked at her, his blue eyes darker yet soft; she could melt into them. She would love to explore this more, but it couldn't be, not now anyway.

He pulled her in even closer, and in a husky voice whispered, "I would love to get to know you better." Reluctantly, he released her.

She wasn't sure she had heard him correctly, but the mere idea of him wanting to know her caused her heart to skip a beat.

The few minutes they shared together were overwhelming. He'd never thought this could happen to him.

In wonder, she looked at him. *You are silly, Anabella. What do you have to offer him? Nothing. Especially the love part. I don't know what love is, and why would he want to know me?*

"But I understand you have to leave. You have a big day tomorrow, and you need your rest," he concluded with a smile.

When he released her, a void filled her heart and body, a void she had never experienced before. She knew there had been something missing in her life and now that she had found it, she didn't want to let go. She stepped closer to him, kissed him in the crook of his neck and walked away. Making her way over to Monica and her parents, she thanked them for a great evening, said her goodbyes to the other guests and walked out the door.

Aldrich was still standing in the same spot where she had left him, still feeling her lips on his neck, shocked at her tender display, when Tim walked over.

"She impressed you, my friend." Tim gave a chuckle, patted him on the shoulder and walked away, saying, "Monica was right about how much you would like her."

As if that brought him back to reality, he quickly took a card out of his pocket, scribbled on it and ran to her car, reaching her as she was about to get in.

She felt a piece of paper being pressed into her hand, and looked up to find it was Aldrich. The message was clear—he wanted to see her again.

Once home and in her bedroom, she unfolded the paper still in her hand. It was his business card.

*Aldrich Hagin*
*Attorney*
*Telephone number: 555 444 0000*

She turned it over, and it read: *Until we meet again.*

Sandra Anthony sat in the hotel room after the conference she and her husband, Jason, had attended over the weekend. She switched on the big screen TV to watch some news while she waited for Jason, who was in the bathroom. They would be attending a charity ball that night for street children. Normally, they didn't attend these kinds of events, but it would help to promote their business. As she flicked through the stations, she stopped at eNews sport. Her daughter had just appeared on the big TV screen, on the starting block for her swimming event; backstroke over two hundred meters.

Her emerald eyes roamed over her eighteen-year-old daughter's young body, a spitting image of herself, except her daughter's body was in very good shape, filled with energy and vibrancy. Her innocence was as clear as daylight. Sandra couldn't help but smirk. She thought it was ridiculous that her only daughter wasn't willing to share their lifestyle; to explore her body's urges. With that body, she could introduce her to many willing customers, bringing in more business. Their lifestyle had opened up a very profitable business, one with various benefits which made life exciting.

It had all started when she was only sixteen years old and met her father's friend, Robert. Robert had been in his early thirties and a beautifully built man with broad shoulders and a heavy chest, narrow waist and firm butt. He was extremely handsome. At sixteen, she'd been very innocent but very curious about sexual intercourse. She and her friends had read all they could on this topic, and secretly experimented with each other. It had thrilled her.

From the moment she met Robert, she knew that he would be her first. One Friday night, her parents had gone out to some function or other, and they stayed at home and watched TV. He was lying on the couch, his well-defined abs clearly visible through his white shirt. She could not help herself; she stared at his broad shoulders and chest unabashedly, and then lower where she could see the bulge in his pants, wondering how it would look.

He caught her staring and grinned, saying, "Do you want to touch?"

Her face has shown her eagerness, so he'd pulled his t-shirt over his head showing off his well-toned, tanned muscular chest.

She licked her lips as her eyes explored him, stopping at the zipper.

Again he spoke, his eyes not missing her actions at all. "How old are you?" he asked in a rough, low voice.

"Sixteen."

"A bit young, but you will not mind if we play, will you?" He leaned closer to her with a devilish smile, her insides twirling with excitement.

She shook her head, not sure what to say, or even what he meant. Her body quivered. Her eyes were still fixed on him, watching as he stood, unbuttoned, and unzipped his jeans slowly, his eyes watching her every move. When her tongue ran over her dry lips, he started stripping in front of her.

"Sweet Jesus..." was the only thing that came out of her mouth. She had never seen anything like it. A thick, long erect member with a glossy tip jutted out and greeted her.

He chuckled. "Come here. Touch me," he demanded, and she crawled to him without a second thought, lifted a trembling finger and touched the length of his shaft; it felt like velvet. She grinned wickedly. With greater eagerness, she wrapped her hand around him and told him how beautiful he was. He thanked her. That night, he coaxed her into touching him as he liked it, and she loved it. Going down on him, he moaned, and when she saw the reaction on his face, she'd felt powerful, grinning at him.

He held her head and told her what to do with her hand and her mouth. She was a typical teenager; curious, eager and full of energy. His taste had been exquisite on her lips, better than any fine wine.

He had just dressed when her parents walked into the house; they drank coffee and went to bed. Sandra kept thinking of the feel of him in her mouth and it was exhilarating. She wished she could have had more as sleep evaded her.

When the house was quiet and her parents in bed for the night, she heard her door open and Robert walked in, whispering, "Are you awake?" She replied with keenness, "Yes." Her heart skipped a few beats.

"Good, now it is my turn."

He only had his boxers on, his body highlighted in the moonlight as she watched him amble closer to her.

He pulled the covers off, removed her panties, and opened her legs. Her eyes never left him. He grinned as he pulled her closer to the edge of the bed and knelt down. She felt exposed, but in a good way, and the next instant, he went down on her.

"I have never had a virgin before," he said softly, just before he drove his mouth deep into her innermost private parts.

She thought she'd died and gone to heaven at that moment. From that night on for the next week, he would come into her room, teaching her, and coaxing her into oral sex. She learned his body and he learned hers; she simply couldn't get enough. After that, he visited often, always introducing her to more pleasure. He always stuck to oral sex until she turned eighteen.

That night, after a party that Robert attended, he brought a friend along to meet her. They had a threesome, a threesome so intoxicating that to this day, she could not forget or ever get enough of. That friend became her husband, Jason Anthony. Robert introduced them to more people, people who opened doors for them, and because of this, they were now extremely wealthy.

Sandra and Robert's relationship continued for many years, until he passed away five years ago. To this day, she missed him because she'd learned to care for him over the years. He had been more than a friend, one who had changed her life profoundly.

She and her husband had continued with this lifestyle—it was the only thing she knew. She had no idea what ordinary couples were doing, or how they managed to stay together. But she knew that it would never appeal to her.

Even their sons had joined in their business, and she would get such a thrill watching them as their young bodies experimented. They were learning to become experts in the field of sex. Only her daughter refused to have anything to do with it. Sandra smirked again. *The little twit doesn't know what she is missing*, she thought.

She watched her daughter gliding through the water as she touched the edge of the pool first, a smile adorning her youthful face.

"Honey?" her husband called out

"Yes?" she queried as she switched the TV off.

"What were you watching?"

"Nothing interesting, are you ready?"

"Yes, let's go," he said, kissing her in the nape of her neck while cupping her firm breast in his hand and teasing her earlobe with his teeth.

She gently pushed him away. "Not now dear, I have special plans for you... later." She smiled seductively.

He moved the piece of material covering her breast with his mouth and said, "I can hardly wait." Biting her, sending shivers running down her body.

Sandra cupped his face, lifted him to her height and kissed him. A kiss filled with such promise, he sighed. "You are the best." She smiled, rearranged the silk shirt and kissed him again before they walked out the door.

Anabella was standing in her dorm room, a familiar business card in her hand, her thoughts very far from the present time.

Aldrich had phoned her the night after the championship to congratulate her on her three gold medal wins. He'd wanted to go over, but she hadn't wanted him at her house. Which was a good thing, since her younger brother had come over with a few friends and seized the living room for themselves. Wild music had filled the air as they played their 'games', as he put it. Games he had learned from their parents, just that this time it was with his own friends. Thankfully, they left her alone as she'd made her way to her bedroom.

The house reeked of sweat, beer and dirty socks by the time she walked in. She was incredibly ashamed of her parents' house, and never allowed any of her friends to visit. Although they weren't home, the evidence of their lifestyle was everywhere to be seen.

Movies with explicit titles were strewn over the coffee tables and TV cabinet, and the art against the walls depicted their lifestyle. Often, the house would smell of smoke, sweat and sex. Not that they lived in a scruffy place, in fact, it was the biggest house in the neighborhood. They were, after all, quite well off.

So, she'd suggested they meet at a restaurant, to which he reluctantly agreed. She was glad he hadn't pressed for an explanation, though she sensed he wanted to say something. They met outside the establishment, kissed each other on the cheek and walked in together, his hand on the small of her back. Opening the door for her, he smiled when she said thank you, looking at him.

He directed her to a quiet spot toward the back, and they took a seat opposite each other. Some of the guests recognized her and congratulated her on her championship wins. Some wanted to take a photo with her and through it all, Aldrich waited patiently for it to settle down while he smiled delightedly. She appreciated that, not realizing how many people had watched her, in turn apologizing to him. But he placed a finger on her lips, saying softly, "I am proud of you."

Small talk ensued while they placed their order, and then silence fell between them—a comfortable relaxed silence. He reached over to her, taking her hand into his, and continued to hold it for the rest of the night. His hand was firm, warm and reassuring; clean hands with long, manicured fingers. Definitely an office jock. However, it suited him. He looked handsome, and was casually dressed in a pair of jeans that did his butt justice, the shirt snuggled around his bulky chest, broad shoulders and thick arms.

"You were on my mind the whole day," he said, his voice proud. "I watched you on TV. You had some stiff competition, but I could see at the last turn of the backstroke event that the other girl was getting tired, and from there on you glided away from her," he praised. He didn't mention the fact that he'd looked at her before she dove into the water, admiring her beautiful body, the one he knew was under the dress she'd been wearing the previous night.

"Thanks. We have swum against each other previously, and I knew she would be my only competition. It all worked in my favor in the end," she said, smiling. She felt good about the championship and the medals; a fitting end to all her hard work.

She managed to steer the conversation away from herself and asked him about his work, which he obviously loved. The evening was pleasant and though they hadn't many things in common, it struck her how he made an effort to get to know her, avoiding the topic of her parents' altogether.

At one point, he bent over her hand and kissed her softly on the knuckles, brushing it with a thumb, and she could not help but blush at this tender display. He was different from the men in her family.

Her father was the silent brooding type, she hardly ever saw him with a smile. The only time he was happy, was when their friends were at home. Only then was he the heart of the party, his dirty jokes a turn-on to many of them. Normally, that would be her queue to leave.

Her brother, Roy, was very quiet, barely saying a thing, and when he was not entertaining the guests, he was mostly in his room reading. The few times she'd gone there, financial magazines were strewn over his desk. But he never talked, and she never asked.

One thing their family could do well was not to speak to one another—they were absolute strangers to each other.

Derek was more like their mother, outgoing, flirty, not a care in the world over what anyone thought of him, a smile always present. He loved their parents' lifestyle and joined eagerly. Roy had to be called before he joined, but Derek was always the one first in line. People loved him.

Their food and drinks arrived, and they enjoyed a pleasant meal together mingled with light bantering.

With dinner finished, they sat back and relaxed, quiet, each busy with their own thoughts. When the waiter returned, he asked if Anabella would like dessert to which she agreed, thanking him. Aldrich then ordered strawberries and cream for both of them.

The conversation continued, and they talked about minute things. Likes and dislikes, books they had read, movies they thought were a mistake to have been made, which ended with them laughing about each other's comments.

When dessert arrived, Aldrich watched as she ate with a toothy grin. She blushed at his continued stare, not knowing she had a dot of cream on her lips. He bent over, and with his finger removed it from her lips, placing it in his mouth. "Delicious," he said, and she blushed crimson. He chuckled as he sat back and finished his own.

That was the most provocative thing ever done to her, and she felt heat rising up her neck but also in the lower half of her body. His closeness was welcoming to her senses, his romantic manners intoxicating to her hungry soul, his voice filled with promises and his eyes, dark pools holding her mesmerized.

It seemed like it took forever to finish their desserts, which for some reason were eaten at a slower pace.

"You enjoy dessert I take it," she said in a husky voice when he put the last spoonful of fruit in her mouth. He nodded, and continued to grin, his eyes never leaving her. She felt beautiful.

There was not much said after that, and the rest of the time they held hands. They didn't want to part and found themselves stretching time, just listening to the music playing.

She couldn't meet his eyes, afraid that he would see her open adoration in them. When he leaned over, he placed his finger under her chin and brought her face up, looking at her. What she saw in his eyes reflected her own desires. He moved closer to her and kissed her very softly on the mouth. Her lips were willing to receive him so she kissed him back; his kiss soft, tender and oh so delicate, as if she were porcelain. It was the first time she had allowed a man so close to her, or even kissed one, but with Aldrich it felt as if she found her home. The idea was so overwhelming that she moaned softly into him, making him chuckle.

Then, very softly he spoke, repeating the words from the previous night, willing her to believe it. "I really would like to spend more time with you, sweetheart. Would you like that?"

She nodded. "Yes, I would love that."

He smiled in return, adding, "You are very interesting."

"I am?"

"Yes, but most of all, I want to be the one to take away your sadness." He kissed her eyes tenderly, the action stirring her deeply.

*How can he see that?* Her thoughts quickened as she savored every word.

"But, I want to give you a chance to experience life, your career has just begun and I don't want to stand in the way of it." Absently, he brushed a strand of hair from her face, meeting her gaze, making sure she understood how serious he was being. "I know we've only known each other for a day, but my heart and mind says that we have something special. I can see you feel the same way."

Tears started to roll down her face at the declaration, and he kissed them away.

The way he said it caused her knees to go weak, and she allowed the words to filter through her mind, repeating them. It was so unexpected, but she, too, would love to get to know him.

He continued to kiss her with soft feather-like brushings, her skin soft to his touch. His tongue explored and caressed her lips as he pulled her closer; excitement grew in the pit of her stomach.

It was true what he said. All of this was very new to her, although she had seen a lot of things others her age hadn't, she knew all about sex, every position and the acts surrounding it, but never had she encountered the feelings that this man was creating within her.

Ever since he touched her, he'd evoked feelings in her she'd never experienced before, and it felt real and complete. He had life experiences she didn't have, and this drew her closer to him.

When their lips met for a proper kiss, she clung to him, eager and desperate. Their breaths heated as they explored with their mouths and tongues. His taste intoxicating to her senses, but all too suddenly he pulled away, taking in a deep breath. His eyes smoldered as he said softly, "I think I need to take you back to your car, sweetheart." He smacked his lips as if he just had the most delicious meal while caressing her back, his breath heavy when he lifted his head, her hands still in his hair, having forgotten where she was.

"Yes," was all she could get out, her voice sounding shaky in her own ears. They left the table after he paid the bill, and together they walked outside to her car. She held on to his arm knowing she couldn't walk on her own, his hand cupping hers possessively. At the car, he pressed her almost into the frame, the intensity building in a passionate kiss. The nightlife quiet around them as time stood still in the adoring embrace. Her arms wrapped around his neck, holding him even closer. When he finally let go she was breathless. She stared up into the handsome face and noticed how his eyes caressed her, telling her all she wanted to know.

No words were uttered between them, because no discussion was necessary. Confirmation was in both their hearts. He opened the door and with one last kiss, closed it.

*He's awakened feelings and emotions in me I didn't know I was capable of, but I'm going to love exploring them some more,* she reflected as she drove back home in a haze.

He followed.

The feel of his lips were still palpable on hers, and when she licked them she could taste him, as if he was still present. When she pulled into her driveway, she blew the horn, and then he was gone. The red taillights coming on at the stop sign, before he pulled away. As her eyes followed his car, the thought of being with him was all too overpowering.

# Chapter Three

As time passed, she saw him again one day during the December holiday season. She happened to be at Monica's house swimming and as she emerged from the water, she found him standing at the patio door, his eyes fixated on her. The smile on his face told her she was a pleasing sight. Elated, she returned the smile.

Monica was helping her mum bake in preparation for the festive season and when Anabella offered to help, Mrs. Richter had chased her out of the house.

She stared at the gorgeous hunk looking relaxed in a pair of khaki pants and black t-shirt, his body toned to perfection. She made her way to the edge of the pool, and had to hang on to the tiles, because the look she saw in his eyes burned her. She smiled, and on shaky legs got out and made her way to where he stood, a huge grin adorning his face. She kissed him on the lips—which was perhaps too forward—but she couldn't resist. He continued to look at her, his eyes dark pools. She had missed him; her days and dreams constantly invaded by him, and now to find him standing there was just too good an opportunity to miss.

"Hi, Aldrich."

"Hi, sweetheart." His voice soft, caressing her, making her smile.

She reached for her towel, which hung on a chair, and then walked to a deck chair and lay down. He followed, sitting down next to her.

"Are you well?"

"School is finally over."

"It is. When do the results come out?"

"On the fifth of January, but I know I have done well."

"That is good news. And the practices?"

"Demanding, but good. I really look forward to varsity. They say the coach is very good."

He smiled as he brushed his fingers against her arm, the feeling sending shivers down her spine. They chatted and she told him more about the practices and a competition she would participate in at the end of the week; just a friendly race at the club.

The air hummed with electric currents and her heart raced. He leaned in closer and semi-whispered, "I have missed you." This was followed by a kiss, which made all the others feel like child's play. They couldn't get enough of each other, her body responding under his touch, his warm hand caressing it gently.

"I've missed you, too," she finally said as his eyes moved over her black bikini appraisingly, smiling at her blush. She felt his warm hand on her ribs, a thumb stroking her skin. She was aware of every touch, so much so her skin was covered in goose bumps. Breathless, she said, "Badly, I can't stop thinking about you."

"You have done something to me, something I've never felt before. You occupy my thoughts every day. I am acting like a lovesick teenager."

"I know how you feel, and I *am* a love sick teenager."

He chuckled at her innocence.

She smiled, pulling him back into her embrace and this time she kissed him, with greater longing. *Damn, he's a good kisser*. Images of swirling bodies flicked through her mind, encouraging her actions as the intensity grew with a burning desire.

Monica cleared her throat, and grinning asked what they would like for lunch.

Aldrich, without lifting his eyes, said, "Strawberries and cream, please." Soft enough that only Anabella could hear, which made them both laugh before he let her go.

It became their private banter, his love for the sweet dessert flavored with Anabella's sweet taste. Aldrich was intoxicated and found himself often eating the dessert just to conjure her image in his mind.

Anabella couldn't believe how reckless she'd become with this man she hardly knew. She watched him from under her eyelashes, with something close to adoration. She couldn't believe how at ease with him she was after what had just taken place. She looked at her friend and blushed upon her curious expression.

Sheepishly, Monica looked at them, not really understanding, when Aldrich said, "Just whatever you usually have for lunch would be great, thank you." His voice was completely under control.

When Monica left, she winked at Anabella over her shoulder; code for wanting to know the whole story once he left.

They sat down to lunch, talking about all kinds of things with Monica, making jokes, teasing each other about silly stuff, their hands always close, his eyes continuously roaming over her appreciatively.

She had never blushed as much as that afternoon. His eyes constantly intense and filled to the brim with emotions. She never thought she could evoke that kind of feeling in a man, and if she and to be honest, coming from him she welcomed it.

Monica left them after her mother called her back, and he pulled her chair closer again and kissed her. Heat emanated from his mouth and his hands, and she loved the feel of it. Her own body responded immediately; he made her forget everything around her, like nothing else mattered. It was a struggle to get away from him, but a phone call interrupted them, which he answered, and soon after, he left. They hadn't seen each other again.

Every night since that afternoon, she'd sat with her cell in her hand, continuously punching in his number then cancelling it. She knew she wasn't ready for Aldrich. The attraction she felt toward him was real and she could relive every second of their time together. Her body responded with equal intensity.

She would love to go to him, but she owed him at least a well-balanced person. She found herself comparing what they had with her parents' relationship. Images and thoughts of intertwined bodies inflicted her mind with doubt and confusion, cluttering it. Her body ached for his touch.

As it was December, her parents were away often, so she barely saw them. During the Christmas week, they'd gone on a cruise, leaving a note on the kitchen table. The holiday was quiet, giving her much time to think about Aldrich and what he meant to her.

Roy met a young woman during this time and brought her home in the second week of the holiday; she never left. The two were inseparable, always in his room, which she was grateful for. As Roy wasn't much into the whole swing thing, as Derek was, he used this time to be himself. A smile frequently adorned his handsome face.

Derek was seldom home, but when she managed to see him it was with a quick acknowledgement before he left again. And every time it was with someone different at hand.

The house felt normal as she wondered around, reading and packing for the following year. She had time to throw old clothes away, rearrange her closet, and make a list of things she would need in her dorm room, doing shopping as required. She acquainted herself with the list she'd received from the dorm, making sure she left nothing out. The boxes in the corner of her room grew steadily with each purchase.

Anabella also took the time to relax at her favorite spot in Camps Bay near the beach and out of the way of the holiday goers, to tan, swim and relax, knowing that the following year would be crazier than this one.

She visited Monica and her family, spending Christmas and New Year with them. The days were searing hot but filled with laughter, loads of play and lots of eating.

"Anabella, where are you?" a shout came from the hallway, bringing Anabella back to the present.

She recognized her friend's voice, stepped out into the busy hallway and called, "Here, I am in room 312," and waved at her friend. Girls were running in the passage, carrying heavy bags and boxes to their individual rooms, and parents followed giving last minute instructions. The place was filled with excitement, energy and eagerness.

"These are the last things from the car," Monica said loud enough for her to hear.

Anabella rushed over to help her with the heavy load. They would be sharing the same dorm room, which was great news to both of them. Though their courses were different, they would still be able to see each other daily. Monica would be studying education as she'd always loved children and had a keen interest in teaching them.

"It is really hot, let's go get a soda before we unpack."

"Okay."

"Were you thinking of Aldrich again?" asked Monica in a soft concerned voice as they strolled away.

"Yes."

"Why don't you call him?"

"I am not ready Moni, too much baggage. My parents aren't the best examples of a relationship; I'm still haunted by the images I've been privy to, and unless I sort them out, I'm not willing to meet or be with any man, especially Aldrich," she replied with a sigh, her breath shuddering as she held back the tears and longing. "He deserves the best." A sorrowful look played over Anabella's face, a far away look of despair.

Monica knew Anabella cared for Aldrich more deeply than she would admit at this point, but she knew not to push the topic further. In her own time, Anabella would tell her, or perhaps she needed to get help in order to work through the nightmares and images that haunted her nightly. She also knew all too well, from past conversations with Anabella, that she didn't lead a regular life. She'd never allowed Monica near her house, so she had no first-hand knowledge of what was really going on inside those four walls. From what she understood, Anabella's parents lived the life of porn stars, swingers and nightclub owners, the ones with very expensive club fees.

Monica had once investigated it on the Internet. Intriguing at first, but the more she read and watched, the more horrified she'd become. Some of the actions diminished people in such a way, they were like animals. How anyone could love *that* was beyond her. There was no ordinary relationship between Anabella's parents, not as she knew it to be with hers, and she loved her parents dearly. As far as she knew, strangers would be at their house every second night, taking part in all kinds of orgies, not bothering to go to the bedroom. The group ranged from four to fifteen at any given time.

The brothers were older and had to participate, and from a young age Anabella had had to watch. She knew they had fights in the house over this, which left Anabella defeated, but they had to give in to their parents' whims. This left serious scarring on her young mind, and Monica was convinced this was the reason Anabella never had any serious relationships, and why she had a hard time allowing any man to get close to her.

Aldrich had come into her life, and without knowing her full story, had backed down giving her space to grow, and to go to him on her terms. Something she appreciated about him. Not many men would be willing to do this.

Anabella was very beautiful and sweet, and Monica had seen the attraction between them; a mutual attraction of understanding and respect, even with the obvious age difference. She'd noticed men's reactions around Anabella, which forced her to retract deeper into her shell. However, with Aldrich it wasn't like that, he really cared about her.

The times her friend was over at her house, Anabella would watch her mum and dad attentively; their interaction toward each other, and toward her and Tim. She couldn't believe that this was just everyday life.

In the beginning of their friendship—they were ten years old back then—Anabella had asked her, "Do they not have other people that share their bed?"

Dumbfounded, she'd looked at Anabella and asked what she meant?

"My parents are never alone," she simply replied.

That response had taken her aback somewhat, and Monica remembered that she'd looked confused, thinking her friend was weird but left it at that.

The more Anabella came into contact with them, the more she observed them with growing resentment, which would lead to tears, bitterness and disgust toward her parents. Observing the interaction and then wanting to say something profound made her think twice. Especially when they had words and she was angry with her mum.

Anabella's wisdom reminded Monica of what she had, which made her appreciate her own parents more.

This was the reason Aldrich had been drawn to her from the very first time he'd seen her. With this deeper understanding, Anabella could see a relationship for what it was, discerning fakes from the authentic ones. She needed help before she would commit herself to Aldrich, and Monica knew how to be a friend. But, her inexperience didn't provide her with the insight or knowledge to deal with this. She loved her friend dearly as they were mostly sisters in every sense of the word. The fact that they shared a dorm room made it easier to observe Anabella closely, and even help her with unwanted attention.

She was well-known; the championships the previous year, and the few articles printed had put her in the limelight, making life difficult. And although she loved the sport, the attention she got wasn't welcomed at all.

Months of hard work followed, days and nights were filled with studying, practices, competitions and campus activities.

Halfway through March, she flew to America where she competed and won several medals. During this time, and although she had a hectic program to follow, she never neglected one single day.

On the Sunday night when she arrived back in South Africa, she walked into the foyer where Aldrich met her with a big bunch of flowers and a huge smile. She was in seventh heaven, stepping right into his waiting arms. A few cameras flashed around them, but they only had eyes for each other.

"Hello, sweetheart. Welcome back," he whispered close to her ear. The bustle of the other passengers as they greeted their loved ones was overwhelming, but she whispered back, "Hello, Aldrich. This is a welcoming sight. How did you know?"

"Monica."

And right on cue, she stepped out of the crowd, arms falling around Anabella's neck, and a big kiss was planted on her cheek.

"I have missed you, my friend," she said loudly, and they continued to talk about the past two weeks while Aldrich gathered her bags on a trolley. Since Anabella's parents weren't home, Monica insisted she stay with her, and she gratefully accepted the offer.

It took them near an hour to get back to her house. Aldrich followed and they visited until late.

She showed them pictures about interesting people she met while Aldrich sat next to her and listened. The Richter family eventually retired for the evening, and they spent an hour alone before he, too, had to leave.

"You had an exciting time over there."

"I loved it, Aldrich, it was so special. To be with people I read about, and being able talk to them as equals was amazing. These are people I never thought I would ever meet, and there I was racing against them. I felt like a kid in a candy shop." She giggled with pleasure as he wrapped her in his arms and held her tightly against his chest. She let him, without any hesitation, just lay her head on his shoulder and enjoyed the solitude his presence brought her.

When he finally left, he kissed her softly on the forehead. She had expected more and was mortified he refrained from kissing her as he'd done before. He chuckled at her pout, got into his vehicle and left her standing.

She was downright fuming. "I mean really, I haven't seen him in ages, and this is how he kissed me?" she sneered to herself as she stomped into the house and up the stairs to Monica's room.

When she was in bed, her phone buzzed softly under her pillow. She removed it; it was Aldrich. At first she didn't want to answer, but when it persisted she answered softly, "Hello." Wearily, she looked to her friend's bed but Monica had burrowed under the covers. She got up and walked out of the room and made her way downstairs to the living area.

"Are you still awake?" he asked.

She huffed, which caused him to chuckle.

"Are you angry with me?"

"And why would you think that, Aldrich?" she replied softly, annoyed with his lack of kissing her passionately.

"Please don't be angry with me, sweetheart. But you are tired, and I didn't want to keep you from your beauty sleep."

She could do nothing but laugh softly with him. "I have missed you," she finally said.

"Me, too. What does the rest of your year look like? You know, so I can make an appointment to see you."

"Why?"

"Don't you want to go out with me?"

"No, you are too old," she whispered on a grin.

He chuckled. "You must go to bed," he demanded, to which she yawned in reply.

"Mmm, I will, but you could have given me one measly kiss," she whined softly.

"Another time, I promise. Sweet dreams."

"Sweet dreams, and Aldrich?"

"Yes, sweetheart?"

"I will send you my itinerary."

On a laugh, Aldrich said, "Okay, go to bed now." The line went dead.

She sighed and did just that. This time, she had no problem and slept till late the next morning.

When she got to her house, she found it devoid of any human life. Her brothers had bought her a big teddy to congratulate her, which they'd left on her bed. The card attached to its huge red ribbon was signed by both. Two days later, they finally showed up, exhausted from whatever they had been doing. The house filled with sounds as music blasted through the sound system. For the next two days, she enjoyed spending time with them. Since graduating from high school, Anabella and her brothers became good friends. Every time they spent a few hours together, she learned something new about them.

Roy signed up for a financial course at college and excitedly told her about his subjects, showing her his books. She watched as he transformed into a new person right before her eyes. His green eyes were lighter than usual, a smile adorned the handsome face. He was relaxed, and the new girl he'd met in December was a constant companion. Wanda was three years older than Anabella; a lively brunette with big, blue eyes who was a student at the same college Roy was going to attend. She, however, would be studying Human Resources. Wanda was open and friendly and chatted non-stop. The best part was that she really cared for Roy, which pleased her tremendously.

Anabella wasn't privy about how much Wanda knew regarding their life, but she truly hoped that Roy had told her before their parents' return from their business trip.

Derek mostly slept, but when he did join the little group, he was full of jokes. Several times, he would leave for the evening, only to return in the early hours of the morning to find her at the swimming pool, busy with her laps. This was a time

Anabella cherished and although not forthcoming with what he was up to, they spoke easily enough; mainly about her career and studies. He'd always been the one to show more interest in her.

He was a tall, blond man, with eyes the same color as hers; exceptionally well-built, his athletic body lean and well-toned. He was intelligent, too, but it seemed he had no desire to study anything further, seemingly satisfied with the life he lived. But yet, she found some changes had taken place within him, not really noticeable but there beneath the surface, regardless.

Anabella saw Aldrich every night as she was on her break. During the day, she would catch up on projects she had to hand in when classes resumed for the next term. He was always considerate of her time, making sure she did not stay out late. He also always greeted her with a kiss on the forehead, as if she were a small child, which aggravated her no end. She didn't know what to think about this new twist, and he said nothing.

She knew she was still young, something they'd discussed several times. However much she appreciated his control, how wrong could it be to ask for one kiss?

During the nights she was plagued with dreams filled with her parents, brothers and strangers' faces. It was always the same dream. Hands would reach for her, dragging her into their world, or they'd be strangling her, pushing the life out of her lungs. And then she would wake up screaming, gasping for breath. During these episodes, Roy would rush in and calm her down.

When classes started again, the dreams continued and Monica would comfort her, allowing her to cry. Sometimes, they would sit and chat afterward, the dreams too terrifying for Anabella to return to sleep.

One dream especially exhausted her physically and mentally, leaving her drained the next day. This particular one didn't happen often, but when it did it scared her. It always started the same; she'd walk up to her parents' house, and her mother would answer the door with a beautiful smile on her face. People within would greet her, her father though, would stand aside not talking to her, the scowl on his face saying he was angry about something. She couldn't understand why. She was then invited to their bedroom to look at a present they'd bought her, and upon stepping into the room, the door shut with a loud bang and she was covered in darkness. Faces appeared, lights shining directly on their eyes, giving them a ghostly effect. Hands groped, taking her closer to a fast, spinning wheel as someone laughed eerily, and a soft voice tried to calm her as she fought against the hold on her.

The more these dreams haunted her, the harder she worked. Swimming was the perfect escape, filling her with joy, calming her, allowing her to be a young eighteen-year-old student enjoying life. If anyone on the outside looked at her, they would see a well-balanced young woman who had everything the world could offer, but those closest to her knew it wasn't so.

After the championships the previous year, and the three gold medals she brought home, she received a letter from the Olympic Committee informing her she'd been invited to compete in the next Olympics, which would take place in four years. She also swam for the university team. Mr. Clark—her new coach—was very strict, which she didn't mind at all. She had a lot of support from the university, her classmates, friends, and Aldrich. His constant encouragement with either a phone call or text message uplifted her, and gave her the assurance to excel. She received a beautiful bouquet of flowers from his firm after her last championship in March, and in return thanked the partners with a handwritten note.

The last year of student life would be a very busy one, filled with studies and the Olympics simultaneously, the same year she would turn twenty-one. Time was of the essence, and the last thing she needed was her personal life interfering with her future.

How she and Aldrich would come together, she didn't know, but she knew that she missed the teddy bear, his warm arms and those gorgeous lips; dreamy. The void when she'd left his arms the night of the dance was still incredibly real to her.

What Anabella didn't know was that Aldrich was always in the background watching her. Monica would phone him to let him know how she was coping, and his heart would ache with the news. Feelings of protection were especially strong, and all he wanted to do was wrap her in his arms and take away all the hurt he saw.

He kept his distance, knowing full well she wasn't the least bit happy about it, but he wanted her to experience life. Her swimming career would only last a short while, so he was willing to step back and give her the space to shine.

Aldrich was struggling with these thoughts while staring out his office window, when there was a knock on his door. He called for whoever it was to enter, and the senior partner's young PA walked into his office, clearing her voice, drawing his attention back to work.

"Yes, Chaney?" He lifted a dark brow, already annoyed.

"Mr. Dorflinger wants to see you immediately, Aldrich," she said in a seductive voice.

"You could have buzzed me," he replied with irritation, rising to his feet.

"I like to come to your office." She giggled.

This woman was really starting to get on his nerves. Ever since she'd started working at the firm, she'd made her intentions known to him. And although at first he'd been flattered, he quickly learned his mistake; she was not his type. He had told her as much, but still she persisted in coming on to him.

"This is an office, not a dating service, Chaney."

"That's not what you said when you kissed me," she purred, batting her eyelashes.

Aldrich's second mistake. She thought that because of one kiss, he belonged to her. Anabella's image came to mind, which made him miss her even more. He could still feel her next to him; her well-formed, tanned body still alive in his mind's eye, and those legs! He'd dreamed about them a few times. Long, shapely legs that seemed to go on forever.

Chaney touched his arm, bringing him out of his reverie. "When are we going on a date again?"

"Not going to happen." He brushed her away, and then walked to the wall to retrieve his jacket from the hook next to the door.

"Why, didn't you have fun with me?" she whined with a pout, her blue eyes looking up at him innocently. By now, he knew that that was far from the truth. He was familiar with her advances toward every man on the floor.

"It was good for one night, nothing more," he replied, and stepped out of his office.

She followed him in her high heels, saying softly, "That hurts, you know."

He looked down at her, not missing the seductive look behind the hurtful stare, and smirked. Without responding, he stepped past her and into Mr. Dorflinger's office, closing the door behind him.

"You wanted to see me," he announced.

"Aldrich, yes, come in." The man waved him closer, and he walked to the large, mahogany desk in the middle of the office. The thin man looked dwarfed behind his desk, but his powerful presence let everyone know he wasn't to be taken lightly. In the courtroom, he was known for his cunning wit, and for being a worthy opponent.

"I'd like you to meet Ms. Giselle Etsibeth."

Aldrich saw a beautiful woman rise. She greeted him in a soft voice, so delicate it was soothing to the ear. Her short, red hair was cut in the latest style, and her smoldering green eyes looked at him with coyness and arrogance.

He stretched out his hand, taking her proffered hand as he introduced himself.

"Ms. Etsibeth has come to see us about a delicate matter, and as you are the best in the field, I have recommended you to the case."

Aldrich acknowledged the praise with a lopsided grin and sat down in the chair directly in front of him.

"What seems to be the problem?" he asked, and Mr. Dorflinger continued to discuss the case. Ms. Etsibeth's close proximity caused him to not give his full attention to what Mr. Dorflinger was saying.

She was a stunner, but the way she observed him openly and with interest made him uneasy. He'd never felt uneasy with a woman before. He listened, making notes, and every so often when she wanted to draw his attention, she would touch his arm or leg. He would look down into the green pools. The look he saw blatantly told him she wanted him, and not as her lawyer. This put him on guard, which made his body tense.

When they stepped out of Dorflinger's office after an hour long debriefing, Tim came to his rescue since the woman had attached herself to his arm the moment they'd stood and walked out. Reluctantly, she let him go after Tim assured her it was a matter of life and death. The devilish smile on his friend's face told him that he knew the woman was a pest. The clinging sort, one he disliked with fervor.

Both Aldrich and Tim left the office building after he'd said goodbye to the woman.

"Thanks, pal," Aldrich said the moment they sat down in the restaurant, "you saved me. I owe you one."

"You know it, friend. Who was she anyway?"

"New client, a Ms. Giselle Etsibeth."

Tim raised an eyebrow. "You know who she is right?"

"No, not really."

"She is the sole heir to her daddy's textile business in the city," he shared, and paused for effect, declaring, "Tex Style Industries."

"Oh..." Aldrich replied, recognizing the name immediately.

"And she is one of your clients!" Tim announced excitedly, looking at him, grinning. "You really have it bad for the young Anabella, don't you?"

This made Aldrich grin.

"I mean, that woman is beautiful and seemed to cling to you, yet you still managed to think about Anabella."

This time, Aldrich blushed. He couldn't remember the last time he'd blushed with embarrassment. Tim just chuckled as he placed his order with the waiter.

Monica phoned him that morning, informing him of the nightmares Anabella had struggled with the previous night. Upon hearing this, all he had wanted to do was be with her.

On previous occasions when he made it to the pool, his heart had ached for the tired and sad lines evident on her face from all the sleepless nights. He would watch her dive into the pool, relentlessly keeping up the pace, and when she was done practicing she would come out of the water as her sparkling self.

This was what he loved most, her ability to bounce back refreshed, as if nothing was wrong in her world. He wished he knew the whole story, but what he did know was that she didn't want him anywhere close to her house. Not that she was ashamed of him. He didn't get that vibe at all. Period.

He'd once mentioned it to Monica, but all she had said was that Anabella would have to tell him herself, as she wasn't allowed to go near her house, either. She never shared anything further, although he had the distinct impression that she knew more than she let on. Monica was a fine and protective friend, and he knew she had her reasons for not telling him the story.

Many times, he wanted to call her just to hear her beautiful voice, tell her how much he missed her, even how much he desired her. He wanted to go over and press her against his body, just to feel her body next to his. He wanted to comfort her, tell how much he cared about her, but he knew it wasn't the right time to do so. He sensed that there were things she was fighting against. Her mind was obviously occupied with troubled images, which made her act differently than the innocent she really was.

"You need to eat, lunch time is almost over, and," Tim said, bringing him back to the present, "did Monica phone you?"

"I spoke to her this morning, but she did call again and left a message. I haven't called her back yet. Why, what's up?"

"She is organizing a birthday party for Anabella on Saturday. You know she is leaving on Monday?"

"I know she is leaving, yes. I'll be there."

"Same time, same place," Tim said, wiping his mouth clean, while he waited for Aldrich to finish his drink.

One more weekend, then she would be leaving for three months with her coach and the team in order to practice and compete, all in preparation for the Olympics in three year's time. He would not miss the opportunity to see her one last time; the chance to touch her, hold her, and hear her laughter. He was besotted with her, but he needed to step back as everything within him wanted to rush the relationship, impatient with the slow progress. He wanted to feel her under him as she gave herself over to him completely. He wanted to drink from her lips and taste her sweetness until she came, screaming his name in ecstasy.

More than that, he wanted to protect her and spend his days with her. She was a very intelligent young woman, one with diverse interests, and not only in sports, which made her an excellent companion.

Over the past few months, he'd examined himself and noticed that she was constantly on his mind. He wanted to share her life, not merely as a spectator anymore, but rather as a team player. He was very proud of her and her accomplishments. She was driven with purpose, and had become a sportswoman younger people admired, and sport magazines wrote about. Anabella had become an ambassador for swimming, and she fulfilled the role with grace and dignity.

Aldrich's firm was exceptionally enthusiastic on her progress, because the senior partner had been a good swimmer back in his day and still loved the sport, something he still followed passionately.

Aldrich was pleased when he'd heard about the announcement of her acceptance into the Olympic team. He'd been at his father's house that night when the announcement came over the speaker, accompanied by her picture. He turned to his father and said, "That will be your new daughter-in-law one day, if she will have me." Excitement and admiration tangible in his voice.

Later, when the realization hit him regarding his open confession to his father, he reflected long and hard upon it. He loved her. When he'd fallen in love with Pauline, the reaction had been the same; instant. His heart, his mind and body had all worked together to let him know that she was the woman for him. But that had been different, they were the same age, both had careers and both shared the same interests.

With Anabella, it was the complete opposite; they had nothing in common except this uncomely attraction they shared. There was also the age difference, and her innocence. The things she struggled with still stood between them, which kept her at arm's length. Her career—one that was only now blossoming—meant she would be away from home for long periods of time. *How was this ever going to work out for them?*

He would definitely be at her birthday party, anything for a chance to hold her again, even if all they did was dance. Aldrich looked forward to the party, which was taking place within the next two days.

# Chapter Four

The Saturday afternoon—the day of her birthday party—Anabella drove to her house from the gym after a hard training session. When she looked at her watch she saw that she had enough time to rest, wash her hair, and shower. She was tired and really not in a good mood, and as soon as she pulled into the driveway leading up to her house, she sighed.

*Back to normal! Don't these people ever get enough,* she asked herself.

The moment she walked in and closed the front door, noises greeted her, noises that she was dreadfully familiar with. She passed the living room where people were parading around half naked, some already on the stairs on their way to the master bedroom. The small group were intertwined with each other, noticing nothing, only aware of their own little world of pleasure.

Disgusted, she looked on. No one noticed her, not even once. "Oh please, get a room!" she muttered. It was always a shock to see the older people in that way. She blushed as she rushed up the stairs and past the couples who were at the top by now, pressed past them and with disgust, closed the door behind her as they shuffled by her door and into her parents' room right next door. It only took her seconds to decide what to do next. With her mind made up, she grabbed all the stuff she would need to finish preparing for the party in order to get out of there as fast as possible. If they noticed her, it would only spell trouble. And in their state, reasoning was out of the question; one could not reason with animals. She didn't see her brothers anywhere. If anything ever happened, they usually came to her rescue, and if they were not around she needed to get out, immediately.

Once outside her room, she noticed that the hallway was thankfully empty, although she could hear the two couples in her parents' room. The door was closed. *At least some of them have modesty.*

When she walked downstairs, a big, hairy man who was only wearing a shirt, stood at the bottom of the staircase in full view, rubbing himself. His eyes focused on someone in the living room.

She had to get past him, as well as make her away around him, but knew it would be futile since he left no room for her to do just that. She clutched her bag tightly against her body, her clothes draped over her arm, holding it all between them in order to obscure her view. She really didn't want to see.

The moment he noticed her, he grabbed her arm with his free hand and pulled her to him with a grin. His breath reeked of smoke and brandy, and his voice was husky with lust. "Come here, doll," he drawled.

Anabella wanted to shrink in total horror. With her bag, she pushed him away to set herself free, but he managed to grab her breast, ripping two buttons from her shirt. Desperately, she fought hard, not letting go of the bag in her hands. But her clothes fell around her feet, almost tripping her in her haste to get away. By now, she knew she was in trouble. She dug her car keys into his hand, and he released immediately. She managed to pull herself free, running to the front door; her only hope of escape and safety, the bag still clutched in her hand.

"Who was that?" The hairy guy asked gruffly to no one in particular.

"Who was who, honey?" Sandra asked in a saccharine voice as she walked up to him, her curvy body swaying with every move.

"The young brunette. She's pretty," he replied as he rubbed his hand with an angry looking scar on top.

"I believe that would be my daughter," purred Sandra, pressing into him.

"Well, I want that hellcat!"

"How much?"

"Ten thousand rand."

"Deal, it is time for Miss Tight-Ass to be introduced to the family business," she said. In a low voice, she looked up at him and asked, "How about we go to her room? I can give you some pleasure."

"You are a real piece of work, Sandra," he muttered into her neck, and she giggled.

"That is what you love about me." She held out her hand, and together they went up the stairs and disappeared into Anabella's room.

Anabella sat in her car for a while in order to calm down; her body shaking with fear and the sudden rush of adrenaline. Her breast still sensitive from the brute's grab. She tried to cover herself as best she could, but the shirt had been torn at the buttonholes, the material stretched. When she'd calmed down, she wiped the wetness from her cheeks and started the car, driving out of the parking area, totally unaware of the plans her mother had made on her behalf.

She decided to book into a hotel in order to finish getting ready for her party. With trembling hands she continued on her way, every movement almost robotic.

As she pulled up to the hotel, she gave her watch a final glance. After parking her car, she made her way inside and booked herself in. Once in her room, she sat on the bed as tears poured down her face. She felt unclean, and was desperate to rid herself of it all. She started searching for the clothes she'd selected, only to realize they were still on the stairs where she'd dropped them. All she had was what she was wearing; jeans and her torn shirt, which was covered by a denim jacket. She stripped off the offending clothing, as if the clothes were at fault, and stood under the shower for a while, crying into the hot rain that cascaded down her face. She rubbed every part of her body vigorously, allowing for no trace of the brute's invasion. When she was done, she stood with the same clothes in her hands, wishing she had something else to wear. But since there wasn't, she put them on, without a final glance in the tall mirror.

Putting on a fake smile, she walked out of the hotel and past customers without making eye contact. Her silver Corsa was parked right out front, but when she reached it, she couldn't get in. She turned back and hurried inside again, only to sit for a few moments to still her quickened heart. When she calmed down, she once again went through the motions, but this time managed to climb into her car and drive away.

As Anabella rushed up the driveway, Monica immediately knew something was wrong. The moment she heard the engine of the familiar vehicle, she walked to the door and opened it.

Still trembling after her ordeal, she slapped a smile on her face as she made her way past all the parked cars. She was late for her own party, but she knew her friend would understand. Due to what had taken place at her parents' house, she hadn't been able to finish getting ready. The incident kept playing over and over in her mind as tears continued to flow steadily down her face.

Aldrich had been watching the driveway when she pulled in, and noticed the fake smile and the slumped shoulders the moment she stepped out of her car, as if she were in pain. He had been standing at the window, waiting since he arrived to get the first look. Immediately seeing something was wrong, he walked to the door, pushed Monica out of the way and took Anabella in his arms.

Monica said nothing.

Aldrich picked Anabella up like a little girl and held her close to him; he could feel her tears soaking his shirt. She was tense and shaking, and his heart clenched in pain for her.

Soft kisses rained over her cheek as he tried to comfort her with encouraging words. "You are safe, Bella, you are safe," he assured her softly. *What has upset her so much for her to be in this state,* he couldn't help wondering.

They went inside and walked to the living room, away from the curious partygoers. The music overwhelmed the air with a steady beat. Monica stood very close to them, speaking to Anabella in a soft voice.

Aldrich could hear everything.

"Are your parents busy again?"

Anabella moved her head in agreement on his shoulder. Aldrich's mind raced, while his eyes held questions as he searched Monica's own blue eyes for understanding. But she looked away. Frustrated, he continued to hold Anabella, rubbing her back to relax her.

Later, after the crying had stopped, Monica motioned for him to put her down. He reluctantly let go, but was flabbergasted over her reaction to the situation.

*Who hurt her so much?* Aldrich was stumped. She looked stressed, fragile and upset, which in turn made him upset.

Monica took her upstairs to freshen up, and silence fell throughout the house, the music was turned down and everyone wanted to know what was going on; the guests speaking softly between each other.

Tim made his way over to Aldrich where he sat bent over, arms resting on his thighs, hands formed into fists. With sorrowful eyes, he looked up at Tim and pleaded, "I don't understand, will someone please tell me what is going on?"

Tim crouched down before his best friend and spoke softly, "When Anabella is ready, she will tell you, but steel yourself as it is not a pretty story. I don't know everything, but the little I do know is that her parents are bastards."

Aldrich's eyes became slits; weary, angry and agitated with these parents he didn't know.

"Meanwhile, you need to be tolerant. She needs a lot of understanding and patience. You are doing a great job, which tells me you are the right man and that you care about her."

"Still, this is upsetting. I mean look at her. In two days, she is leaving for America. I can't let her go if she looks like that."

"Maybe this is perfect timing for her," Tim reasoned, "as she will have the chance to be herself again, and be safe. Anywhere away from her house is safe at this point."

"Okay, Tim. If you say so, I have no choice but to believe you." He sighed.

*What have I become involved in?*

Mr. Richter managed to inject life back into the party after he'd discussed it with Anabella, who'd assured him that they mustn't stop. The music vibrated throughout the house once again and a little later, Monica and Anabella came down and chatted; her beautiful face radiant with a bright smile.

Anabella looked stunning in a sleeveless, rich-cream dress that hit just above the knees, and black sandals, which showed off her tan. She was slenderly built, something that confused her competitors who underestimated the strength in that body. Overall, she created a beautiful picture.

Everyone greeted her the moment she joined them; the Anabella they knew and liked. Although they were curious, they kept their questions at bay, and for that she was grateful. She searched through the crowd for one particular man, and when she finally found him, she sparkled. A blush spread over her face; ashamed of the state he had found her in, but when Aldrich opened his arms there was no judgment.

Willingly, she stepped into his warm embrace, the same arms that had held her protectively earlier, and he gave her a kiss on the forehead. It had become his custom since they met. He battled with this for a long time and knew that if he continued to want to take her as he wanted, it would just complicate things more. Which she didn't need.

She lifted her face to receive more than just a peck, but he brushed her face instead with his thumb, studying her as his eyes roamed over it. Eyes layered with questions he shielded carefully.

However, reading him correctly, she reached up and whispered, "I am okay, thank you."

He smiled faintly. Aldrich was thankful for the transformation; in the place of a sad and fearful little girl was a beautiful young lady full of confidence. He still wanted to know what had upset her, but he would have to be patient with her until she was willing to open up to him. He'd had a traumatic past, something he never talked about. Therefore, he respected her silence. After all, they had known each other for only a year, and it was not as if they spent a lot of time with each other to talk about personal issues.

One thing that stood out very strongly in Aldrich, was the need to protect her against whatever it was she faced. She had grown more mature in the past year, making her more attractive and looking older than her nineteen years. She still had a long way to go in growing up, and he wasn't getting any younger.

For a brief moment, the redhead, Giselle Etsibeth, filtered through his thoughts. Just the day before she'd been at his office, clinging to his arm as they'd discussed the case she wanted him to handle. She was everything that Anabella wasn't. She was his age, was even willing and ready, but something about her prevented him from becoming too acquainted with her, as she would have liked.

Giselle had invited him for lunch at her apartment in the city as soon as business was wrapped up. He'd gone reluctantly, but was glad to find her father there, although that hadn't stopped her. She'd given him all of her attention, practically sitting on his lap the entire time her father spoke to him. Aldrich couldn't find it in himself to be rude to her, but he'd definitely been uncomfortable.

And today, he found Anabella in a state, and the question he'd asked himself earlier raised itself once again. *What have I involved myself in?*

He came from a loving family, and he had hoped that he, too, would someday have the same relationship as his parents had had up until his mother passed away ten years ago. His father hadn't been, and was not interested in anyone else. There were many women who'd tried to catch his attention because his dad was a first-class catch, but for him it had always been Sarah. His two sisters' marriages were solid, and they were very happy. So far, that same happiness eluded him, but he was more than ready to settle down.

For the rest of the night, he made sure he stayed close to her. His urge to protect her against anything that tried to go against her was enormous. He was enjoying watching her every movement, every flex of her muscles, and the delightful smile curled around her lips. He enjoyed watching her small hand pick up a strand of hair, and then placing it behind her ear. Elegant and graceful; she was everything he wanted. At times, he had to control himself and refrain from touching her, because if he did, he would forget all about his self-discipline. He just couldn't be the hard-ass attorney he was known for in the court room; indifferent and uncaring when handling a case.

This is how she affected him, brought out his true nature so that he acted differently. He was sure his emotions were openly on display, and did Aldrich care that everyone knew? No, would be the correct deduction.

Anabella noticed that Aldrich was distant, as if his thoughts were preoccupied, but he watched her every move with brooding eyes. Every time she looked around their eyes would meet, and she would give him a shy smile. She enjoyed the quiet strength that emanated from him, his manly smell and his sound, authoritative voice. People listened intensively when he spoke. *Gorgeous*, she always thought.

Monica had been watching the interaction between the two; Aldrich's reluctance to get closer as he stayed in the background, though the attraction between the two was evidently mutual. His eyes were tentative and brooding as he followed Anabella's movements. She could understand why. Whatever was going on, it didn't hide the fact that they would make a lovely couple.

Tim had told her that Aldrich was taking it very slow because of the age difference, and because he wanted her to enjoy varsity without any complications from his side. He'd also mentioned that the situation at Anabella's house confused him, and he wasn't sure what to think about it all.

Monica couldn't blame Aldrich. It was hard to understand her friend's life and the way they lived. Anabella would have to trust him first, and then she would bring him up to speed and as her friend, she couldn't break the valuable trust they'd had in each other for years. But after today, things could change for the better. She hoped. Except for the nightmares, Aldrich knew nothing at all. She wondered how long he would tolerate being in the dark. He was ready to move on, that much she knew, and she wondered if he'd leave Anabella if someone better came along. She really hoped not as they were perfect for each other. There was definite electricity between them, and it would be no problem to help them along in the right direction if need be.

Again, Monica gave Tim the queue and a song started immediately.

She watched as Aldrich held out his hand to Anabella, and how she accepted without hesitation. She smiled at the couple until they were swept away on to the dance floor, and then she lost sight of them.

Aldrich didn't let her go during the songs, but instead pulled her closer to him. His soft, shaven skin brushed against her cheek and she loved the feel of him. His masculine smell filled her senses; crisp, clean and all him. His shiny hair begged her to run her fingers through its thickness, and without thought she did just that. She drew his head closer, and he responded to her by placing a kiss on her cheek; soft and gentle and full of emotion behind it. However, he wasn't yet able to reveal his true feelings.

Again, Anabella found herself in his arms, just like the first time they'd danced together, a year ago, as she trailed a finger down his neck. His heart thumped against her, and she heard him take a sharp, deep breath.

Her forwardness startled her at times, but she was enthralled with everything about him. That he didn't move away gave her the confidence to explore more, enjoying the proximity the music and night provided. For the next few songs, they didn't break contact and enjoyed each other's closeness, content to just be; both knowing the feeling was mutual.

Whoever happened to look at them sensed the growing attraction. As a couple they complimented each other very well, she the dark-haired brunette, and he the dark blond hunk of a man. They melted together as one.

Aldrich found it hard to control himself around the young woman in his arms. Her warm breath on his neck, the feel of her fingers in his hair and skin. He had to concentrate, or he'd drag her away and do with her as he pleased. His body screamed for gratification. It had been a while since he'd had a woman, and ever since she entered the picture, the mere thought of finding someone else, even temporarily to relieve the ache, didn't enter his mind.

By no means had he become a monk after Pauline's death, but to hold back was gratifying, knowing that the wait would be worth it in the end. Although she relaxed in his arms, he had the common sense to know that she wasn't ready for anything more than what they were doing right then. To hasten her in any act of lovemaking would have the opposite effect. But, because he was still a man who loved to have a beautiful woman in his arms, he couldn't let the opportunity pass; he had to have one last kiss before she went away.

By the fourth song, the lights were dimmed, and Aldrich pulled her closer, steering her to a dark spot in the corner of the patio. He wanted to be alone with her for a while. He wanted to kiss her, time was wasting away. With a finger, he lifted her head and found her lips waiting for his. He kissed her, at first soft, lingering kisses. A year had passed since the last time he'd given himself the luxury of doing this. He wanted her to be comfortable around him. As the mood changed from familiarity to passion, the kiss grew in intensity. The taste of her mouth intoxicated him and his hands wandered, resting on and gripping her slender hips. He couldn't draw her close enough, his eagerness overwhelming them both.

Anabella enjoyed every stroke of his tongue, making soft, pleasurable noises as it explored her sensual lips. She had longed to kiss him for so long. His arms held her tight against his body, his broad chest concealing them from curious looks. She felt his hands move, then coming to rest on her hips. To feel his strong hands and fingers on her only encouraged her to explore him in return. He intoxicated her senses.

Minutes passed where they were totally lost in each other's embrace, but Aldrich knew he had to stop. His mind and body, however, were not in agreement. He needed her. He buried a hand in her long, dark tresses and held her head so that he could see how far he'd be allowed to explore her body. He needed to know what was acceptable to her.

He cared for her, that much he knew. And as she gave of herself to him, the desire in his heart grew. His hand probed until it touched her breast; she didn't move away. He touched it softly, as if it were something very delicate, enjoying the feelings it invoked in him, and her, as she approved. Ever so softly, she released a moan as she wrapped her arms around his neck, and he knew that she felt the same. Still, he knew it had to stop. Deep down, he knew he required more than just this fleeting moment with her and as hard as it was, he had to push her away.

"We need to stop," he whispered in her ear, his mind in control once again. She smiled at him, and he grinned in return. "If we keep this up, I can only think of one place I want to take you." He sounded out of breath and a chuckle escaped her.

Anabella's heart pounded in her ears, she wanted to get lost in him. For a year she'd thought he'd turned cold toward her, making her unsure, but tonight he'd shown her that whatever was between them was still as powerful as the first time they'd met.

The images of the man stroking himself and what had happened that afternoon were vivid in her mind, and although she'd been disgusted by it all, it had planted a seed of want in her, and here in Aldrich's arms it was playing havoc with her body. The soft moans of the woman in her father's arms had excited her, and she could feel the need to open up to the man in her arms. She wanted to feel what that woman felt, but then he spoke, breaking the perfect moment. The images came to an abrupt stop. She stepped away and turned to leave, ashamed and embarrassed with herself and what she had allowed him to do. Her mind was in turmoil.

He reached out, but when she looked up at him, desire was written all over her face, her eyes dark pools, inviting him in. Her innocence had made way for something perverse, a look he didn't understand. Startled, he tried to grasp her again, but before he said a word, she stepped back, her eyes downcast, leaving him at a loss for words once again. His arms fell to his sides, and he had to take a few deep breaths to get himself under control. He followed the slender figure past the guests, into the living room, baffled with the change he was seeing, as well as her sudden departure. He hoped he hadn't done anything wrong to have affected her this way.

Anabella knew she had to leave. The visuals of her parents and their friends, as well as what they were doing, was still very much alive within her. It flooded her mind; she wanted what they had. Her body screamed for satisfaction. She wanted to hold him; her hands had already examined his narrow hips and his broad shoulders, the thickness of his hair, the feel of his skin; all now ingrained in her. He wanted her, of that she was sure, she'd felt his reaction toward her.

But that wasn't how she wanted it. The fight for control to regain her composure had left her shaken. She would not allow herself to give into her want, simply because it was born out of lust—not love. She knew the difference between the two, even if she didn't understand. When she eventually gave herself, it would be out of love. To be out of control like her parents were would mean that they had won, and she'd never give them that satisfaction. Their lifestyle disgusted her. Her first need was to clear her head and determine where Aldrich fitted in. She cared about him, but was it the real thing? One thing she wasn't interested in was to compromise over anything except real love. She wasn't interested in a relationship like her parents'. Anabella wanted what she had seen between Mr. and Mrs. Richter, the deep abiding love of mutual respect and devotion to one another.

It was late anyway, and she had to get back to her hotel room, needing some time to think about her feelings for Aldrich.

The moment she left, Monica followed. She could see the conflicted emotions playing over her face, and the heartache in Aldrich's features. Both were in pain for whatever had transpired between them. Monica caught up with her in the living room. She could not let her leave before she was convinced everything was okay with her friend. She remembered the conversation they had that afternoon and asked, "Where are you staying tonight? I take it you will not go back to your parents' house?" Anabella was very proud, and Monica knew she'd better not to ask her to stay, but she had to be certain that she would be safe.

"I have booked into a hotel close by," she whispered softly, at the same time avoiding her eyes.

Just then, she realized Aldrich had followed her and overheard the hotel part. His brow was furrowed with concern.

"What is this I hear about a hotel?" He queried sternly, annoyed, but kept his voice low. A few people stood around them, so he took her aside. Startled, she turned to face him and paled. For a moment, she'd forgotten about Aldrich, not even thinking he'd follow but there he was, right behind her.

"It's nothing," she stammered. She didn't want him to know and now that he did, she felt even more ashamed. Her eyes pleaded with him, but she could see it was futile.

Aldrich stood there with a very determined look on his face, the grip on her arm unyielding as he waited for an answer.

She wanted to shrink away with embarrassment. She looked to Monica helplessly.

"Answer me, please," Aldrich demanded, impatiently.

"She has booked into a hotel for the night." Monica gave in.

Stunned, Anabella looked at her, and Monica returned her look with *sorry* written all over her face.

"Why, sweetheart?" Still, he demanded an answer, and as the endearment slipped out, her eyes met his, shimmering with unshed tears.

"Please, I don't want to talk about this."

He watched her closely and saw that the sadness and desperation he'd seen that afternoon had returned. He knew that this wasn't mere rebellion of a spoiled teenager; what he saw was fear. He couldn't help but wonder why a woman as young as Anabella was against returning to her parents' house. Something was definitely wrong. However, he decided that this wasn't the time to be soft. "There is no way you will stay in a hotel. You will stay with me, and that's final." Forcefully, he allowed no room for any backchat. "Come, get your things, you are going home with me, sweetheart."

She wanted to object, but he was very clear that this wasn't open for discussion.

With a firm grip, he pulled her along and up the stairs in order to retrieve the bag she'd brought with her, and once done he pushed her to the door with a soft nudge in the small of her back after they said goodbye to everyone.

"I will follow you in my car. Lead the way, please."

He walked with her to her Clio and when she was inside, he turned to a black BMW, one of the newer models she couldn't make out because of the darkness. The electronic watch on the dashboard showed it was 12:30am.

She couldn't believe what had taken place. He'd taken charge, and for once she was okay with it. She had allowed another person to decide for her. A man who only had her safety in mind; it was a comfortable feeling, albeit one she wasn't used to.

He followed her to the hotel. Once inside, his features were unchanged as he walked into the lobby with her and waited. Looking around, Aldrich thought it looked decent enough, but he was adamant that this wasn't the place for her. He grimaced at the thought of her being here all alone as a drunk stumbled against him. While she went upstairs, he paid her bill and once she was back, her complexion looked fragile and forlorn. He wanted to wrap her in his arms to comfort her, but he kept to himself as they made their way back to their respective cars.

At her open window, he bent down to speak with her. "Just follow me, sweetheart." She nodded, although he could see she was trying really hard to be brave. He touched her cheek in reassurance. "Give me a smile."

She looked up at him, giving him a lopsided grin, but her eyes were swimming with tears.

"That's my girl." His eyes scanned her lovely face, missing nothing before he walked to his own car, which was parked right behind hers. He pulled out first, with Anabella not far behind as she followed him to his home.

She watched the dark figure closely, and observed his every move.

He did the same, his eyes occasionally flicking to the rearview mirror, making sure she followed.

She still didn't know much about him; only that he was older than she was, unmarried, a lawyer, and a good friend of Tim's. She had to admit that because they didn't spend a lot of time with each other, they didn't know one another as they should have. She thought that she was probably to be blamed for it, because she hadn't exactly made it easy for him, plus her schedule had kept her busy. On Sunday night she'd be on her way again for three months, and once again they would be apart, each busy with their own lives.

She couldn't help but ask herself if Aldrich would be fine with it.

Thinking about Aldrich and how the evening had gone, she knew he wanted more, but she wasn't ready. Her schedule was going to prevent them from growing any closer, or even become a couple. *Are we a couple,* she pondered. *Can I hope for more?* She knew he liked her and made an effort to visit her when he could, but other than that they were just acquaintances. Nothing more.

After what seemed like only ten minutes, they stopped in front of a five-story, modern brick building briefly, and then Aldrich turned into an underground garage, passing two rows of cars before he turned and stopped in the furthest corner. She parked next to him. The lift was two parking lots away. A dim light marked it clearly.

Aldrich got out, closed his door and walked to her side where he opened the door for her. He then took out her bags and directed her to the lift.

She felt awkward, so avoided his eyes.

He was silent. The stern look on his face told her he wasn't happy.

Anabella could only imagine what was going through his mind.

He pressed the button, but they didn't wait long before the doors opened and they stepped in. He pressed the P on the panel, and the doors closed behind them. He did, however, take her hand in his while they waited, the bag over his shoulder.

"Are you okay?" he asked softly.

Anabella nodded, not trusting her voice. She leaned into him seeking his warmth and shelter. His calmness was working wonders for her frail emotions.

When the doors opened, it led them directly inside a spacious apartment.

Aldrich looked down at her and smiled. "Welcome to my home."

# Chapter Five

At first, she could see that this was a man's apartment; no woman's touch was evident. It was decorated with comfort and class in mind, no expense spared. He walked ahead of her to the door on their left and opened it, putting her bag inside, and then switched on the lights. The soft light revealed a beautiful room decorated in cream. It looked peaceful and tranquil, and the bed invited her into its soft embrace.

This was the closest she had ever been to him and she liked it, even if it was under these circumstances. To see first-hand where he lived, and to be more acquainted with the man she deeply cared for was important to her.

"Do you want some tea before we turn in for the night?"

"Yes, that will be nice."

Together, they walked to the modern open plan kitchen with dark, wooden cabinets, which were well-stocked with modern stainless steel appliances, all in the correct places; everything of the best on the market.

"You have a lovely apartment," she said, and for the first time since they'd left the party, she smiled brightly with a keen interest to learn more about him. "Did you do all the decorating yourself?"

"Thanks, and no, my sisters helped but they assured me they wouldn't do the 'womanly thing'. There was a time in my life I wanted no reminders of anything feminine." For a few seconds, a sad look covered his face before it was gone.

Anabella wondered who had hurt him so much. "Well, it is beautiful and cozy," she admitted softly.

Aldrich smiled appreciatively as he finished with the tea. "Let's go and sit down." He directed her to the living room where they sat down. When they were comfortable, he handed her a cup of tea while taking a seat opposite her.

He distanced himself from her, and she felt alone for the first time since they'd met. Gone was the playful banter, the gentle touch of his embrace. This was a new turning point in their relationship, meaning, if they had one at all after tonight. Her insecurities flared up, preventing her from meeting his eyes as he searched for answers. An uncomfortable silence fell between them. All she could do was stare at the cup in her hand. She wasn't ready for the conversation she was sure would come, or for the rejection that would follow. She couldn't bear the thought if he walked away, and right out of her life.

"Are you cold?" he asked, his tone not reflecting his inner turmoil as he watched her from where he sat.

"No, I am fine. The tea is lovely."

Although he seemed relaxed, she saw the muscle in his jaw flex. There were obviously questions going through his mind, and she swallowed back the fear that threatened to overwhelm her.

When Aldrich finished his tea, he placed the cup on the table and sat back, looking pointedly at her. He then said, "Tell me about your parents."

It was the one question she feared most. She'd always managed to avoid the question with others, but with Aldrich it wouldn't be possible. Maybe it was because of what they felt for each other—the kiss they had shared still on her lips—or maybe it was because of what he did for a living. Either way, she had to answer, but that wasn't quite correct. She wanted to respond. She wanted him to understand what she was up against. She needed to share her secrets with him, and hopefully he would stay. If he did, they could then start this relationship free of any baggage, and on a clean slate. Still, it took her time to gather all her courage in order to open up to him and explain what her parents were about, but most importantly; the impact they had made in her life.

"Tell me about your parents, sweetheart. You never talk about them. I need to understand this, whatever this is. What happened tonight to upset you so much?" He leaned forward, giving her his undivided attention, his eyes narrowed in concentration, and Anabella wondered if this was the look he afforded all his clients. It was a look that brooked no nonsense.

She swallowed once again, her throat already dry and she hadn't even spoken yet.

Aldrich saw raw emotion on her face as she struggled to find the right words. He wanted to go to her, sit next to her and assure her that it would be fine. However, he had to keep his distance in order to help her, and when she was done he would discern how best to help. It didn't matter what her story was, his feelings would not change. He cared for her deeply. He did not repeat the question again but waited for her to talk, determined to hear what was bothering her.

When she started to speak, it was very soft, and he had to lean forward to hear her.

"At the age of ten, I realized that our home life wasn't the same as other kids. Things happened in my house that I didn't understand, or could explain. I never saw it at Monica's house, and I was confused at the differences in our homes.

Over weekends, and some weeknights, when people came over, I wasn't allowed to go down and visit with them. Usually, they were groups of twenty people or less that filled the living room. When it was smaller groups, they would disappear into my parents' bedroom. I never met these people. I heard their voices accompanied by unfamiliar sounds. I was mostly kept in the dark and never allowed to ask questions, because Mother and Father would reprimand me in their sternest voices. It was my two elder brothers' task to keep me busy and put me to bed.

In the mornings when I'd go down, the house was a complete mess, and I smelled the most disgusting odors I didn't like. Even when I tried to speak to my brothers they wouldn't explain a thing." Her hands clamped together as he kept a close watch, his face blank.

By now her hands were shakier, and he noticed how she kept clenching them together, but he left her and waited for her to continue. He sensed her willingness, even though he knew how hard opening up must be. Never before had she talked about this, and it was time for her to open herself up in order to let them in.

"By the time I was fifteen, I was told to join them and sit quietly on a chair in the corner of the living room. I had to watch and learn, but wasn't allowed to ask questions. My parents and brothers, and every person that was present, would strip naked and kiss one another. By then Roy was twenty years old, and Derek eighteen.

I was shocked at the display, and found myself openly staring at these people, especially my parents and brothers whom I had never seen naked before; their casualness with each other as they enjoyed one another's bodies was mind boggling. I was embarrassed, didn't want to continue looking, but at the same time I was curious. Sometimes, Father would leave with a couple, other times it was Mother. I remember gasping in shock when my brother and father both took a young redhead together as they pleasured her, while she did the same with them.

When the sounds became intense, I tried to cover my eyes with my hands, but either my mother or father would remove them, assuring me that it was all right, that it was natural and beautiful. These people, along with my parents, orally pleasured each other, their faces eventually turning from pleasure to beastly lust; they were ugly to me. It was the first time I'd seen it, but recognized it for what it was." Anabella paused, taking a few deep breaths.

"The first time I threw up next to the chair was when I saw my Mother tied up as they spanked her while she screamed. I tried to stop them, but one man told me that it was okay, that that was exactly what she wanted. When I looked at her face, I watched in horror as one of the men laughed at her, and she pleaded for more while grinning. I wanted to run and when I tried to do just that, people would block my path, leaving me no choice but to watch as they played the scene out.

That entire weekend, they kept up the same pace. From time to time, I would fall asleep on the couch while they were busy. During their breaks, they drank of the liquor provided, ate food that was brought in, and smoked weed." She grew silent as tears rolled down her face.

Aldrich ached to comfort her, fists clenched at the enormity of the shocking things she'd had to endure. He had heard of these things, was even curious at times, but he never thought that her parents had forced her to watch. That was sick.

"I had no ordinary teenage life. It was ripped from me, and these images were and are imprinted within me. My dreams are haunted by them non-stop."

She shivered uncontrollably and he realized the enormous strain she was under. He saw how very uncomfortable she was as the tears continued to stream down her face. Because he couldn't stand it any longer, he stood up and went to sit next to her, although he still had to restrain himself from reaching out to gather her into his arms. Instead, he took hold of her hands and held them. By now, he was angry and disgusted at these people, but was careful not to show her what he was feeling.

*What kind of people are these? Who does this to children?* He was all for kinky stuff, like any average person, but to force a child to watch as their parents had sex with multiple partners harbored on abuse, and it was unacceptable.

From deep down, she gathered strength and continued with her story. The fact that Aldrich had moved closer eased her frantic heart and gave her hope. "By the time I turned sixteen, they wanted me to join by removing my clothes so that someone could touch me. However, my brothers came to my rescue, forcefully stopping them. They told these people that I was only fourteen, although I looked older. Mother never argued the point, but by then she was usually too far in a haze to care." She grinned crookedly, and met his eyes for a moment.

He smiled reassuringly.

"By then, I was involved with sports—an escape from the life at home, when at all possible. I did anything to avoid the house, especially over weekends. When I was home, I would lock my door, preventing drunken men from trying their luck, but my brothers were always nearby to save me. My parents were never open for discussion about this lifestyle. As a result, we stopped speaking to one another a long time ago."

It became quiet in the room as yet more tears poured down her cheeks. She cried softly, placing her hands on her face. It went without saying that she felt ashamed and filthy, and she couldn't look at him out of fear of his rejection.

With difficulty, he continued to hold himself back and asked, "What happened this afternoon?" He kept his voice even.

A heavy sigh escaped her, and she continued in a shaky voice. "I walked into the house to get ready for the party; an orgy was taking place. Not once did they acknowledge my presence. It's been a year since I've been home; apparently, they didn't miss me." A dry sob left her lips at their apparent rejection, and at that point she looked older than most teenagers her age. That she had remained innocent was a godsend.

"When I came down the stairs, a naked man—older than my father—stood at the bottom masturbating as he watched another couple. I tried to bypass him, but he grabbed me. I struggled to free myself while holding my bag between us. During the struggle, he grabbed my breast with a paw-like grip and pain ripped through me, so I jabbed my car keys into his hand and he let go. I ran, hearing him yell something about a hellcat, but I closed the door quickly, shutting him down effectively."

By now, she was crying uncontrollably. Aldrich couldn't handle it anymore and in one smooth motion, moved her on to his lap and held her firmly. Her head was buried in his neck and with every sob, she shuddered against him. They sat like that until his legs became numb, but he didn't care, he wanted to remove all those memories and comfort her.

Eventually, she became silent and sat up straight, brushing away the tears, by now completely self-conscious and filled with doubt while trying to avoid looking at him as best she could. She felt small and lost, like a child who didn't know where he or she belonged, dispossessed of all her carefully built walls as they tumbled down around her with a silent crash. She was tired, weary, and ashamed.

*What will he do? Will he leave me?*

Panicked, she could only watch as he placed her back on the couch without a word, stood and walked toward a closed door, opened it and went inside. After a few minutes, he came back with a warm cloth and wiped her face. He wiped away all the filth and shame she felt. His actions were tender, his eyes showing how much he cared, and she felt relieved. He held out his hand, and the moment she placed her hand in his he lifted her and wrapped her in his arms. Her heart pounded as she nestled into him, appreciating the safety he offered, making her relax. This was a safe haven.

Aldrich knew he had to hold her, yet at the same time hide the rage he felt within; his body shook with wrath toward these people. Instead of love and support, they had rejected her, and she had desperately tried to hold on. He had to be that someone. Now, more than ever, he was convinced that he cared for her, just having her at his house felt right. Her body was pressed against his, and he held her closer, inhaling her sweet fragrance. With her head on his shoulder, he placed chaste kisses on her forehead and face. He wanted to be the one to protect her. With all his heart, he wanted to be that special someone in her life.

"Bella," his voice sounded hoarse to his own ears. He lifted her chin and looked at her with so much love that tears began to run down her face again; quiet tears. He comforted her with soft-spoken words, her eyes fixated on his lips as she heard every word he said.

"You know I care about you?"

She nodded in confirmation.

"I want us to be more than just friends." He kissed the tip of her nose, and she smiled her thoughts joyously.

*There is no rejection... he cares for me.* Relief vibrated through on that thought; his sincerity enveloping her heart and soul in happiness. Elated, she reached up and touched his face in disbelief. He stopped and looked at her, and Anabella melted into him. Their souls became one in that instant.

"I want to know if this will be acceptable to you."

"Yes, more than anything, Aldi," she whispered, and then giggled openly. "Are you my boyfriend now?"

To which he grinned. He enjoyed the youthful teasing and the smile that now adorned her face.

"It seems that I am. I really like you."

He kissed her first on the lips and then on her eyelids, from her cheeks back to her lips, all feather-like, but she wanted more and pressed in closer, opening her mouth and kissing him passionately. She enjoyed him so much, knowing with absolute certainty that he was the man she would give herself to. She loved him. The thought caused her to swoon in his arms. She turned so that she straddled his body with the greatest of ease, opening herself up. Her blood rushed through her veins at what seemed like 120 km an hour; her ears ringing with pure pleasure. She felt him as he reacted beneath her, his hands gliding over her bottom, warm to the touch.

His mouth was intoxicating as she delved in. Never had she kissed a man before. Not like this. It was a pure act that connected them deeply. This kiss was like hunger pangs that needed to be fed. Her body, her mind, and her heart were into it fully. She wanted to feel his bare skin on hers, and with one hand she began to loosen some of the buttons on his shirt, anxious to get close. When she touched his skin, warm sensations flooded her whole body, and she could feel warmth build up between her inner thighs; she became moist with pleasure.

Images flooded her mind, and she wanted to award herself with the temptations of them. She wanted to experience it, to feel a man deep inside her. She forced herself upon him with greater desire, as if someone else had taken over. Her body was pumping with energy as she moved rhythmically on him. She was all over him, showering him with kisses as she touched every part of him that she could. She wanted this, needed this, was desperate to get closer to him.

Aldrich had his own struggles; at first he enjoyed the onslaught of her hungry mouth, which only fueled his own desire. He indulged in the fire and pace she set for a while. It had been a long time since he had been with any woman, and he was definitely not cold toward her. He'd wanted her from the moment he'd seen her for the first time.

But something was not right, his gut was sending off warning bells, yelling for him to stop. It continued persistently. *This is not the way!*

He could sense a different person in his arms, not the innocent and sweet Anabella, the one he deeply cared for. This person was almost cold and distant, without real passion, something that didn't fit her at all. She was all over him, and it drove him to places he didn't want to explore at this moment. Not like this. He had to stop; he couldn't maintain his fiery emotions any longer. It wouldn't be the best thing for either of them. She needed to heal first before they could continue. He would only make love to the woman he cared for; this wasn't his Anabella.

He grabbed her arms, pushing her from him gently. Out of breath, they looked at each other as desire continued to smolder in their eyes. His shirt hung open, pulled loose from his trousers; her dress was unzipped, revealing a lacy undergarment that looked simply stunning on her. He wanted to pull her back, but knew it would be futile. He had to let go of her, and besides the intensity of the moment, she was after all a guest in his house. He'd taken her away from her situation to help her, not to complicate things further.

He cupped her face, and said in a strained voice, "Please know I am not rejecting you. You understand why we had to stop, don't you?"

Anabella took in a deep breath, her eyes becoming a clear green. She looked at her surroundings and blushed. With a nod, she said, "Yes, I do understand." Her voice was strained, and her body felt like it had turned red from head to toe.

Aldrich smiled as he appreciated the sight of his sweet Bella. To him, she was adorable like this.

How could he resist? Foolish he knew, but this was for the best. "It's time we both get a good nights sleep, and then we will discuss this further in the morning. All right, Bella?"

The term of endearment warmed her heart, especially after what had just taken place. He could have taken advantage of the situation and been with her in that way. After all, she could still feel his arousal against her, but he hadn't and she loved him all the more for it. "It is. Thank you, Aldrich." Shyly, she stood up and stepped back, holding her dress against her body. She turned around and walked to her room, closing the door behind her. Leaning her head against the door, she just stood there in order to still her heart and mind, yet relaxed in the knowledge that she was with him, and that he hadn't abandoned her as she thought he would. Not even after he heard her story. She smiled, all giddy with his assurance and commitment toward her.

Aldrich sat back once Anabella's bedroom door closed, his breath still uneven. What just happened had been too close for comfort, and as a result his body still ached. He couldn't remember the last time he had wanted a woman so much; there was nothing for it but a cold shower. He smiled into the darkness, thinking about how fiery she was, and that he couldn't wait to have her, to finally unleash the passion within her and take her places he knew they both would love. He heard her move around inside her room, and when he noticed the light go off from underneath the door, he got up and made his way to his own bedroom.

Both lay in bed with thoughts rushing through their minds. Anabella very much ashamed with her behavior, and Aldrich angry toward the people he'd never met. Never had he thought that people such as they were, could ever be aloud to have children. Did they not have a clue as to how much damage they were doing? He couldn't help but wonder about something this important. Frustrated, he punched his pillow, turned on his side and willed himself to sleep.

Eventually, Anabella fell asleep, only to fall into a deep pit where hands pulled her into its black depths, deeper and deeper with a laugh so wretched, it scared her. She felt trapped, fought desperately against the pull, grabbing at thin air. She screamed when lips covered her body. She tried desperately to push them away, but then hands grabbed her once again, wanting to hold her down, making her thrash around. She was shaken with fear.

"Anabella? Anabella, it's me."

She heard a voice through the eerie laughter and screams, but couldn't place it.

"It's me, wake up, Bella, wake up."

A strong, determined voice called to her from the depths in which she found herself. Finally opening her eyes, although terrified at first, she focused and looked up into Aldrich's face; the face she loved dearly.

"Shhh, now. It was only a dream. It's okay, *you're* okay. Don't be scared, Bella, I'm here. I'll protect you," Aldrich whispered. He got onto the bed and continued to speak softly, not wanting to scare her even further. He drew her closer so that she now rested in the crook of his arm, her body soft and warm against his, the tank top she'd worn to bed all wrinkled and rolled up around her midriff as she pressed against him. Her skin covered in a sheen of perspiration.

To him, all that mattered was calming her down, even though seeing her in his arms in this manner set his heart galloping. "Go to sleep, little one. I'll stay with you."

She relaxed against him and fell asleep soon after.

When he was sure she was truly asleep, he whispered, "I love you..." in her hair before he placed a kiss on the top of her head. He fell asleep with her still in his arms.

The sun streamed into the room, painting it a bright amber, its rays touching the bed Aldrich and Anabella lay on. Simultaneously, they woke and felt each other's presence at once, but stayed in the same position, too afraid to disturb the closeness they shared. His arm was draped over her body as he held her close, and shyly Anabella followed the muscles stringing up it with the tips of her fingers. In response, Aldrich's long fingers traced the length of her arm, making her snuggle deeper into his neck.

She smiled. "Hi, boyfriend of mine."

He chuckled, the bed vibrating as a result.

Anabella grinned, and kissed his fingers softly. The closeness they had shared was the most special experience she had ever had. Never in a million years would she have thought she'd lay in bed with him. Not like this. He was everything she wanted in a man, ever the handsome hunk with his tousled hair and day old stubble. Simply irresistible.

Their eyes met, and she could only stare at the flecks of different shades of blues she saw there. She traced his jawline, ending up on his lips, mesmerized. He softly kissed her fingertips, then gave her a mouthwatering smile.

It was a lovely day. She couldn't remember the last time the sun had caught her in bed; by this time she would already be in the swimming pool, hard at work. This was a luxury she definitely could get used to. Her cell started to ring and when she saw it was Monica, she answered. "Hi Moni," she greeted, rolling onto her back with a satisfied smile.

"Are you okay, Anabella?"

"Yes, I most certainly am. Slept like a baby." She smiled up at Aldrich, who returned the smile as he came up and rested on his elbow.

"Are you still at Aldrich's?"

"I am. I will leave in about two to three hours. There are a few things we need to discuss before I leave tonight."

"Do you need any help?"

"Nope, I packed a few things already. Don't need much."

"Okay. Then I guess I will see you at the airport."

She could hear her friend's disappointment. They'd planned to spend the day together before she left. But this was more important, and she knew Monica would understand.

"Moni, thank you. You're a good friend... the best."

"Bye, Bella, see you later my friend."

Aldrich watched as she spoke to Monica. She looked well-rested and refreshed after the good night's sleep. He smiled while enjoying the sight of her disheveled look; her long hair all messy around her shoulders, yet this made her even more attractive to him.

When she was done, he kissed her on the forehead and moved away. He had no choice but to put some distance between them as his body demanded attention with hers so close to his own. "What would you like to drink?"

"Orange juice, if you have it, please."

"I do. Bought some yesterday." He smiled, affording himself a final look while she still lay against the cream sheets that framed her dark, tousled hair, eyes bright and a soft smile playing on her curvy lips.

*Be strong, man! She is an innocent… remember that,* he admonished himself. "You finish up, and I will start with breakfast."

He could see she was well rested, even if they had only got to bed at 4:30 that morning. He wanted to talk to her about counseling; he knew people who could help her during this time. He loved her. Startled, it dawned on him with brilliant clarity, and it made him more determined to help her. He loved everything about her, and last night had just cemented it in his heart. For now, he had to be cool-headed and practical about this.

Since he was older, he would have to show restrain and allow her to grow into the woman who lurked inside. The one who was struggling to get out from all the confusion she had experienced. He could not afford himself the luxury of touching her, which seemed to be difficult at times. She wasn't making it easy, either. He wanted to explore her passionate side and bring it to fulfillment. With those thoughts and more, he made his way to the kitchen. One of them being that her distracting presence wasn't allowing him to think soberly. She was proving to be a handful. Aldrich couldn't help but grin.

Once she'd freshened up, Anabella came out of her room full of bounce and energy. It had been a long time since she'd felt this peaceful and safe, welcoming it, as if she truly belonged there. A feeling which had been unfamiliar to her until now, one she could get used to with this man.

Aldrich was at the kitchen counter, cutting up cheese. He looked relaxed and at ease as he prepared their meal.

She'd put on a pair of tight, fitted jeans that displayed her bottom beautifully, and a bright-pink tank top. She looked innocent and youthful, her long hair pulled back into a ponytail swayed gently as she moved toward him.

He watched her as she neared him; a child wrapped in a woman's body, and what a body. His hands had been all over it the previous night. He walked around the kitchen top, meeting her halfway, also dressed in jeans and a white t-shirt, which showed off his upper body muscles beautifully.

*He is beautiful,* she thought. She walked straight into his waiting arms, their lips meeting softly, lingering just there as they inhaled each other's scen —but ignoring the passion their bodies craved.

"You look beautiful, Bella." A new softness that hadn't been there before was now present in his eyes. "I love you very much," he whispered, as if in prayer against her lips, sincerity written all over his handsome face.

Anabella stared at him, stunned at the words as a tear ran down her cheek. Her throat clogged up with the sudden lump.

"Don't cry, Bella, please don't cry, I can't take it," his voice broke.

She wiped her tear away. Innocent, sincere, and full of trust, her green eyes focused on him; hope embedded in their depths.

He cleared his throat and invited her to the table. "Come, sit down, breakfast is ready." With a kiss on her lips, he turned her toward the table where a feast awaited them.

They enjoyed breakfast in silence, content in the knowledge that this was the place to be, the right place. After breakfast, they cleaned the kitchen and Aldrich directed her to the couch again, making himself comfortable next to her.

"I know people who can help you with your nightmares, Bella. Will you allow me to make an appointment with them as soon as possible?" He watched her carefully, hoping he hadn't overstepped his boundaries. "I know you are leaving, but if you are willing, counseling is easily done over Skype. You know I have your best interests at heart, so all we'd need to do is figure out what the best time for you would be.

She knew this was important, not only to her but him as well. She owed him that much. If they were to have a future, she needed to heal, and just to feel normal again would be a good start.

Silence met him, and he wondered if he'd been too hasty with his request.

And then she answered with, "You can make the call, Aldrich. I'll meet them. It will be good not to be plagued by these nightmares any more. They control me, and I want my life back. Sometimes, when we embrace..." Upon starting with this confession, a blush crept up her neck and then her face, but she continued, regardless. "...I have visions of naked bodies penetrating my mind, the moans and groans encouraging me into their world." She sighed heavily. This was the best way she could describe it and she hoped he would understand.

He squeezed her hand and smiled. There was no judgment or resentment, just understanding glowing from the blue depths, encouraging her to go on.

"I will have to send you my itinerary for the next few months. Let me warn you in advance though, it is hectic, but I will make the time. This is necessary," she said with conviction.

"Good, I'll wait for that. I want my Bella whole and all to myself. Meanwhile, I need to take you back home."

Franticly, she rose from her chair. "I don't want you to come with me, Aldrich. Please. I don't want you anywhere near my house."

He frowned, and it appeared as if he would argue the point, but then he agreed, smiling at her.

She looked into his eyes, and cupped his face; there was so much love and genuineness in them. She bent down and kissed him first on the lips, and then in the creek of his neck. This was one spot on him she really adored, only because it was closest to his heart. In that moment, the realization of her love for this teddy bear woke her up, and she would do anything to take this relationship to the next level. She wanted him with all that was within her; her heart and body ached for him, but she knew that it would not be fair to him if she were not 'restored'. Then, and only then, would she go to him without any hesitation at all. Nevertheless, for now, to be able to feel his heart beating under her lips was adequate enough for her. When she finally stopped pouring kisses over him, she said softly, "I need to go."

"I will see you at the airport tonight."

"Thank you for everything, Aldrich."

"I love you," he whispered.

"And I love you," she echoed, her heart woven into every word and action.

The moment Anabella stepped into her house, she came upon her mother waiting for her at the stairs with a soft smile on her face.

"Oh, sweetie…" she started in her fake manner.

Anabella watched her blankly, that plastered farce of a smile didn't fool her one bit; no emotion showed on the youthful face. She moved to step past her mother, placing her foot on the first stair.

Sandra, not about to be ignored by her little uptight daughter, grabbed her arm.

"Let me go, Mother," Anabella demanded, pushing her mother away, but Sandra held on.

"Now, you listen here, missy. André just wanted to get to know you better. There was no need to treat him as you did," Sandra said, disapprovingly.

"He tried to rip my clothes off, and groped me, Mother. That is not being friendly, or how you get to know someone. What he did was molest me, which borders on rape!" Anabella snarled in disgust, her voice rising in pitch.

"Is that so? Well, that's not what he told me," she replied in an angry tone.

This would have previously stopped her in her tracks, but not this time. Anabella couldn't believe what she heard.

"He is a friend of the family, and all he wanted was to kiss you. What is so wrong with that?"

*She's defending the creep. Why is she doing this?* Anabella's thoughts were of shock. She stomped her foot and took another step up, but turned and looked down at her mother with defiance written all over her face. "Do you ever listen to yourself, Mother? I will not be groped by any man, if I haven't given him my consent!" She stormed up the remaining stairs.

"Where are you going?" her mother called out, following her. "I am not finished talking to you."

As far as Anabella was concerned, that was the problem. They never talked, so this would be the first in years.

"I am going away, or did you forget?" Anabella asked the moment she turned around to face her mother from the first floor.

"Where are you going?"

"Maybe if you cared enough, you would have read the papers I left on your desk about a month ago, Mother. I am going to America for three months." She raised her brow questioningly. "Did you even bother reading it before you signed?"

On the verge of saying something, her mother stopped and looked at her father as he joined them.

"What is going on here?" he asked, looking at his watch, not really interested in the conversation.

She would bet anything he was waiting for someone.

"Anabella says she is leaving for America," her mother snarled.

"When?" he asked, only partly interested.

"Tonight," Anabella replied, the confusion on her mother's face said it all. She had no idea.

"You must enjoy it. Do you have enough money?"

"Yes, Father."

"That's nice." On that note, the doorbell rang loudly throughout the house. Her father smiled, hurrying off as she had expected, and just like that the conversation was over, before it had even started.

Anabella hadn't expected more. She returned her gaze to her mother, who studied her intently, and the moment a couple greeted her father with a loud "Darling!" her mother's attention went immediately to her father. Anabella sighed. There was no point in even feeling disappointed, not anymore. Their life was just too important to them to even realize what they were doing.

"There you are, my darlings"—her father practically sang—"let me escort you to the living room, refreshments are waiting."

"Oh, I hope that isn't all that is waiting?" the woman said with a syrupy giggle.

Anabella looked down at the redhead, who clung like a vine to her father.

Her mother piped up cheerfully, as if Anabella cared. "It is a new couple we met last week, and we invited them over."

Anabella looked at her with the same blankness, turned and walked into her room, slamming the door behind her.

*This is going to cause a problem,* thought Sandra as she walked down the last stairs. André had all but demanded to have her daughter and soon, and now a replacement had to be found to satisfy him. She chewed on her lip for a second, a frown between the eyes. But the moment she stepped down and walked into the living room, she slapped a grin on her face. It was a problem they would need to sort out later. For now, her eyes roamed over the perfect specimen of the man standing next to her husband.

"Delicious," she purred, and looped her arm in his with a grin on her face. He was strong and muscled, just as she liked them. She looked up into the steel-gray eyes; the promise of pleasure lingered in his appreciative stare.

# Chapter Six

"I will miss you," Aldrich said softly, holding her close to him. People bumped and passed them at the departure terminal. The rest of the group had already said their farewells.

"I will miss you, too. I love you," she whispered against his lips, not willing to let go. He kissed her, his whole body tensing as he held her for the longest moment. Their hearts ached, but yet thumped repeatedly knowing that this was not forever.

"I love you, sweetheart. I will phone as often as I can."

"Yes, me too."

"Come, Anabella!" Mr. Clark called out.

They looked at each other, parting reluctantly. She placed the strap of her bag over her shoulder and with one final look, walked away leaving him standing between Monica and Roy.

He waved as she went through the gates and joined the large group on the other side.

Vibrant energy radiated from them as they laughed with one another, the underlying tension tangible. It was a completely new experience for many of them, the euphoria and adrenaline running high on their youthful faces.

He breathed deeply and brought his emotions under control before he turned to the younger people next to him. "Would you like to go and have a drink?" he asked them, more out of politeness than for any other reason.

"No, but thank you, Aldrich. We need to leave," Monica replied. "My parents have family visiting, and I promised mum to help her before classes resume tomorrow."

"Same here, but it was great meeting you," Roy added in a deep voice.

He was the same height as Aldrich, with similar green eyes to Anabella's; a strong man.

Aldrich had to admit he liked the younger, quieter man. The same look of abandonment Anabella carried reflected in him. The innocence was long gone.

"Okay then, best I get home."

They bid their goodbyes and made their way to their respective cars.

Aldrich's phone buzzed, and with one glance, he groaned in exasperation. Since he'd taken on the case, the woman had become a consistent pain. Her subtle come-ons were not appreciated, which now made him regret taking on the case. He let the call go to voicemail, and climbed into his sports car when his phone rang again. He couldn't help but sigh. He knew he was going to regret answering, but he didn't have a choice.

"Good evening, Ms. Etsibeth," he answered as politely as he could.

"Giselle, please, Aldrich. Ms. Etsibeth sounds so formal," she insisted in a syrupy voice.

"How can I be of help, Ms. Etsibeth?" he continued, rolling his eyes as he leaned back into his leather seat.

"I am at the hotel, alone and missing you. Would you join me?"

He looked at his watch and frowned. It read 10:15pm. "No, this would not be an appropriate time for me."

"Please, just one nightcap," she pressed.

Aldrich could already envision the pout on her plush, red lips. She was beautiful, of that there was no doubt, but since he'd started with her case, two of his co-workers had already asked for her contact details; he'd had no choice but to reprimand them about their folly.

"My apologies, Ms. Etsibeth, but it is late and I still have work to do."

"How about if I come to your place?"

"I'm sorry, but that wouldn't work either," he forced out sharply.

She chuckled. "You don't like me do you, Aldrich?"

"You are my client. It's not about what I like."

"Don't you find me pretty?"

He rolled his eyes once again; the woman was arrogant, too full of herself and bored.

"Is there anything remotely urgent you want to discuss now over the phone, Ms. Etsibeth?"

This time, she humphed into the phone, and the call ended abruptly.

He smirked, powered up his machine, and drove to his penthouse. His thoughts back on the young woman he'd just left at the airport. There was just no competition. Anabella was the woman for him; kind, innocent, and drop-dead gorgeous. She was also strong-willed and passionate, and no one else could compare.

"Mr. Dorflinger wants to see you, Aldrich," the pretty blond said with a bright smile. Her eyes lingered on his chest before lowering south, licking her pink lips as a grin crept over them.

He groaned in agony and pushed his chair back, frustrated with this woman's persistence, too.

"Chaney, you could have simply called," he quipped as he made his way past her.

"And miss the chance to see you? No way," she retorted on a chuckle.

Aldrich had gone out with her once, and this is what he got, a young clinging doll who didn't understand the word, no. He turned to say something, but thought better of it, and walked out not waiting for the little snit. He knocked once on the senior partner's door, and when he heard the familiar "Enter", he stepped in and closed the door behind him.

Mr. Dorflinger looked at him, and directed him to a chair in front of his desk as he put down the phone. His face was solemn as always.

"Aldrich, it has come to my attention that you have been avoiding Ms. Etsibeth."

The frown between his eyes alluded to the fact that he was not in the best of moods, and Aldrich decided he'd better keep his thoughts to himself, stopping a groan before it escaped from his lips.

"We take great care in providing our clients the best service at all times, do I make myself clear?"

"Yes, I understand, sir."

"She can direct several clients our way, so it goes without saying that we cannot afford to aggravate either her, or her father."

"Yes, sir." Aldrich kept his expression blank as the older man studied him.

Mr. Dorflinger let down his guard for a second, and asked, "How is the swimmer?"

"She is doing well. Left for America last night," he added the little tidbit. It had the desired affect.

Mr. Dorflinger cleared his throat, and pushed his papers around before looking back at Aldrich. "Yes, right. See that this case is handled with your usual efficiency."

"Yes, sir. Will that be all?"

"Yes. You may leave, Aldrich."

Aldrich walked out, closing the door behind him, just to bump into the little snit standing there with a bright smile.

"Is everything okay?" she asked, batting her long, black eyelashes.

"Don't you have work to do, Chaney?"

She just looked at him, almost as if he were the last morsel left in a packet of something scrumptious she'd been devouring.

Annoyed, he uttered, "Please excuse me."

However, she stood unwavering.

To bypass her, he would have to brush up against her, which she was obviously aiming for, and that would not happen, ever.

"When will we go out again?" she asked in a low, seductive voice, her finger trailing down his jacket's lapel sensually, her eyes fixed on his lips.

"Not going to happen, Chaney," he said abruptly, "besides, I am seeing someone." *Yes,* he thought, *get it out there and make it official.*

She raised a perfectly manicured eyebrow, her curved lips forming a pout. She stepped closer, and what with his back against the door, there was no way of escape unless he was rude to her. But his parents had taught him to always respect those of the female persuasion, so he kept himself in control.

"Since when, Aldrich? I thought I was your girl." Her hands danced over him, and it almost seemed that she was aiming to kiss him, but he turned his head to the side slightly.

His tall body towered over her. "Dream on, girl," he sneered under his breath, and with a firm grip on her shoulder he pushed her aside, saying firmly, "No, Chaney." As he walked to his office, she humphed loudly, like a naughty child about to have a tantrum.

Aldrich sighed; he couldn't believe that he had thought her attractive once. The one night he'd gone out with her had been the longest two hours he had ever spent with a woman. She was self-obsessed, couldn't hold a decent conversation, and ate like a bird. She may be beautiful to look at, but a man could only be satisfied with so much beauty before he would look for something substantially meaningful.

Anabella was exactly the opposite. She cared more for others than herself, and her general knowledge allowed them to speak about different topics. She enjoyed a good meal, always putting it away with exuberance. She was sharp, witty, and beautiful. He grinned as he sat down behind his desk. Just the thought of her made his heart beat faster. Thoughts of the previous night, and what they had shared on his couch were still vivid in his mind. Three months he'd have to wait. It would be excruciating.

Just then, his phone rang, which brought him out of his reverie. Letting out a sigh, he continued with his day.

"I didn't know about the trip, André," Sandra said in a low voice.

Upon his arrival and not finding Anabella, he'd been in a foul mood. Sandra's day at the office had been a long one, and all she wanted to do was relax and have some fun with the new couple, who would be joining them shortly.

Derek shifted his weight from one foot to the other, not quite looking forward to what was expected of him. His mother had told him that he would be entertaining the man tonight, and although he didn't like him, he had no choice in the matter. He'd warned his mother that this man would not get his claws into Anabella; he'd told her this, not once, but a few times. As a result, she then demanded Derek take Anabella's place. Begrudgingly, he'd agreed.

Once again, he found himself in a place he didn't want to be. The older man was rough, and hard to settle down. He had an endurance that could go on all night. Derek noticed how strung up he was with pent-up frustrations, and he would be the one to pay. He groaned inwardly, knowing that tomorrow his body would scream with the onslaught he was about to go through.

Just then, the doorbell rang, and happy to get away from André's thunderous stares, he walked to the door. He opened it to Lucy, a small brunette who was new on the scene. He liked her, a lot. A client of their parents' had brought her along one night. She hadn't been at all ashamed, got right into it, and enjoyed every minute. Her eagerness was a turn on, though. She always dressed in black leather and long, black boots that showed off her well-toned legs to the maximum.

Tonight she wore a leather corset, which she had paired with a leather skirt, one that covered just enough to entice every man and woman in the area. Her ensemble included her familiar boots. They never allowed her to remove them whilst at their house, and she was happy to oblige. Her hair was pulled high up on her head in a ponytail; when she moved, it gently swayed with every step as it enticed them closer—like a fly to a spider web.

"Derek, how are you, darling?" she purred, stepping into his arms and kissing him.

"Just fine, thanks," he replied, and hugged her tightly. Tonight they would be a team, hopefully able to appease the angry man.

"Is it Lucy, Derek?" his mother asked in her typical, stern voice.

"Yes, Mother."

Sandra shot him a dirty look, but he just chuckled. She didn't like to be called *Mother* in front of the guests, but sometimes he couldn't help himself. Derek continued to grin, holding Lucy tightly to his side as they strolled lazily toward the older couple.

"André, I want you to meet Lucy Fritz." Lucy's eyes swept over the older man, and he returned her look shamelessly.

Derek frowned. He knew that look; it was not a good sign for either of them.

"She is new to the group, but agreed to come tonight." Sweetness dripped from Sandra's sultry voice.

Derek loathed his mother.

André was an excellent client, and Sandra didn't want to lose him because of Anabella. She was angry with her. The nerve to drop her like this and leave was totally unacceptable where Sandra was concerned.

"Turn!" he demanded in his usual abrupt way. Lucy complied with a sashay in her step. His dark, brown eyes swept over the appealing package. "When will the hellcat be back?" he asked, not taking his eyes from her, already brushing her exposed skin with a thick finger, lust shimmering in his eyes.

"Three months," Sandra answered, to which he growled.

"I want her room," he demanded, and wouldn't take no for an answer.

"Yes, of course, you are more than welcome to use it." She turned to Derek and said in a low voice, "Derek, please escort André to Anabella's room."

Derek sighed. *Yes, it was most definitely going be a long night.* He walked up the steps, with André and Lucy following closely behind.

Lucy was already hanging on to André's arm, doing her utmost to calm the man down. Her soft voice soothed him and by the time they reached the room, he had a smile on his sweaty face. He was also out of breath, which was always odd to Derek. The man was lazy and overweight, but yet had the stamina of a bull when it came to orgies.

When they entered, André's eyes fell on a framed photo of Anabella, which only made his sour mood return.

Derek and Lucy exchanged a look of sceptisism.

Lucy quickly got to work and reached out to him, drew his lips down to hers and kissed him deeply. He groaned as he wrapped her in his arms.

Derek watched as the two got acquainted before joining the couple, already shirtless. His tanned chest clean-shaven, just as André liked.

Aldrich was frustrated with the case. As a matter of fact he did not think it was even a case at all. It was a petty thing Ms. Etsibeth had got involved with, and instead of handling it like a grown up, she used her connections to scare the young man, and took the little bit he had for her own gain. Their greed knew no bounds and his resentment grew toward both her and her father. Between the case and Ms. Etsibeth, his time was occupied. She constantly demanded he must be ready for her whenever it pleased her, and that had been every night for the last eight days.

Since Anabella left, he had had no time to call her. He received an email from her, to which he'd quickly replied. He missed her innocent youth and energy.

"Aldrich, pay attention, please." Giselle Etsibeth pouted, drawing him out of his thoughts. She had insisted he accompany her to the ballet that night. During the interval, she introduced him to some of her friends, who unsurprisingly were as vain and dimwitted as she was.

"Yes, Ms. Etsibeth," he replied, irritated with her.

She rolled her eyes at his response, which always frustrated her.

Aldrich just smiled. "Please forgive me, what did you say?" Satisfaction beamed on his face. The fact that he had annoyed her pleased him tremendously.

"Leon and Bianca have invited us for a night cap after the ballet."

He raised a brow and sighed in frustration. He was tired and in no mood to continue this farce of a night out, but her pouty mouth and look told him he'd better not refuse. Reluctantly, he accepted the offer with a half-hearted grin. "Okay, but only one drink, and then I take you home, Giselle." The night had already dragged along; all three's mundane chatter not holding his interest in the least.

"One drink, that is all," she purred up at him.

Aldrich sighed as her hands clasped around his arm possessively. With the interval at an end, they walked back into the theatre. She continued to clutch his arm, as if her life depended on it. To him, the grip felt like a trap set for an animal.

Finally, after what seemed like hours, he got into his sports car and took her home. Her hand made itself at home on his thigh, making him cringe; the woman just didn't stop. He'd told her several times that he wasn't interested in any sort of relationship with her, platonic or otherwise. However, she continued to pester him with her not-so-subtle flirting.

It was the longest ride to her house in Camps Bay. When he finally stopped, he couldn't walk her to the door quickly enough.

"Don't you want to come in?" she asked, when they'd reached her front door.

"No, Giselle, it's late."

"Please, Aldrich," she pleaded in a seductive whisper, her hand brushing against his shirt-clad body. She stood very close to him, her red lips ready and waiting.

He grabbed her hand, holding it firmly in place. "I have told you many times, Giselle. We will never be an item. I feel nothing for you."

"But, Aldrich... I am lonely," she hiccupped, crying softly, her shoulders slumped, and her bottom lip trembling.

He hated it. She used this tool often to get what she wanted. It worked for her father, and for Mr. Dorflinger, but it didn't work for him. Bored, he folded his arms and waited for the next stage of her act.

The green eyes flickered in anger. Her stance changed within seconds and she became ugly. The porch light did nothing to hide her anger toward him and frankly, he didn't care.

"You have to do as I say." And she grinned victoriously up to him. "Daddy said you work for me, and that you have to do as I say." She stomped her high-heeled foot arrogantly.

He clenched his hands into fists, angry at her little show, and hissed softly, "I am your lawyer, Ms. Etsibeth, nothing more and nothing less. You pay my fee, as any other client would do. I haven't been hired to occupy your bed."

"What will it cost to get your attention?" She brushed up against his arm, her eyes gleaming under her dark lashes.

"That will never happen. I have told you on numerous occasions that my heart belongs to another. I've nothing further to say in this respect." He stepped back to leave.

"I like you, Aldrich, and I thought—"

But he stopped her.

"You thought wrong, Giselle. I only endure your friendship because of the case, nothing more. Now, I'll bid you a good night." Turning, he walked to his car, but the persistent little thing ran after him, and the moment he reached his door, she pressed herself into him. He could feel her perfect breasts rubbing up against his back. *Really, woman,* he shouted within the confines of his head. Aggravated, he turned and looked down at her. Her body invited him in, of that there was no doubt; curves in all the right places, but she didn't do it for him. Not by a long shot. He felt no excitement, or arousal, and she all but left him cold.

"Aldrich, I need you," she whispered as she traced his mouth with her tongue, biting his lower lip seductively. He pushed her away, but like a clasp, her hand reached for him, making contact; he felt his body stirring. The sudden attention awakened him, and he knew where it could lead, although he'd fought hard against it. He tried to brush her hand away, but she was so close to him, and adamant in her stand, that he found it difficult not to be pulled in. Only brute force would help, but he was not a violent man, especially toward women.

When she cupped his face and drew their lips together, he allowed the touch for a brief moment. His body demanded attention as her succulent lips parted under his, her tongue snaking into his mouth. She moaned softly as her hands moved against his crotch, stroking him through the material. With a sudden jolt, he reversed their positions and pressed her against the steel frame. With demanded urgency, his mouth came down on hers. She giggled with delight the moment she got his zipper down.

That snapped him out of his stupid daze and he stepped back. As her hand was caught in his pants, it only pulled her with him. He removed it, looked at her with revulsion, and without a word moved her aside, got in his car and left.

He watched her in his rearview mirror as she stood rooted to the spot where he'd left her, a soft smile playing on her face. He slammed the steering wheel in frustration. A pain shot up his arm, which made him grunt in agony. He shook his hand, chastising himself harshly. *Fool, that is what you are, Aldrich Hagin! There can never be anything between me and that witch. I can't even stand her!* He loved Anabella, and with a glance at his clock, promised himself that he would make contact with her, soon. He needed to hear her sweet voice.

Finally, they got out of the water and for the first time in a very long time, Anabella was stiff, her legs and arms numb. They were all exhausted, but Mr. Clark demanded the best and refined their skills meticulously, which inevitably took its toll on them all.

Tersia had been sick the night before, and couldn't get out of bed that morning. Josh had cramps, and would be with a physiotherapist for the rest of the day. Ann had come down with a stomach bug, and was now sleeping after spending a night in hospital.

She shook her hair free of the cap, letting it fall over her shoulders; it needed a wash. Tomorrow was their day off, so she planned to pamper herself.

"There she is, the most beautiful girl in the water," Charles' voice boomed across the swimming pool. Anabella groaned softly, turning her back to gather her towel and without a word, walked to the dressing rooms.

"Are you avoiding me, Anabella?" the man asked as he stopped her.

She growled softly, not knowing how he'd gotten to her so quickly, yet there he was, standing right in front of her. She was forced to look at him. Charles was a swimmer for the American team; his tall, lean body told her that this man was lethal, and dangerous. But most assuredly, a talented and skilful opponent. They had briefly met during practices but so far, hadn't found the opportunity to become better acquainted. That didn't mean he hadn't tried every chance he got, like now.

From the start, his attention had been on her, and although she'd never given him any reason in this department, he would send her a soda if they were in the cafeteria, or a note with his cell number. She even received a single red rose on one occasion, which she replied to with a thank you note. Whenever they were in the same group, he would stand close to her, and as time passed it unnerved her more. With time, she felt her resolve breaking down, and couldn't get him out of her head.

His face always lit up in a handsome grin, and his blue eyes sparkled. The papers called him the American Dream. She could see why. The man was gorgeous and with a body like that, all kinds of imagined thoughts rushed through her head. She took a step back; couldn't trust herself around him.

Last night, she had dreamed about that body intertwined with her own. However, Aldrich's face had penetrated through the mist she found herself in, his soft voice whispering how much he loved her, and she'd found herself wide-awake. She also found herself blushing when she woke this morning, and now with him so close, she could feel the familiar heat rush to the surface.

"Hello, Charles," she greeted softly, stepping around him, but he was quick and blocked her way.

"Where are you going?" He lifted her chin with a long finger, and she shivered with anticipation.

She had to get away. "I want to get changed. I am tired, Charles."

"Come now, not too tired to go out with me tonight, surely." His thumb stroked her cheek.

She removed it with more force than intended. "Please don't do that!"

"Why?" A roguish smile played over his features, making her heart thud in her ears as excitement coursed through her veins. He was now the second man her body was reacting to, and she didn't like it, or did she? Her brain felt frozen, as if all reason had left her, and she couldn't respond as she knew she must.

"Don't, okay," was all she said, trying to move past him, but he blocked her yet again.

"I will not let you pass unless you agree to go out with me tonight. You need some serious relaxation, Anabella."

He was so close to her that she could feel his warm breath against her face. She closed her eyes to regain control. He mistook it for an invitation, and placed a kiss on her closed eyelids. It was delicate and soft, and her body craved the intimacy he promised with the brush of his lips.

"You are so beautiful, please say you will," he whispered, and again kissed her nose, followed by a brush of his lips over hers.

It felt purpose driven, as if he knew exactly what he was doing to her, privy to her dreams and thoughts.

"Please," he begged softly.

The feather-like touch made her knees turn to jelly, forcing her to hold on to his arm. He was so close, she could smell him; his skin taught over his wide frame and sprinkled with small freckles begging for her touch. Her fingers itched to explore the expanse of his chiseled chest—their bodies only separated by a mere inch.

"Yes," she whispered without a second thought.

Charles smiled as he cupped her face, and whispered, "Make yourself pretty. I want to show you Houston's nightlife." He let her go, and she stumbled as he walked away.

She grabbed onto the rail to steady herself once again.

"Pick you up at seven." He had stopped to say this loud enough for all to hear; several heads turned toward her as he then spoke to a fellow swimmer, delight evident in his voice.

She groaned in frustration. She couldn't believe the effect he had on her. *How am I going behave myself around this man?* The sexual dream infiltrated her mind once again, along with other more graphic scenes. Scenes she was trying hard to ignore. Ever since Charles had come into the picture and confronted her, she'd felt her treacherous body responding.

To make matters worse, she'd seen a young couple making out the very first night she had arrived, which had only made her arousal peak. As she'd made her way around a corner, she bumped into the couple. The man cursed her to bugger off in a heavy English accent. He'd been thoroughly annoyed that she dared interrupt them.

It seemed that everything was working together to make her body react with each stimulus she received. It was like a drug she could no longer ignore; her body was constantly tense. She felt Charles' lingering presence, his lips on her face, her body trembling with want for more contact. She inhaled sharply, closing her eyes when the guilt and shame penetrated her mind. Frustrated, she chastised herself. *What is wrong with you, Anabella? Aldrich, remember him? He loves you, and you love him. How can you be so shameless? You are not your mother!*

After the long discussion she had with herself, she left. She knew she needed to unwind. Besides, there would be other swimmers with them, so it wasn't like she'd be alone with Charles.

She met him at the corner he'd suggested. Two of her teammates, Izak and Jeffrey, joined them, together with several of his team, and she found that she could finally relax. Charles never left her side as he led her into the darkened alley of the club, the beat of the music thrumming through her body the moment she stepped onto the first steel, steep staircase. They made their way up, meeting a huge bouncer with arms the same thickness as her waist. He stared down at her from his towering height with a menacing look. His shirt was an extremely tight fit over his beefy chest, of which the buttons fought to hold it together. His hair was styled in a crew-cut, and he sported a stud in his right ear; it glittered in the reflection of the roof's light.

It was all business with him. He acknowledged Charles with a nod when they walked past him the moment he opened the steel door leading into a hallway. It was lit up with a fluorescent, blue light that gave the place an eerie appearance. With each step, they got closer to the booming sound, making everything within her vibrate. Funnily enough, it somehow forced Anabella to overlook all her troubles and just relax in its overwhelming presence.

The further they walked in, the more people they passed, some blatantly ignoring them. Some checked them out lazily until they reached a wide hall. By now, the music was in her body, making her heart thump to the rhythmic beat.

Charles bent down, speaking directly into her ear, "Take a seat." He pointed to an empty table where bottles and glasses were still scattered over its surface, as if the cleaning staff had forgotten their job. "I will be right back with drinks!" he announced loudly, and before she could protest, he was gone.

She walked to the empty table and looked at the mess in disgust.

Izak, who had followed her, swept the table clean in one fluid motion, sending its contents cluttering down, the sound drowned by the music.

Grateful, she nodded her appreciation, and he grinned at her. Any attempt to talk was out of the question. When she sat down, she looked toward the dance floor where bodies were bashed together. People were gyrating to the pounding music, as if in a trance. Scantily-clad women and men moved together, some making out, and others holding drinks while they moved to the beat. The chaotic rhythm pulsed through their veins. Everyone was having a good time.

Around her, people stood at railings or tables, some sat on couches making out; one young woman's breast was on the verge of being exposed as the man touched and kissed her in total oblivion. Another couple was definitely doing it, the woman's head bounced and swayed from side to side. Anabella started to feel the usual dread when she saw these things, generally within the confines of her house. She looked away, closing her eyes momentarily in futile hope that this would be over soon.

Charles and the rest of the group had returned with drinks. He touched her lightly on the shoulder, and she opened her eyes. "Here you go," he said, close to her ear, his presence near enough that she could smell his woody cologne, his warm breath tickling her ear. "Relax, Anabella. Enjoy!" he called out, encouraging her to drink the offered glass, but all she did was stare at it hesitantly. He shrugged, and with a tilt of the head poured the liquid down his throat and swallowed. Looking at Anabella, he smiled, smacking his lips in appreciation.

Charles openly looked at her with desire, a desire so strong, she was certain she had to leave.

*This is not good. I don't belong here*, she thought, as she worried her lip in concern. She felt his hand brush against her bare arm. This did nothing to soothe her concerns, and in fact had the opposite effect. She had become aware of everything he was doing.

When he squeezed her arm, she jumped, looked at him and took the offered glass. With one swig, its contents were gone. It burned as far as it went making her shiver, and her face contort in an ugly grin. Rapidly, her heartbeat thumped in her chest. She had to calm down.

Anabella had just enough time to place the glass on the table, when she was pulled up and dragged away. As she was behind Charles, his lean body sheltered her so she could bypass the throng easily.

Without warning, he turned and pulled her against him. "Let's dance!" he shouted.

With her body plastered against his, she could feel his every contour, and when he placed his knee between her legs, she felt his arousal; she knew she was in trouble. She tried to push him away, but his grip was firm around her, pinning her against his body in a tight embrace. Anabella could smell the mint on his breath from the drink he'd had, as well as his fragrance intermingled with the sweat in the air. Everything about him aroused her and standing so close, she could see the pulse at his throat.

She turned her head away, and saw a couple having a tongue duel next to them. Their bodies moved to the beat as he held her provocatively against his groin. The young woman was obviously into it as her leg was wrapped around his hip, her hands in his hair holding him close.

Quickly, she returned her gaze to Charles' chest, and released a groan. This wasn't good, not good at all. Searching for her team members, she found Izak. He was already following a raven-haired girl on his way to the overcrowded dance floor. Jeffery was trying to get the attention of an auburn-haired female who smiled brightly up at him the moment she turned around. They weren't going to be any help.

Charles continued to hold her tightly to him, swaying to the beat. "Relax," he mouthed, as his lips brushed her ear, sending shivers down her spine. His hands moved her hips against his, his erection so hard she couldn't help but be affected by it.

The moment she closed her eyes, she experienced the dream, and felt her body responding to his wandering hands. Their lips met briefly, her breath hitching as their tongues met. Anabella was lost in the moment he offered, but when his hands landed on her buttocks, she pushed him away. Charles, not yet ready to let her go, grabbed her arm and pulled her back.

"Come on, sweet thing," he whispered seductively, holding her tight.

"No. Please, Charles!" she shouted, but he only smiled down at her.

"You will love it." He slanted his mouth over hers, entering with his tongue.

Her body tingled, but she knew she had to get away. She pushed once again, this time harder than before, and the moment she felt his release, she moved away. She bumped and brushed against several people as she made her way past, until she reached an empty spot. Scanning the crowd, her two teammates were nowhere to be found. Regardless, she had to leave the club as soon as possible. Spotting the entrance, she took the first step toward it, but Charles was at her side, holding her arm.

"Are you afraid of me?" he asked, so close to her, she could see every line on his face pulled into a grimace.

*Yes* would have been her first response, followed by her admittance as to how much he affected her, and this she could never do. He would only continue to try, so it was in her best interest to be open with him about Aldrich.

She shook her head. "No, but I can't do what you want. I'm in love someone else!" she shouted in his ear.

Stunned, he looked at her for a minute. "Okay. If I were to promise to behave, would you stay?"

He seemed sincere, which made her smile. Somewhat mollified, she willed her heart to slow down. "You, behave?" She raised an eyebrow in question.

"Yes. I promise. Scout's honor."

She laughed and asked skeptically, "Were you even in the scouts?"

"Yes, for four years," he said with a rueful smile, while holding four fingers in the air. Turning slightly away, he added, "I'm sorry, Anabella, but I like you. I just wanted to be close to you." He watched the dancing cluster, his face unreadable before he turned back to her. "Do you want to do something else?"

"Yes, if you don't mind," she replied, "you did promise to show me Houston, remember?"

"Yes, I did. Okay then, let's go." He took her hand, leaving the rest of the group behind.

The remainder of the evening was spent at a restaurant, where the ambiance was quieter; couples sat in small groups, enjoying themselves. Soft music played from the speakers, which was nice as they could talk. Since they were both swimmers with a love for the sport, they had a lot to discuss.

They were still close, though; the table setting not allowing for more personal space. Anabella was constantly aware of his proximity, but gained more control as the evening progressed, was relaxed, and even managed to enjoy herself. He seemed to respect her enough by giving her the breathing space she needed, something she appreciated.

When it was time to call it a night, he bade her farewell with a light peck on the cheek.

"Thanks for the night, Anabella. I hope we can do this again."

"I would love that," she replied. "Thanks for understanding, Charles."

He lifted a hand, and said with a grin, "Hey, when a lady says no, I accept it. The only pity is that you are taken." He sighed. "You are beautiful," he whispered. "Are you really sure there is no hope for me?"

"I really love him, Charles."

"He is one lucky guy." With that, he walked away.

"You're back early," Thomas remarked the moment Charles stepped into his room.

"Yeah." He shrugged his jacket off, threw it on the couch and plopped down.

"Didn't you go out with that bombshell, Anabella?"

"Yeah." He crossed his long legs before him and released a frustrated sigh.

"And?"

"And, nothing," he hissed. "She's as tight as a can!" He punched the cushion in frustration, but looked at Thomas with absolute determination. "But she will open. One of these days, she will open, and I'll be there ready and waiting." He grinned devilishly, turning his attention to the show Thomas was watching.

"Are you planning something?"

"I am. She will be in my bed before she goes home. I'll just have to work better at it." He smiled a crooked smile that promised a lot of action for him, but nothing good for Anabella.

"Need some help?" Thomas asked, eagerly.

His friend and teammate glanced at him, smiling once again. "I like where you are going with this."

"She will be putty in our hands when we're done."

Both grinned, high-fiving in camaraderie.

"You want water?"

"Yeah, thanks."

Thomas walked to the small refrigerator. "When are you planning on having your way with her?" he asked, handing Charles a bottle of water.

"Soon. I want her soon."

"In the meantime, do you want to get some?"

"Yeah, why not?"

"Good. I saw a pretty blond booking in tonight. Let me work my magic and see if I can get her to join us."

"Okay, but hurry up!" Charles yelled as Thomas stepped out of their room.

A frown appeared between his eyes as he thought about Anabella and the kiss they had shared for only a brief second. Charles growled in frustration, shouting to the now empty room, "You are mine, Anabella Anthony. You can bet your sweet little ass on that!" Lifting his bottle in salute, he downed the contents.

# Chapter Seven

Anabella had just gotten back to her room when her laptop beeped with an incoming call on Skype. She rushed over to her desk and sat down with her heart in her throat. It was Aldrich on the line. His sweet, handsome face looked back at her; she almost cried. She had missed him every day.

"Hi, sweetheart," he said, "were you out?"

"Hello, Aldrich. Yes, with friends."

"You look beautiful." He smiled.

She loved his smile. It was charged with adoration and it warmed her.

"Thank you, Aldrich." She blushed under his appreciative stare.

"Where did you go?"

"A friend took me clubbing, but I didn't like it, so we ended up at a restaurant instead. It was nice. I missed having you with me, though." She didn't want to have to explain to him how her night had gone, or the feelings Charles had evoked within her. He would end up thinking that she'd moved on, which wasn't the case at all. In fact, it showed her that she was head over heels in love with him.

"I miss you too, sweetheart. You look good, Bella."

She knew he wouldn't miss anything up close. The down lights placed her in the spotlight, giving him a clear view. She informed him of her schedule, and their next couple of events. They talked for a further twenty minutes before he received a call. With a promise that he would watch her, they concluded their call.

He seldom missed any of her events, and although he didn't say much, she knew he loved to observe her in and out of the pool.

Later, when she eventually made it to bed, exhausted from her day, his words entered her mind, making her smile. He'd assured her of his love for her, and she'd returned the same declaration. She really missed his quiet strength, and his solid, protective presence that put her at ease every time they were together. He was everything she wanted in a man.

"I love you," she whispered, before she fell asleep. With her pillow tucked beneath her head, she slept peacefully. But all too soon the evening's events took its toll, and she started to move around in her bed. Her dream became real, and she dreaded the effect it was having on her.

*A hand brushed up against her inner thigh, parted her legs and she moaned with pleasure. Her lover's mouth expertly kissed her. Her breath was sucked out of her lungs as she devoured the exploring tongue. It tasted divine; she could feel herself melt into the kiss, enjoying the feel of the hard body pressed against hers.*

*She felt her Pj's being lifted and removed, the coolness easing the heat on her skin in the warm room. More hands joined in, which added to the already sensuous sensations she was feeling, her legs opening wider. She heard a groan the moment he touched her core. Her body lifting as hands played with her.*

*Arousal flared in her veins at the pursuit of tongues and hands, warm, hard bodies lying next to her and on top of her. The scene aroused her, but soon made way for panic as the hands turned to vice-like grips. She kicked out, but her legs were tightly constrained. Someone chuckled when she wiggled in an attempt to move away, the grasp becoming more determined, fiercer. She pushed, to no avail.*

Finally, she screamed out loud.

"Anabella, wake up," a small voice repeated several times, while she fought against the pillow and sheets.

"Anabella, it's me, Tersia. Come on friend, wake up."

Finally, she opened her eyes and looked at the blond who hovered over her. Her big, blue eyes wide with fear as she shook Anabella's shoulder.

"You scared me," she said, in a low soothing voice, concern etched in her huge eyes.

"I'm sorry," Anabella replied hoarsely, struggling to sit up straight. She switched on the bedside lamp, and looked at her clock, groaning. It was 5:00am.

"Are you okay?"

"Yes. Thanks, Tersia." She met her eyes briefly, but no smile formed in her misty eyes. Tired and weary, they felt scratchy and Anabella rubbed at them.

"Try and get back to sleep," Tersia suggested around a yawn.

"No, I might as well get up, it's almost time to anyway." Anabella swung her legs off the bed. "I'm going for a run."

"Okay, see you later."

She left as Anabella reached for her running clothes. Her thoughts were in complete shambles due to the dream. She always remembered the dreams she had, because they made such an impression and impact on her, dreams she would never forget.

*Again, the same dream. What is wrong with me,* she asked herself.

This time, she enjoyed the dream, she knew it, and she could feel it—her body was still aroused with the intensity she had experienced.

The dreams usually left her listless and numb, but this one had most definitely excited her. She knew they didn't involve Aldrich. It was always someone else; someone whose face she could never make out. Only this time, there had been more than one face, all unknown, but familiar all the same. She shivered, and her muscles throbbed with a need she was becoming accustomed to. She had never been with a man before, but the deeply embedded experiences she had witnessed whilst growing up had caused her body to crave the touch.

She quivered. As yet, she hadn't spoken to the professional Aldrich suggested. She'd thought she had it under control. Apparently not, because they kept on coming back. It was time to talk with this person. Her resolve crumbled with each passing day.

When she returned from her run, and after taking a shower, she sent an email to Mrs. Smit, the councilor Aldrich had suggested. She explained her situation, and asked when it would be suitable to call her via Skype.

At 6am, Anabella was in the water before anyone else, and by the time the team arrived, she had done five laps.

The days moved on. Both Anabella's and Aldrich's thoughts never strayed too far from the other, but his workload and her practices kept them from communicating most of the time.

Giselle Etsibeth was determined to have Aldrich as her prize, inviting him to yet more ballets and dinner parties at her house. Somehow, she had gotten his address, and twice she'd arrived unannounced at his door. The last visit she'd paid him, she'd been scantily dressed, again, making it hard for him to push her away.

Her case was finally coming to an end, since the plaintiff was willing to settle outside of court. For Aldrich, this was great news, which meant he would finally be rid of her. Meanwhile, he had to continue to listen to all her lame come-ons. Since the night she'd kissed him, he'd made it his mission to avoid any close contact with her. As often as he could, he made sure he was never alone with her, even on a so-called date. Her mouth remained a permanent pout of displeasure, but he allowed her no freedom.

Chaney was also adamant they go on a second date. Her actions started rumors in the office, which greatly annoyed him. She would invite herself to business lunches, making sure she was always seated next to him. Like the gentleman he was, Aldrich said nothing, but Tim noticed his friend's tense posture throughout.

Tim had asked her out on several occasions in order to discourage her, but she was no fun to have around. She was empty-headed, and her life only revolved around herself. He thought that she could very well be great in bed, but it would, without a doubt, stop there. Some men needed more than just a good tussle.

A huge swimming event was taking place at the end of November, and Aldrich decided to spend the day with his father so that they could watch it on Super Sport. He was looking forward to seeing her, even if it was only in a live broadcast.

The last time he'd spoken to her, she'd sounded exhausted, but she assured him that it was all due to not getting enough sleep. Aldrich, however, knew that the nightmares continued to haunt her.

Because of the fact that she was overseas, Mrs. Smit was not able to council her efficiently enough, and although Anabella didn't elaborate on her dreams and nightmares, he knew she struggled with sleep. With her vigorous training schedule and on-going championships, it didn't help much.

On the last Saturday of the month, Aldrich and his father watched as she dove into the crystal, blue water; fit and beautiful as ever, but the lines around her eyes showed how tired she really was, and her usually glowing skin now seemed pale.

There was nothing wrong with her technique, or form, as it had all been drilled into the very fabric of her being. She glided through the water with swift strokes, her feet paddling behind her. At the turn, she was first and excelled in speed, ending with a win in the first heat. When she climbed out, her smile seemed plastered on her face as she waved to the crowd, and then congratulated the runner up.

The camera followed her to her seat, and that's when Aldrich noticed a young man standing very close to her. He also couldn't help but notice her body tense up, and then the camera moved to the next heat.

He looked at his father and frowned.

"What was that about?" Mr. Hagin asked curiously, having picked up on the exact same thing.

"Not sure, Dad, but I'm going to find out, and if she won't tell me, I will call her coach," he replied in a stern voice.

*Why did she act that way,* wondered Aldrich. Anabella loved swimming. It was her life. It always calmed her, but what he'd seen was completely out of the ordinary where she was concerned. Moreover, who was the young man fawning all over her, smiling pathetically, and touching her? One thing Aldrich was sure of was that she hadn't welcomed the guy's attention, hence the reason why her body had tensed up. Picking up his cell phone, he typed out a message and sent her the text. Then, he waited.

"Please leave," Anabella hissed at Charles. The man was constantly at her side. For some reason, he didn't understand what no meant, and after last night, she never wanted to see him, or his friend again.

She grabbed her towel off the chair and dried herself, unaware that the camera was still on her.

"No, sugar," he said in a low voice, "you are mine."

"I'm not yours, and never will be. Have you forgotten a very important piece of information I shared with you not so long ago? Someone by the name of Aldrich? The man I love? This conversation is over, Charles!" she hissed, walking away with another forced smile on her face as she waved to supporters in the arena.

When she got to her locker, she heard her phone ring. Grabbing her bag, she rummaged around in it until she found her cell. The message she read left her breathless.

*Aldi, if you only knew how much I needed you right now.* Anabella released a soft groan of pure frustration. She wished she could go home, because these three months were turning into one big nightmare. And last night had been the final straw.

She'd never thought that she'd be one to fall into a trap, but she had. She walked right into the trap set up by Charles and Thomas, and she literally walked out with bruises on her body. Anabella couldn't believe his audacity in telling her—after what happened—that she was his. It wasn't going to happen.

The first two months had been fine. Charles would always ask her if she'd like to join him and go clubbing, or accompany him to parties. Of course, as he had kept true to his word, she had gone. A few of his friends always joined them, especially Thomas, whom she had liked at first. Moreover, for some reason, she always ended up sandwiched between the two; either at a table, or on the dance floor. Something she found odd, but never said anything about, or even queried. However, as far as the last two times were concerned, they had become more daring, and at one point she had had no choice but to ask them to back off. Up until then, they'd given her enough breathing room and the friendship had blossomed, that was, until last night.

In the pool they were great competitors, and out of it they fooled around. She always enjoyed their lively conversations and light banter with the rest of the participants, which allowed Anabella to relax with her peers.

As per usual, they invited her out again the previous night. They'd gone to a club she wasn't at all familiar with, one very different from the previous clubs she'd attended with them; louder—and evidently—with absolutely no regard for moral rules. She watched young people letting go of all their inhibitions, not at all ashamed of their behavior.

From the start, she'd been nervous.

Drinks flowed as they introduced Anabella to many of their friends, their faces blurred in the flashing lights. The music was so loud that conversation was impossible, not that anyone was interested in talking.

As the night progressed, the party became more energetic. She knew she was inebriated, and one only had to look at the amount of empty glasses that stood before her. Dancing between Thomas and Charles again, they were squished together due to the throng of dancers all around them, so she'd had no choice but to allow the proximity. Their hands made themselves at home all over her body, and when she wanted to say something, all they did was shrug, continuing to move with the crowd.

It was stifling hot, but no one noticed, too lost in the beat of the pulsing music. Due to the amount of alcohol she'd consumed, she'd had no choice but to hold on to Charles in order to stay on her feet. Her high heels hadn't helped either. With Thomas supporting her back, she rested her head on his shoulder.

She could feel the tightly-fitted dress move, and realized hands were now on her inner thighs, brushing against her constantly. This was followed by her mouth being captured by Charles' lips and tongue; the heat of his mouth ensnaring her with delight. She could taste the cocktail he'd had earlier on his tongue; sweet, with a spicy flavor, and it turned her on. Soft moans escaped her lips. She knew, somewhere in the far recesses of her mind, that this was wrong, but the sensations which coursed through her body were not willing to be ignored, and she gave into them.

Their hands held her even closer, exploring her body. She lifted one of her legs, wrapping it around his hip, moaning with pleasure when they brushed against her. Minutes—or was it hours—passed where she gave in to the attention. The music made them alive as their heartbeats thumped to the same rhythm. Her senses were heightened as they explored every inch of her. She forgot her surroundings, loving the vibrations her body was exuding. They would tease her, over and over, their warm breaths always present on her. Her hands explored on their own initiative.

At one point, she became aware of Charles' erection in her hand; his own groans filling her ears. Her body lifted, and she was open. Thomas' hand had prepared her to receive Charles. Her heart rate picked up as she was thrust against them, bumping, grinding, and rubbing. And then there was the slap. Its vibration woke her.

Finally, it all came crashing down, forcing her to come to her senses. Mortified, she realized where she was, as well as the closeness of the two men who were still deep in their haze. She released Charles' member, and pushed them both away. The music around them still keeping up the persistent pace as she tried to right her dress. Anabella was wasting her time, because they became more adamant as their hands turned into claws, hurting her. She felt her dress rip in the process.

Charles and Thomas had her pressed so tightly between them, she could barely move. Nevertheless, she continued to struggle, even biting down on Charles' lower lip. It seemed to have worked, because on a curse he released her. He touched his bleeding lip, his eyes dark and fierce, the look he gave her menacing. Fear clutched at her heart in a death grip. He said something, but she didn't hear him. Again, he grabbed her, with Thomas holding up the rear, pressing her tightly between them once more. She wanted to scream. Frantic and panicking, she continued to struggle against them, until two bouncers arrived and lugged them away.

She was grateful to the two men. Anabella stood there on shaking legs due to the sudden loss of their weight. How they'd gotten to her she didn't know, but she didn't question it and left the club in one piece. Prior to leaving, they'd asked her if she wanted to press charges, but she decided against it and allowed them to be released. One thing Anabella didn't want was for the police to get involved.

Her torn dress lay in the rubbish bin. Her body was covered in haphazard bruises, which ached the moment she hit the water. She couldn't believe how far she'd let them go. The most frightening was the fact that she'd been very close to losing her virginity. Shame and fear became her constant companion since that night.

When she saw them the next morning, the daggers that shot from their eyes and the looks on their faces, told her they weren't close to being done with her.

She struggled through her event, but kept her composure. Determination and a strong will kept her head in the game. She had come too far to quit now and it paid off. Anabella achieved first place, beating Andria by the tips of her fingers. However, her coach awaited her at the finish line, and he was not at all happy. After a few words were exchanged, she messaged Aldrich, telling him she was fine. She knew it wouldn't help by sharing with him what had taken place, because there was nothing he could do.

This was yet another obstacle she would have to face alone. As with everything else in her life.

"What does she say, Son?" his father asked the moment the phone buzzed with her reply. He read it and frowned.

"She says she is fine, and that I shouldn't worry about her. So typical of her," he mumbled as he walked away. Determined to find the underlying cause of this he added, "I need to make a quick call, Dad. I'll be right back to help with the fire."

"Fine, Son." Mr. Hagin disappeared into the kitchen, deep in thought.

Aldrich just knew something more was going on with Anabella, and since he couldn't help her, there were other ways to achieve this. He decided to give Mr. Clark a call. He'd met the older man a few times during practices; a very practical and paternal man, one who cared about the well-being of his team, especially Anabella's. They spoke for a few minutes, a conversation which left both men disturbed. Mr. Clark agreed to look into it, and would get in touch with what he managed to discover.

Aldrich made his way back to the patio where he immediately set about starting the fire for the barbeque. A permanent frown was etched on his face.

"She will be fine, Son. You just need to put her in the hands of the Lord. He is able to watch over her, and send in the troops if need be."

Aldrich chuckled. "Yes, Dad, I'd forgotten that."

"No harm done, Son, she will be fine. I'm sure she's strong, and will overcome whatever is bothering her. You are doing a great job so far yourself."

"Thanks, Dad."

"Are you serious about her?"

Aldrich looked at his father, somewhat perplexed, as if the absurdity of the question was out of line.

"Yes, Dad, I am. She's definitely the next Mrs. Aldrich Hagin." He chuckled. "She calls me her boyfriend. That's so sweet."

It was Thomas Hagin's turn to chuckle. His son was smitten with the young girl, and although he had not as yet met her, his son talked about her constantly. Just by watching him when Anabella had swum during her race was evidence enough that Aldrich was lost.

His heart was on his sleeve, and he was happy for him. It was about time he found the happiness he deserved, one which was long overdue.

"You owe me," Charles' whining voice told her when she answered a call on her cell. She'd already been in bed.

"I owe you nothing!" she balked, outraged at his assumption. *How dared he?*

"I have spent a lot of money on you, and in return you ran out on me, on us," Charles accused.

"Well, I never!" she huffed, seething, her fist hitting the mattress with a low thud out of frustration.

"Come on, Anabella, don't tell me you didn't enjoy it." He smirked, remembering her willingness for a few seconds as she'd relaxed against them during the dance. Her hand wrapped around him in those scorching moments, moments when he'd thought he would finally achieve a home run.

"I. Did. Not. You owe me a dress," she clipped out, and in return he laughed. It felt like ice-cold water running down her back, and she shivered.

"No, darling, I don't. By the way, we are in your hotel right about now, and you will open the door so that we can finish our dance, if you know what I mean."

"Not going to happen," she snapped.

Charles continued to laugh, adding, "We will see. There are ways to get into your room."

"No!" she shouted in frustration, hearing him snigger before the phone went dead.

She felt sick. Her heart raced uncontrollably. *What am I going to do,* she asked herself. A knock on her door interrupted her thoughts. Her heart stopped in that moment and she clutched the blankets close to her. Her knuckles white, her eyes big and scared as she watched the door, terrified of the men on the other side.

"Anabella? It's Mr. Clark," the male voice called out, relief flooding her body as she sagged against the mattress.

"Oh, thank you," she whispered, rushing to the door, not bothering to cover herself. She looked through the peephole and saw Mr. Clark accompanied by his wife.

She took deep breaths to ease her racing heart and with shaky hands, opened the door. "Mr. Clark, is something the matter?"

"No, dear, we just wanted to visit with you a few minutes if that's acceptable?"

"Yes, of course." She opened the door wider for them to enter, and then rushed back to her bed to pull on her sweat pants and sweater.

"Please, have a seat," Anabella invited with a welcoming smile.

Mrs. Clark complimented her on her win, and they chatted about that for a while. She offered them water from her bar fridge, which they gladly accepted. Anabella had always loved this couple; both were coaches, with all three of their children showing promise as swimmers. They loved the sport and its participants equally. Something that set them apart from many she knew.

Mr. Clark was strict—as any good coach should be—but he showed a good deal more care for them. He was interested in all aspects of their lives, and his door was always open for a chat. Their conduct resembled the Richter couple, whom she respected just as much.

"I noticed you were tense this afternoon, Anabella. Is there a problem you'd like to talk about?" Mr. Clark asked, his tone relaxed, although she detected a hint of urgency.

*How much can I tell them?* She didn't want to get the two men into trouble, which would inevitably cause problems in their sporting career. As they were extremely good swimmers, their country supported them and expected them to deliver Olympic gold in two years time.

With her decision made, she told them about the sleepless nights, but didn't elaborate, or give them too much information.

They listened and nodded in understanding.

"I am receiving counseling," she assured him, "for the nightmares. I think it's perhaps the intensity of constant competition that's making me tense, but I can assure you, Mr. Clark, that it will not influence my abilities in the water." This was delivered with confidence, her gaze unwavering under his strict stare.

"You do know that if there is anything else, anything at all, bothering you, you can speak to me, or Doreen?"

"Yes, sir, I do. Thank you."

"Are you ready for tomorrow?"

"I most certainly am, sir."

"Okay then, we shall leave you in peace. Goodnight, Anabella."

"Goodnight, Mr. and Mrs. Clark."

They walked out, pondering over Anabella's words.

Charles and Thomas passed them, each sporting a smirk, and greeted her coach. Shocked, she closed the door and locked it. She rushed over to the window, making sure it was locked, preventing them from entering via that route. With her cell phone in hand, she was back in bed in a flash, her heart racing a mile a minute.

Suddenly, her cell rang. It showed an unknown number, but she was certain of who the caller was. Answering, against her better judgment, and before she could say anything, she heard, "I hope you didn't rat us out, little girl, because if you did..." The warning hung in the air.

"No, I didn't," she said, concentrating on her voice to keep it under control. Under no circumstance would he ever know how much he affected her. Fear wouldn't rule her; exactly what Mrs. Smit had said in her last email to Anabella. She would remember that. She wouldn't be a slave to fear. She would overcome this, not only for herself, but also for her future with Aldrich. He was definitely her future, that much she knew, and she would protect it at all costs.

"You'd better hope so. Sleep tight, sugar."

The connection went silent, and with a sense of foreboding, she shivered.

She lay back in bed and whispered, "Lord, tonight you protected me from harm, and I thank you for that. Despite the fact that I don't know you that well, You were a shield around me."

She fell into a dreamless sleep, awakening the next morning refreshed.

The month of December passed quickly for Anabella without any problems from either Charles, or Thomas, although their constant stares all but informed her that they were not done with her. She kept her distance, and accepted no invitation from the group in general.

The constant snickering when she entered a room couldn't be avoided. The glances from fellow swimmers—which showed disgust or simply curiosity—were ones she didn't return. The way the men looked at her, though, was something else entirely. Some went as far as to ask her out; she didn't respond.

Through all of this, she made one friend. Marjorie Simms was an excellent swimmer for the English team. Her raven hair, huge, green eyes and beautiful body caused stirs wherever she went. Her pale, freckled complexion reminded Anabella of marble, and she spoke with a heavy Yorkshire accent. At first, she couldn't understand a thing Marjorie said, but as time progressed, Marjorie spoke slower and they eventually formed a friendship.

The competition was stiff and the practices grueling, but the results were seen in the number of medals they all received.

Two days before Christmas, they were invited to a party at the home of Mr. Townsend, Charles' father. Anabella—for obvious reasons—was reluctant to go, but her friend assured her that she would stay close, and that Charles wouldn't dare try anything at his father's house.

As they were staying for the whole weekend, Anabella and Marjorie shared a bedroom suite, which had been assigned to them by the butler. Anabella spent her time laughing at Marjorie's antics as she mimicked the ramrod butler with his English twang. She relished the house's luxury, if you could call it one. It was a three-story, brick home with a large wraparound porch in a southern style, so Anabella was informed. The blue shutters against the white-washed walls glimmered impressively against the late afternoon sun.

Their room was called the Pink Lady because of the huge portrait of a woman that hung against one wall. Her white dress was trimmed in pink lace, which showed off her slender body, and the parasol she delicately held in her left hand was all white lace. Her expression was serene as she stared into space, with only a glimmer of a smile on her face. The room resembled the same tones of pinks and whites as the frame; everything looked exquisite, and expensive.

The house reeked of history in every corner, nook and room, and they were told that the house had been in the family for five generations.

That night, as they finished dressing, Marjorie suddenly left without a word. Anabella couldn't understand her friend's flustered behavior. She had acted tense all day, but Anabella brushed it off as tiredness. The previous day's championship had taken a lot out of them, with Marjorie needing extensive physiotherapy for a stiff muscle.

Anabella didn't give it further thought and disappeared into the bathroom to add her finishing touches. With a last glance in the full length mirror, she smiled at herself. She looked good in the black number she had bought. The dress fit her like a glove, but covered enough not to reveal too much skin. The spaghetti straps highlighted her toned shoulders, and she wore no jewelry, as always. The black pumps showed off her tanned legs and she lifted one in pure enjoyment. It had been a while since Anabella had gone out, and this was a good opportunity to get to know all the other swimmers.

Muffled music flowed through the walls and she sung to the familiar tune while swaying her hips. Fifteen minutes later, she entered her room.

Charles and Thomas were waiting for her.

She gasped at the unexpected visitors. Both wore a devilish grin on their handsome faces. She paled and felt her blood oozing through her veins with rapid velocity.

Charles stood lazily at the door studying her from underneath his thick lashes, his shirt unbuttoned, showing glimpses of his chest and hard abdominal muscles.

Thomas was on the bed, his shirt on the floor, his tanned body shimmering under the soft light.

"Well, well," Charles finally said, arrogant and self-assured as always. "Sugar has made an entrance." His snarling tone sent shivers down her spine.

Thomas chuckled, sat straight up on the bed, and watched her with brooding eyes.

"She sure has taken her time, but look at her."

They spoke to each other as if she wasn't in the room. At first, it angered her, but as awareness crept in, she realized she was in trouble.

"It was worth the wait." Thomas' brooding eyes skimmed over her in lust.

She tried to conceal herself with her arms as best she could, but knew it was fruitless.

"Yes, it was," Charles remarked, having moved closer, and now stood towering over her.

"What do you want?" she finally asked, when she got her voice back. She tried to stay calm, but her body trembled in fear, although she tried to hide it by taking on a no-nonsense stance. Finding a way to get away from them was imperative. Her eyes darted around the room, looking for an escape route, but she was trapped.

"Oh, sugar, we'll finally get what we've always wanted," Charles quipped. "You." He wrapped his arms around her.

Anabella struggled with all her might, but he held her securely. "Please… don't," she pleaded as she kept her head away from him, but all he did was chuckle.

"Yes, sugar, we will."

With one hand, he gripped her face and slanted his mouth over hers with force, his thumb working her mouth open for him. Its force hurt her and she struggled, trying to push him away, but nothing worked. He was more determined than ever. In the process of struggling, he'd turned her around where Thomas now boxed her in from the front. She shouted in his face, pushed her butt out to push Charles away, but he just laughed in her ear.

"Feisty little thing, aren't you?"

It was a rhetorical question. Their grip intensified on her body.

"Don't worry, sugar, you will have me soon," Thomas whispered.

She struggled some more, but the only result she got was feeling her dress being lifted, exposing her thighs. She kicked out, but again it was fruitless and had absolutely no effect on either of them. They all but continued to smother her between them.

Everything within her fought. Anabella knew she had to get out and quickly, her nails scraping a cheek, which was followed by a growl.

The sting of a slap against her cheek caused her to stop. Determined eyes bored into hers. Charles smirked, satisfied with the fear he saw in her green depths.

He hissed softly, "This time, there is no one to save you, sugar. The sooner you comply, the sooner we can leave."

"Never," she hissed, and spat in his face.

He continued to smirk. At that point, her head was jerked back as Thomas slammed it against his shoulder, his tongue leaving a trail of wet kisses behind her ear.

Charles wiped away her spit, before his mouth found her chest. He bunched her dress up further in a fist, ready to rip it.

Her heart pounded in her ears and she knew she had to move quickly, sacrificing the dress in the process, but rather the dress than her. She pushed back with all her strength.

Meanwhile, back in South Africa, Aldrich woke from a bad dream. Startled, he rubbed his eyes, the feeling of unease not willing to leave him. He glanced at the clock; it showed 2:24am. He lay back and closed his eyes, but sleep evaded him. He tried to remember what had woken him, going over the dream. He'd dreamed of Anabella running free in a field, her dark-brown hair waving behind her, all sunshine and radiant. Then, she'd stopped as stormy clouds covered the sky. She looked behind her, her face contorted as she screamed. He remembered the feeling of helplessness which seemed to swallow her.

*What does it mean, and why was Anabella screaming?* It didn't make any sense to him. That's when Aldrich remembered the few moments he'd seen her reaction when the young man had stood close by. She had tensed up. Aldrich frowned. He'd never had warnings like these, but the uneasiness continued to plague him. He sat up straight and his eyes fell on the Bible's cover next to the clock, the fluorescent green light highlighting the gold lettering on the black leather.

Picking it up, he said a few words. "Father, I don't know what this all means, but I will pray for Anabella; for her protection in whatever situation she's found herself in. Please, bring back the bright smile to her face. Let me make her happy. Let her come to me unharmed." He fell silent and waited.

"Let. Me. Go!" She finally managed to break free as Charles' seething eyes looked down at her.

"You are a bitch." He touched his cheek where two long, red marks ran down it.

Her hand shot forward, scraping the other side, and she felt satisfied with her handiwork.

"Look what you've done!" he growled, ripping at her clothes as she fought against him.

Thomas grabbed and held her tightly to his body, but she stomped on his foot with her heel and ran.

Thundering knocks echoed in the room, the door giving in under the onslaught. She could hear Mr. Clark calling out her name. She ran to the door and unlocked it, not realizing the disheveled appearance she presented. Behind him, stood Marjorie, her eyes red and puffy, attempting but failing to avert Anabella's gaze.

"What is going on here?" Mr. Clark demanded, looking past her to the two men standing directly behind her, both smirking in defiance.

They didn't answer, so he looked at her.

"Anabella?" He pulled her closer to him the moment the tears ran freely down her face.

"What have you done?" he hurled at the younger men.

"I am so sorry, Anabella," Marjorie said between sobs. "They forced me to leave you alone. I had no choice." She fell to her knees and sobbed, her shoulders trembling uncontrollably.

"What is going on here?" The same question was parroted in the hallway. This time, it was Mr. Townsend, whose voice boomed throughout the house. He stepped into the room.

Thomas and Charles were pale, the smirks gone, all but fear remained in the depths of their eyes.

"Get dressed!" he barked at them.

They scurried to retrieve their shirts. Charles tried to speak in their defense, but Mr. Townsend was having none of it and held up his hand, stopping him mid-sentence.

"Whatever's gone on in here, I can guarantee will not happen again," he seethed, turning his attention back to Anabella who was being cradled by Mr. Clark.

It took them a while to calm her down enough to get the truth out of her.

Marjorie confirmed her story by what she knew in a very ragged voice.

Mr. Townsend immediately took control of the situation. He phoned Thomas' parents, and their coach. He sent the two girls to their rooms, and the party was called off.

Both Mrs. Clark, and Mrs. Townsend, tended to the young women, and after a doctor examined Anabella, she received a mild sedative, which thankfully sent her to sleep. Marjorie had been given something milder in the form of a relaxant, and although she'd tried to explain the situation again, she wasn't able to get one coherent word out.

She, too, eventually fell into a deep sleep, one nevertheless filled with shuddering sobs.

# Chapter Eight

Eventually, at around 3am, Aldrich fell asleep, exhausted after the vigil watch. Finally at peace, he dreamed of his beloved running through the sun-filled field, carefree and happy. Her ability to bounce back always left him in awe. He wished he had the same gift.

Although the Etsibeth case had been finalized, the woman continued to pester him non-stop. Once again, Mr. Dorflinger called him in after yet another brush off he'd had with her, demanding that Aldrich be kind; his reason being that they had brought their entire portfolio over to the partnership. They—the partners—couldn't allow petty things to spoil their newfound business.

Begrudgingly, he agreed to be more attentive to her needs, knowing full well what she had in mind as far as they were concerned. When she had introduced him to her friends, she'd told them he was her 'special friend' while fluttering her eyelashes and putting on an innocent face, something that aggravated Aldrich beyond belief. When he'd reprimanded her, she'd simply implied that he had it all wrong. Shortly thereafter, he had been placed on the 'red carpet', so to speak. She couldn't fool him, but was resolute in her conquest to claim him as hers. Since then, she'd hung on to him like cling wrap every time they went out.

The night before, she had attempted to kiss him. Allowing the temporary contact, she had come alive in his arms, and because he was hungry for touch himself, he'd enjoyed the warmth of her mouth and the feelings it evoked within his own body. When her hands touched his bare skin, sanity had stopped him. As if he'd been stung, he remembered where he was and with whom, letting go immediately. Back in his car, he'd been furious with his raging hormones, buttoning his shirt with shaky hands. He could not believe he had been so stupid. But, having been restrained from physical contact for such a long time, his body had demanded attention. It argued with him that Bella wouldn't know. That it wouldn't be a betrayal if he enjoyed the plate that was offered, but his heart had disagreed with that reasoning. The meaningless encounters with Ms. Etsibeth had left him cold.

She was not Bella.

He didn't experience the sweetness of strawberries with Etsibeth. His body reacted differently when Bella touched him. She gave him the vitality and ecstasy he had craved since Pauline passed away, to be one with her and only her. He had known Anabella's intention from the moment they met. Her sweetness and love was tangible with each innocent touch, and he could only imagine what their bond would be like when they finally consummated their union. That was what he craved.

He missed Bella tremendously; his thoughts never far from her. Diligently, he would check her schedule, making sure he had access to a TV to get a glimpse of her adorable face. His hungry eyes would rake over her slender body moving gracefully on the screen; her smile ever present.

"Not too long now, my love," he whispered, "then you'll be back in my arms."

He had lain in bed for a while, his thoughts scrambling around after he had woken.

Just after Christmas, the swimming committee held a hearing. Anabella hadn't pressed charges against them, but Charles' father had been adamant that his son wouldn't walk away without punishment. Charles and Thomas had been heavily fined; both fathers refused to pay it for them. Both had to dig deep in order to pay the committee in a timely manner, and both received stern warnings. They couldn't approach either Anabella or Marjorie, who had testified against them.

Marjorie told the court of their manipulation in getting women into bed and using them for their own pleasures. The parents had been shocked with the news. She also told them about her involvement; how she befriended the women she took to them. Greatly disturbed, she'd sobbed during her testimony. It also came out that when she'd tried to stop they threatened to expose her drug use when, or if, she didn't comply with their wishes. Although they regretted her part in it all, the committee felt it pertinent that she be expelled from the competition, which led to her suspension from the English team.

Adding fuel to the fire, this caused an avalanche of trouble for both Thomas and Charles; thinking they had been cleared once their fines were paid. One member of the board, a Ms. Anne Steward, spoke up and said that their fines weren't acceptable punishment and that they, too, deserved to be suspended. This caused much debate amongst the remaining board members, which consisted largely of men. However, she kept at it for two days, managing to sway the board that a clear message must be given that men cannot and must not be excused in something as grave as rape. Finally, the board relented and they were suspended.

When a reporter caught a whiff of the story and managed to acquire further information, the committee diverted his attention by giving him related news to the well-being of the group. They decided it would in no way benefit the swimmers if any other details were to be released.

The ordeal left Anabella unsteady and disorientated, her dreams returning tenfold. She'd always end up in bed, butt-naked, with bodies she couldn't identify groping her private parts. Some hurt her so that she would scream herself awake. Other times, she actually enjoyed it, but it left her numb, loathing herself the next day. For some reason, the smell of garlic was always present.

She had spoken to Mrs. Smit about her body's reactions, and the counselor had explained the normalcy of it. Anabella was a vibrant young woman, whose body had responded to the natural cravings of sexual intercourse, and that the act of lovemaking in itself had not been wrong or despicable, but was meant to be enjoyed between two consenting adults. She needed to distinguish between the two, and not allow apprehension to cloud her judgment. Because in the process, she could miss the most beautiful act between a man and a woman.

That had given her the peace she desperately needed, the assurance that she was a normal young woman with normal desires to be with a man, and not just any man, but Aldrich. She missed him dearly, now more than ever. In keeping up with appearances, she continued with her participation, but inside she ached for her beloved.

Shortly after the hearing, Marjorie flew back to England. Although she tried to contact her friend, Anabella hadn't attempted to return the many messages her friend had left.

André stood in his customary fashion, towering over Sandra with brooding, glazed eyes. The night had been tiring and no one had slept. On top of that, Sandra was moody herself; something that had never happened after one of their marathon nights. She would never admit to herself or anyone else that she was getting older, that she had to calm down. It never even occurred to her.

The group was larger than on most nights, and it took her a while to attend to everyone. During any of her parties, she never left a person untouched, or unexplored. She'd had too much to drink, she realized that; her head felt heavy and her eyes burned from the smoke.

The hot, sea breeze filtered through the spacious living room when someone had opened the windows earlier that morning. It was New Year's Day.

André's constant whining about her daughter had been grating on her nerves. He was the source of her tiredness from the time he arrived, which ended up being just after midnight. Her patience brooked on empty.

"I've told you, André, that she will be back on the fifth," she said brusquely, rubbing her eyes.

A growl was the only response she received.

She introduced him to younger women and men, trying in vain to keep him entertained, but still he had whined about Miss Uptight the whole damm night. How pitiful.

Whenever he stayed over, he insisted staying in her room. Why? Only he knew. Derek had told her that he'd stared at Bella's photos continuously whilst they'd been in her room.

Sandra had only smirked. Really! Anabella was pretty, no one could argue with that. However, did he have to behave like a lovesick puppy?

"The fifth," he growled once again.

"Yes, Thursday," she replied.

"Then she will be mine?" A grin appeared for the first time.

Sandra appeased him by saying, "Yes, all yours. For as long as you want."

And his grin had grown, showing off a white, toothy smile. "I would like that... she is pretty."

Sheepishly, the grin continued to spread over his face; it had been quite comical to watch. She would have laughed if she hadn't been tired. He'd lost weight, too, she realized, not for the first time. He had also started working out, making an effort to look respectable for Anabella, and Sandra had to admit she liked the new look.

Forgetting her tiredness, she smiled, wrapping her arms around him. Her heart softened toward him and tapping him on his shoulder, she said softly, "Yes, she is. I will make sure she is waiting for you in her room."

To that, he laughed boisterously. "She will love me, yes?" All the while rubbing his body sensually.

Sandra couldn't believe that this man, with all his accomplishments and stand in society, would wonder if her daughter cared for him. It was quite pathetic, to say the least. She stopped herself just in time from rolling her eyes in exasperation.

"Yes, of course. What is not to love?" She brushed against his bare torso, which was covered in gray hair. His once protruding belly was now less significant, and his chest more defined; clearly he had put a lot of effort into exercising.

He groaned when her hand brushed over his erect member, making him shiver in anticipation. Capturing her hand, he whispered seductively, "How about another round, only me and you?"

She chuckled as her tiredness quickly evaporated, leaving her feeling energized and open for a bit of gentle sex after the night they had. André could be a tender lover when he wanted to be. She looked around. Her husband had fallen asleep with his favorite blond on the couch, a pleased grin displayed on his face. She grinned with satisfaction. He had enjoyed his birthday party thoroughly.

"Why not?" Leading him upstairs, Sandra bumped into him as he stopped at the landing and motioned, almost pleading her with puppy eyes.

"In there."

She agreed, sighing. She followed him to Anabella's room, closing the door behind them.

Finally, the day the young couple had been waiting for arrived. The plane had landed a few minutes ago.

Aldrich stood at the glass doors, waiting impatiently for his Anabella. The last three months felt extremely long, never-ending almost, and he had been lonely. Now the wait was over, and he looked forward to being reunited with her again.

He couldn't believe how lost he'd felt without her; his days and nights filled with dreams of their union. A final decision had been made; she would be his wife, if she would have him. He wasn't concerned over their age difference, or the many obstacles they would undoubtedly face. For everything, there was always a solution, and the rest could be taken care of as and when they presented themselves. Waiting any longer was not an option; he never wanted to be apart from her again. He also knew he'd been acting like a lovesick teenager—his father and friends often pointed it out on several occasions—but their opinions hadn't bothered him.

Anabella had become his life, the very air he breathed; she had become the most important person in his universe. No other woman would be good enough, this period of separation had taught him that.

No. Giselle, and definitely not Chaney, would do. Anabella had something that set her apart from any other woman, and he wanted to make her his, soon.

Monica had joined him ten minutes ago, followed by Derek, Roy, and his friend, Wanda. The conversation flowed easily between them until they spotted Anabella through the glass doors.

She beamed brightly in their direction, waving excitedly, and the moment she was standing before Aldrich, he wrapped her in his arms, kissing her as if she was the giver of life. They completely forgot about the entire group of people pushing and shoveling against them, as well as her brothers and best friend. Patiently, they waited their turn, each with a grin on their faces, watching the couple's union with great interest.

Finally, out of breath, she pushed him away, glowing up at him, whispering, "I missed you."

"Oh, sweetheart, you have no idea," he responded, his heart reflected in his eyes, while he cupped her face and took in every tiny detail.

"You are so beautiful," he continued to whisper, stroking her cheek with his thumb.

A tear rolled down her cheek, which he tenderly wiped away.

"Ms. Anthony can we have a bit of your time?" someone called, ending their moment, although the air between them was still electrified.

Remaining in his embrace, she turned to see the reporter standing close; he had been watching them with curiosity. Anabella blushed, realizing she'd given the man quite a show when greeting Aldrich. At this stage, it no longer mattered to her; the world could see how infatuated she was with him. She wasn't ashamed of her feelings for him.

With wide-eyed anticipation, the young man smiled at her, making her sigh softly as Aldrich released her.

"Sorry," she apologized with a rueful smile.

He stated dryly, "It comes with you having those two medals, I suppose." He referred to the gold medals hanging around her neck.

Bella chuckled. "I will be back soon."

"Hurry, my love," he pleaded.

"Ms. Anthony, I am from the Sunday Times. We'd love to take a picture of you." The young man continued with his introduction. "I am Jerry Visagie." He stretched out a proffered hand, which she accepted with a bright smile. They walked to a quiet corner in the lobby where he asked her a few questions, as well as the rest of the group. A photo shoot followed.

And then, Izak, and Tersia—who had brought back more medals—were gathered together with a proud Mr. Clark. He'd stood watching in the background.

People stopped and stared at the commotion they'd created. A few recognized them and waited eagerly in the hopes of getting their autographs.

Aldrich, Monica, Roy, Wanda, and Derek, were waiting patiently to one side for them to conclude the interview.

"She's lost weight," Monica pointed out, studying her friend.

"Yes, I noticed," Aldrich replied, his probing gaze hadn't left her for a minute, taking in her delicate features, her gracious posture, shoulders straight but tensed. She towered over most of the people around her. Her long hair was tied in a high ponytail, glossy as always. However, the dark rings under her eyes told a different story, the fine lines around her mouth harder. Something of the old Anabella had been lost on the trip.

It took Aldrich only seconds to decipher her; he was not pleased with what he saw. What now immerged was a more mature woman, one with a guarded expression as she scanned the people in front of her, hesitant in her approach. He realized with trepidation that her innocence had been tampered with. Her eyes were shielded, and it was more than the weight that she lost, he perceived. Watching her closely, he had to admit that this Anabella appealed to him more. A strength and purpose emanated from her, making her more beautiful, if that was even possible. The young nineteen-year-old woman he'd left at departure gate three months ago had matured.

More than that, her turmoil—that anyone could see if they really took the time to look at her—pulled at his heartstrings. The only desire he had was to pull her closer, and shield her as much as possible.

Several times, Roy cleared his throat in an attempt to talk to Aldrich, but his attention was fixed on Anabella. Finally, with a touch on his shoulder, Roy managed to gain his attention. Perplexed, Aldrich looked at Roy. He hadn't heard Roy speaking the first time, and raised a dark brow in question.

Roy repeated his question. "Are you serious about my sister?" He kept his voice low as his eyes flickered between Aldrich and Bella.

Aldrich's eyes narrowed before he promptly looked to Anabella again. "Yes, I am. I want her to be my wife."

Monica squealed with pleasure, clapping her hands excitedly. Many eyes turned toward her, but she ignored them.

"I knew it!" she exclaimed in a soft whisper. "I told Tim you were going to do this; you were too smitten with her." Bubbles of giggles were bursting over her lips as she gave him a quick hug.

Smiling sheepishly, he looked down at her whispering, "Was I that obvious?"

"Yes, duh," she replied, her smile growing.

"There is something you need to know," Roy interjected, his voice serious, devoid of laughter.

Startled, Aldrich glanced back at him as alarm bells went off.

Derek paled and was trying to get his brother's attention.

"What?" Aldrich asked sharply.

"Roy, you will be a dead man." Derek tried to pull him aside, speaking softly into his ear, "What are you doing?"

Roy would have nothing of that, standing firm as he stated, "He has the right to know, Derek."

"Can you two tell me what in blazes is going on?" Aldrich asked as a deep crease formed between his already narrowing eyes.

Roy shuffled his feet uncomfortably as he glanced wearily between Aldrich and Anabella. It was clear that he was in a tough spot. *Should I keep my mouth shut, or warn Aldrich?*

Both Monica and Aldrich watched him, dread growing in the pit of their stomachs.

"Don't do this, man," Derek warned.

"Don't do what?" Aldrich demanded, now totally stunned over the behavior of the two brothers.

Roy was looking at his brother in utter despair, but turned to Aldrich and said, "You need to keep her safe." Briskly, he turned around and walked away. However, it hadn't been quick enough; they'd seen tears rolling down his face.

Wanda followed him, and when she caught up to him, she held him to her as a mother holding a wounded child.

Aldrich watched in absolute stunned silence. He looked at the couple, and then at Monica who was equally dumbstruck at his words.

Their eyes settled on Derek. He shrugged, saying, "We can't talk about this. Tell Anabella we will see her later." He rushed after his brother, leaving Monica and Aldrich with a lot of questions, and no apparent answers.

"What did he mean by *you need to keep her safe,*" Monica whispered. She looked at him fearfully, and then at Anabella who was still busy with her team, the reporter, and a few fans still hovering around her.

"I have no idea," he finally replied, returning his eyes to Anabella, totally unaware of the tumult surrounding her.

*Why must I keep her safe?* Fisting his hand in anger, he watched her closely as the questions crushed through him. *What does it mean?* He planned to take her to dinner before seeing her home, but how could he relax knowing what he had just learned. His inner questions continued. *What did Roy want to tell him? Why had his brother stopped him? Why would she be in trouble? She had just arrived, so what possible things could have happened since she she'd left that would put her life in danger?* The look on her eldest brother's face had been frightening and it scared Aldrich. He couldn't dismiss the fear and pain he had seen in Roy's eyes, nor could he ignore the anxiety in Derek's whole demeanor.

*But, save her from what, or whom?* That was the question.

Still beaming, Anabella looked at him, puzzled with her brothers' disappearances.

He met her questioning gaze, smiling back at her with a steady gaze, all the while willing his beating heart into silence.

She mouthed, "Where are my brothers?" For a brief second, a frown appeared on her face shadowing his own discomfort as he shrugged.

He didn't understand. Nothing made sense.

"Are you going to tell her?" Monica whispered close enough for him to hear.

He tore his eyes from her, briefly looked at Monica, then nodded. He had to talk to her before he dropped her off at home. How he'd go about that, he had no idea, but this was not something he could keep to himself.

Maybe she would understand.

"How could you?" Derek demanded. "Sandra would be furious if she knew you thwarted her plans." His eyes darkened, and broodingly he glared at his older brother.

"Can you honestly tell me that you are okay with what she has planned for our sister?" Roy snapped at him. They had been on the highway for a few minutes now, heading home. Wanda clutched his leg in an effort to keep him calm.

"No, but if we interfere, we will pay the price. I'm done with that man. I still hurt from the last time. I can't take this anymore." He could hardly sit straight. He rubbed his face in frustration as he watched the dark landscape outside flashing past.

"We need to protect Anabella," Roy stated. "That man will tear her apart. Did you see the look on his face tonight?"

"Yes, I did," Derek replied in a low voice. "Can't we go somewhere else?" His body ached; fear causing his heart to thump hard in his chest. The man was a beast in bed. Since Anabella had gone overseas, Derek had had to stand in, giving in to every sick whim the man demanded. He was tired, his body numb, and all he wanted to do was to curl up in his lover's arms tonight. The one good thing that had come from all of this.

André invited him to a party a month ago, which is where he met Frank. He was gorgeous male perfection and stood six-foot, three inches tall in his boots, his body muscularly carved in all the right places, and handsome as sin. They clicked the moment they lay eyes on each other. Frank brought the best out in him. He missed him.

"I promised we would be back," Roy said as he clutched Wanda's hand. She smiled up at him. "But first, we take Wanda home."

"I want to stay with you," she said softly.

"No, my darling, not tonight," he replied as he touched her cheek briefly, before returning his attention back to the road.

"You never let me stay when your parents are home."

"It is for the best, darling, we have spoken about this many times," he said, his voice laced with warning.

"But… Roy."

"I said, no, Wanda, and that's final." He gave her an icy stare. She shrunk back into the leather seat of his Audi, staring at the dark exterior.

"Take me to Frank's house," Derek intervened.

Roy looked at him in the rearview mirror. His younger brother's eyes sparkled with pleasure before turning his attention to Wanda once again, who was clearly still angry with him. He hated when she was angry with him. *Perhaps I can spend the night with her instead,* he thought, smiling.

"I am sorry, darling," he apologized softly, lifting her hand to his lips. "Can I spend the night with you rather?"

She turned her beautiful face up to him, grinned and said softly, "Yes, I would love that."

"Okay, then I will drop lover-boy off, and we can go home."

"Yes!" Derek shouted, making Wanda giggle as she planted a kiss on Roy's cheek.

"I love you," she said in a low voice, and he groaned in delight.

"I love you, too, my darling."

"Are you absolutely sure that that's what he said?" Anabella asked. They were seated at their favorite restaurant in Cape Town; already done with their meal, dishes cleared before them, and her face contorted in shocked confusion.

"But… why?"

"I don't know, sweetheart." Aldrich sighed heavily. During their meal, he'd argued with himself about the information. He'd had no idea how to go about mentioning it, except to get straight to the point, and knew it would come as a shock. He still couldn't believe it himself. He had thought of every possible scenario, but nothing had stuck. In all honesty, he'd been fearful of the unknown, a position he didn't like at all.

Silence fell between them; each contemplating the news. He gathered her in his arms and stared at the dark clump of rock in the distance, as if the mountain was the answer to this dilemma. Their minds blank.

When she covered a yawn, he asked, "Do you want to go home tonight?"

"Yes. I have nowhere else to go."

"You can always come home with me." He smiled into her hazy green eyes, the spark of moments ago gone, the shield back. He could understand why; she was protecting herself from whatever was out there causing her harm. He had missed her, so to just sit there with her in his arms was heaven. He wanted to protect her from the unknown. From the moment they'd walked in and were seated at their favorite spot, he hadn't let her go. He fed her just so the contact couldn't be broken, and it had caused a few blissful minutes of pure pleasure.

"You'd love that," she said softly, blushing when she saw his desire, which mirrored hers.

"You are irresistible," he murmured, planting a kiss on her forehead. They sat like that for a few seconds, each busy in their own thoughts.

"Do you think your parents would harm you?" He finally asked the one question he refused to take seriously. His heart clenched. This one question had haunted him through the night whilst watching her.

She looked up at him, her eyes big and scared.

He hated this.

She hesitated for a moment before she replied in a shaky voice, "I don't think so." Nothing had prepared her for this. She'd never been fearful of her parents before, even in their drunken state. She had no energy to cope with this. All she longed for was a bed, and a few days of rest before she needed to return to her regular routine. Nevertheless, Roy had warned Aldrich, and then rushed away without waiting for her.

*Could it be?* Once again, she covered her yawn and giggled from pure exhaustion.

"Must I take you home?" he asked ruefully.

"If you don't mind, Aldi. I am tired. I could do with a good night's sleep."

"Okay, I will bring you your car tomorrow."

"No." She stopped him. "I will take my car tonight." She looked at him, hoping he would understand. "It's better this way."

He was quiet for a long time. "I don't like it," he finally admitted.

"Yes, I know, Aldrich, but it's how it is, don't fight me on this."

He sighed in defeat. "Okay. Come, let me take you home."

When he moved to stand, she stopped him. "Thank you for understanding, Aldrich," she whispered.

"I don't like this, just so we're clear." His voice became hard with his own displeasure.

"I know," she said softly.

"I would never forgive myself if something happened to you, sweetheart." The edge of anger and disappointment still evident as he cupped her face.

"Nothing will happen to me, I promise," she replied, her lips so close to his that he could feel her warm breath brushing up against his mouth.

He kissed her softly. "I love you, Anabella Anthony."

Her face lit up. "I love you, Aldrich Hagin."

"Will you?" He stopped, staring down into her eyes. The hardness made way for a soft glow as he took her in, swallowing at the lump forming in his throat. Anabella was all fragile and beautiful, so very much his.

She squeezed his leg. The brilliance in her eyes had returned while she watched him tenderly, expectation written on her glowing face under the subtle light.

They forgot about all the commotion around them, it was just them in that moment of time. No one mattered, and when she licked her lips from the sudden dryness her breath caused, Aldrich asked again, "Will you consider becoming my wife?" Finally, the words that had been burning into his mind since she'd left had now been said. His body trembled. "I know this is too soon, and I'm willing to wait until you finish with varsity and the Olympics, but I want everyone to know you are mine."

She gulped in surprise, and her breath caught in her throat. With her face beaming her absolute pleasure, she leaned closer to him and said, "I will consider it."

A few moments passed where all he did was watch her face closely. His heart was thundering in his chest, silencing the music emanating from the speakers. Her eyes were an open window to her soul; he could see her every emotion clearly displayed. She changed from a thoughtful expression to a bright smile in seconds as they sparkled with pure joy. Aldrich just grinned.

"Yes, I will," she replied, and kissed him with unashamed enthusiasm.

"You are mine, Bella," he groaned.

"Always," she returned passionately, and they were lost in the burning kiss long overdue.

At first, their mouths touched tentatively—almost in reverence—innocently, tenderly, and hopeful, but soon desire took them into an explored adventure of discovery. Their world was opening to the vastness of their love. Reacquainting themselves with each other, their individual tastes became one with every brush of the tongue and lips.

Anabella pulled him closer to her, her hands twisting in his soft, dark hair. She moaned in delight as their lips crushed with intensified pleasure.

He groaned softly into her mouth, and her body pressed against him so that he felt every delicious curve of her slender body.

"You are stunning," he finally said, releasing her, her lips swollen from his passionate kiss, "and you are mine." His touch worship-like as he adored her with every loving caress. From his pocket, a small, red box appeared and when he opened it, a small, princess style, diamante ring winked at her.

Her heart leaped with joy as he placed it on her ring finger. Perfect wasn't the word she would use to describe it, but for the moment it had to do.

When their lips touched, she couldn't help but release another moan, one that told him all he wanted to know, and more. He devoured her with his eyes, his mouth, his hands, and his mind. He filled himself with her fragrance, her softness, and her splendor; took her in, making her a part of himself. His body responded as he swept his tongue over her skin, his hands wandering over every delicious curve. He wanted her. Badly.

Out of breath, he whispered, "I'd better take you home." He released her, and Anabella pouted her already swollen lips.

Aldrich chuckled with delight. "Come on, you minx, it's time to put you to bed."

Those words made her smile seductively, her mouth curling with pleasure.

"In your own bed, young lady," he corrected with a grin.

Anabella laughed, not quite believing how straight forward she was being with him, goading him for more. Her dreams had been vivid and alive when she was in his arms. She wanted him more than she thought possible, her body demanding his attention. She had missed him. To have been so near, and yet so far from him had been frustrating. She needed him, desperately. But he was right, not in this way. It didn't stop her lips from trailing down his neck, pausing at the spot she loved so much, enjoying the pulsating beat against her tongue; his pulse quickened with every stroke.

"Don't temp me, sweetheart," he warned in her ear, releasing her as he sat back.

She snickered, "Or what, Aldi?"

The waiter appeared. Aldrich paid the bill without saying a word, but his eyes gleamed with want. The moment they stepped out into the cooler January night, he swatted her on her bottom. She giggled, and he couldn't help but smile himself.

With their arms linked and bodies melded together, they walked to his parked car. The night sky was filled with millions of stars, and small critters were out and about making their own music, highlighting the beautiful night. He was perfect in every sense, and she couldn't help but look up at him with all the desire she felt, only to find his eyes burning on her.

He pushed her up against the BMW and kissed her. Her arms circled his neck as she gave herself to him. He groaned his want, and his hands got busy exploring her body. He delved into every curve, hovering over her neck, her breasts, and finally her bottom as he held her tight against him.

"You are delicious," he groaned into her ear.

"You're delicious yourself," she said as her body quivered with want.

Aldrich chuckled. "Let me take you home." He opened the door and helped her in. When he closed the door behind her, he took a deep breath in order to compose himself. Whistling softly, he walked to his side of the car and quickly got behind the steering wheel. The yielding leather's familiarity was welcoming to him. When he reached for the start button, he stopped in mid-air as her soft voice floated to him.

"I need to tell you what happened while I was gone." She didn't want to break the serenity between them. It was amazing to be back in Aldrich's arms, and most importantly, his intentions still hadn't changed. She loved him even more now that there weren't any doubts between them. He'd confirmed it tonight by asking her to be his wife. She found herself looking at the ring again, already such a huge part of her.

He raised a brow, briefly looking in her direction. He started the car in silence as his jaw clenched, then turned his attention back to the road. They passed cliffs, sentinel in the dark, and the vast ocean to their right. The sliver of a moonbeam glittered on the calm, inky sea, giving off a surreal feeling as it welcomed her home. The magnificence of Table Mountain loomed over the city, its presence overshadowing the sleeping town, keeping it safe in its rocky embrace. She loved her city, one vibrant and full of life; never dull for one moment, but yet had the awareness and tranquility of the country to create the perfect atmosphere for the mother city.

"What do you want to tell me?" He broke into her thoughts. His hand rested on hers, warm and comforting, their fingers entwined as he steered the car along the winding road.

Anabella took a deep breath, resolute in what she had to tell him. She recounted her time and experiences, continuing with what Charles and Thomas had tried to do to her. She concealed nothing; she wanted him to know so that there would be no secrets between them. Painstakingly, she continued to recount every detail of her three months, while her heart beat in her chest as she watched his passive face.

Mrs. Smit had told her that in order for a relationship to survive, honesty and trust was valuable. This was new territory for her since she'd never talked to anyone before, never trusted grown-ups, and Aldrich fell into that category. As time passed, they had learned more about each other, and she now knew she could trust him. The way he'd greeted her at the airport, unashamed of what she represented, amidst the flashing lights and throngs of people had shown her how open his heart really was.

She felt him tense for a second before he relaxed, listening without interrupting her once. When she was finished, silence fell inside the car, and when they passed an overlaid section, he stopped, the car's nose overlooking the ocean as it moved in the moonlight.

He turned and opened his arms for her.

Anabella beamed up at him, grateful for his acceptance. As she moved into his warm embrace, he said softly, "Thank you for telling me, sweetheart." He placed a kiss on her forehead.

"I want you to know everything about me," she said as she nestled against him, her eyes fixed on the moving sea; its calming influence soothing her in its own way.

"I am glad you trust me enough," he replied, his embrace reassuring her as she surrendered to it.

"Really?" She looked up at him, hadn't known what to expect, but the understanding he was giving warmed her heart immensely.

"Yes, sweetheart. I guess I better tell you what happened to me." He grinned as he placed another kiss on her forehead.

Their eyes met, and she smiled tenderly up to the handsome face.

"What could possibly have happened to you?" she asked, unbelieving.

"Women find me irresistible," he said with a soft chuckle.

"You are conceited, Mr. Hagin."

He smiled at her innocence before the seriousness of the moment returned. This was a breakthrough for them. They could speak to each other unashamed and without fear of rejection.

"Seriously, there was this woman…"

And he told her about Ms. Etsibeth's relentless advances while she listened with growing trepidation. Aldrich was much older than her; ready for commitment and kids, and here she was holding him back. Her youth, her career, and her life seemed to work against them. Wouldn't it be fair to rather let Aldrich go? She blinked away the sudden pooling of tears. She could never give him up, could she?

"Hey, what are you thinking?" he asked, when he noticed her attention wasn't with him anymore, shattering her thoughts.

She looked at the scenery as she pulled away. The mere thought of letting him go lay heavy on her heart.

Aldrich had to have sensed her mood as he lifted her chin, forcing her to look at him.

"Hey, sweetheart, you know I love you, right?"

"I do," she confirmed, not wanting to meet his steady gaze.

"You are everything I want, and I'm willing to wait for you," he said in answer to her thoughts.

"Are you sure?"

"Of course I'm sure. Never doubt me." He kissed her again, first on the eyelids and then on the cheeks, eventually claiming her lips as she moaned with pleasure. He was a good kisser; no scrap that, an excellent kisser.

"I don't want to hold you back," she said, after catching her breath.

"No, Bella, never. Besides, I asked you to be my wife, which is serious stuff." His eyes pierced her soul, burning away her heavy thoughts. "Do you believe me?"

She swallowed. She had no choice. It was stupid of her, she knew. "Yes," she managed, barely audible.

"Now kiss your fiancé," he demanded softly, and she laughed as his mouth captured hers once again, leaving her breathless. "How are the nightmares?" he finally asked, after a long silence.

"They're better."

"Are you sure?"

"Yes."

He looked at her, his eyes searching her face. Convinced she had told him the truth, he finally let her go, sitting back in the plush seat. He asked softly, "You will tell me if the nightmares continue, won't you?"

"I will," she admitted after she again glanced at the scenery, swallowed, and closed her eyes. The images flashed before her frequently, willing her to give in to the desire that they fed. She squeezed his hand, eager for the thoughts to go away, whilst the ever-present call to join them was strong; they promised her rapture in their midst.

After the failed attempt with Charles and Thomas, she'd found herself asking the 'what if' question. Her parents lived it, her brothers participated in it, and she had to admit, it had felt good on the dance floor with the two boys; the total abandonment as they enjoyed her, her body's response to them, and the pleasure of knowing them in such an intimate place. But deep inside, she knew it wasn't the way she wanted to live. That it was wrong for her as a person. Ever since the incident, she had deliberately avoided any contact with anyone, and her swimming had received all the attention it deserved. Having worked hard to accomplish that, her goal was in reach. That was what she wanted to do, besides being in Aldrich's arms.

She remembered one of two quotes Mrs. Smit often referred to in the mails she sent her:

*For the mouth speaks what the heart is full of.*
*Our thoughts determined our way of life.*

The wisdom was so profound, but so simple to follow. This kept her quiet, afraid to say what was on her mind, running the risk that he would think she was like her parents; that her desires would drive them apart.

Aldrich was her focus—other than swimming—and he deserved the best. This time with him had just emphasized her heart's desire yet again. She had missed him, there was no doubt in her mind. He was her future. She was committed to him and her swimming equally in her life. That was what needed to spill over into her heart and thoughts, becoming a part of her life. Her life changing for the better. It was her choice.

When they finally got to his apartment and he stopped next to her parked Clio, he placed her luggage in the trunk of her car. They parted with a long kiss. She was tired. Reluctantly, she let him go, and drove away. Once again, he assured her of his love, thrilled that she had trusted him enough to tell him what had taken place.

A weight had been lifted off her shoulders. At first, she hadn't wanted to tell him, but as soon as she saw him, she knew it was for the best. She didn't want to jeopardize what they had, and keeping secrets only caused more pain in the end. That much she knew.

It was well after eleven when she pulled into and stopped on her parents' driveway. Her brother Roy's vehicle was nowhere to be seen; only two other cars had been parked in the driveway, next to the oversized fountain spewing its water in an arch to cascade into the pond below. The light breeze ruffled the shrubs as she walked in with her overnight bag in hand. She'd unpack tomorrow. Just before she'd gotten out, she had slipped the ring from her finger, kissed it tenderly and placed it in her jacket pocket. After the last discussion she'd had with her parents, she knew they would not be happy with her engagement, and she was not in the mood for any confrontations.

Nothing had changed, she noticed, in the three months she'd been abroad as she opened the huge, wooden door and walked into the foyer with its oversized chandelier.

"Ah, there you are, darling!" her mother's smooth, syrupy voice echoed throughout the foyer.

Startled, Anabella stared at her as she took in the whole picture. Number one, the woman was fully dressed, which was a shock in itself. Number two, the woman was sober; and number three, the most shocking of all—she had no male ornament clinging to her.

Surprisingly, number four was that the house's welcoming warmth was refreshing, something she had never experienced before. She had to admit that she was at a loss for words over this change. Was it only for tonight, or could she dare hope for more?

Just then, her father and an older man joined them, their smiling faces beaming at her. They were fully dressed. *Okay, now this really creeps me out,* Anabella thought, flustered, but plastered a smile on her face and greeted them. The older man was familiar, but she couldn't place him at that moment. Maybe it had to do with the black, well-cut suit he wore, making him seem all businesslike and serious. However, the interest in his eyes was unmistakable, raking over her body as if she was his possession, which made her uncomfortable.

"Mother. Father." She nodded, looking briefly at the older man.

"You remember, André, darling?" her mother asked, cheerfully.

"I can't say I do." She nodded in his direction as well, and he returned her greeting with a brilliant smile.

Anabella wasn't willing to meet his stare.

"We are so glad you are back, honey," her dad said, giving her a hug.

*Okay, now this really gives me the jitters. What's happened to my father?* With difficulty, she hugged him back. It left her uneasy and unsure; being as this was the first time her father had given her a hug spontaneously.

"Thanks, Dad," she replied, and stepped back.

Her father, fifteen years her mother's senior, had more gray in his dark hair—her beneficiary in hair color and eyes, only her hair was crisper and her eyes a brighter, clearer green than her father's, which showed her youthful innocence. Years of a hard life were evident on his face, but it never allowed the smile to falter on the handsome face. His tall, lean frame was still in peak condition, another attribute she could thank her father for. He was dressed in a white shirt and charcoal, dress pants, proof of a life spent in the gym and well-balanced diets. His life centered on his business, his wife and the pleasures they shared. The children and house were last on the list, which meant that after nineteen years, she barely knew him.

"You were on the news briefly tonight," her mother said, with a hint of pride.

Anabella couldn't help but look at her curiously. "Yes, reporters met us at the airport," she informed them.

"Congratulations on the medals," the older man said as he moved closer, invading her personal space.

She stepped back once again.

"Thank you, sir." Her smile faltered. The whole scenario just didn't seem right, and she felt extremely uncomfortable. The momentary welcome she had felt was gone, now replaced by a strange nagging feeling. Not all was as it seemed to be.

"Please excuse me, I need to go to my room," she said, moving to the side, but Sandra stopped her escape to the stairs.

"No, darling, first let's have a drink. This is a celebration, after all. We are delighted you're back." She pushed her to the living room where a couple was seated. Sandra introduced them as Lizzy and Dan Porter.

Anabella shook their proffered hands. The man's appreciative glare deepening her reservations.

They sat down on the couch, with André next to her, her mother and father directly in front of her, holding hands. André turned to her, his eyes fixed on her. On the smaller couch, which was to her left, the other couple could barely contain themselves. Lizzy sat on Dan's lap, rather than on the couch, quite happy, apparently, to be together.

Her father asked about her experiences in America, and through stifled yawns, she answered him as politely as possible. André sat listening to every word she said, which made her squirm. Not once had he interrupted her, just listened intently, his hands folded in his lap in a relaxed posture. Avoiding his eyes, she fixed hers on either her father, or the painting behind him.

His closeness unnerved her, and she didn't know what to think of this profound interest, both from her parents and this man. The other two were too involved with each other to care what she said. After half an hour of relentless questions, and no drinks, Anabella called it a night. Determined, she walked away after excusing herself on yet another covered yawn.

Inside her room, she fell onto her bed, exhausted after the long flight, ready to do the sleep-thing when a paper crunched under her body. She lifted herself on to her elbow to retrieve the A5, brown envelope underneath her. She turned it around, but saw no name had been written on either side. She threw it to the floor, jumped from the bed to shower, which she followed with a good night's sleep.

# Chapter Nine

"What do you think, André?" Sandra asked attentively. Her daughter had left the living room ten minutes ago, silencing the room affectively. Jason had followed suit, taking the couple to the pool for a late night swim. The January night was humid and warm, and they all felt sweaty after the long, hot day.

Sandra told them she would join them later, after noticing that André was deep in his own thoughts. She couldn't leave him like that, so stuck around to pour a drink for them both, hoping he would snap out of whatever was bugging him and soon.

He looked at her quizzically, his smile rueful. Not something you would associate with the normally arrogant man. André, three years older than Jason, had a killer smile that destroyed her resolve, melting her insides, always. He was a strenuous lover, but she always walked away sated, even if she swore she wouldn't allow him to get close for a time. Which never lasted long; he was potent in bed, and almost like a drug, caused her to go back quicker, hypnotizing her affectively with his charms.

Watching him, she couldn't help but see the similarities between him and her first lover, Robert. With just a smile or a touch, Robert would take her places in seconds, allowing her to fly in his embrace, taking her to nirvana and back. Not even Jason had that affect on her, and he was an excellent lover.

"I'm enamored with her," he finally said, his declaration bringing her back to the present. "She is everything I want in a woman."

Sandra smiled. He seemed to blush at his own statement, which she found adorable on him. The man had been a self-proclaimed bachelor for years, one who never committed to any sort of relationship. Besides that, no woman could keep up with his demands in bed, never willing to partake of it on a long-term basis. For him to say those words, could only mean that he was serious. She had thought he just lusted after Anabella, but the declaration said so much more.

"What do you mean, André?" She had to be sure she'd understood him correctly.

"I want her as my mistress," he quickly replied, confirming her suspicions.

She gasped for air, stunned at the statement. Anabella was still—for all intended purposes—child, an innocent young woman. Maybe too innocent, but still, the idea of him and her being together had her shaking her head in disbelief. "Anabella will never go for it, besides, she is too young for you."

"Nonsense. She's at the right age to learn, she is ready for plucking, and I will be her teacher," he said, matter-of-factly, his tone changing ominously, which seemed to unnerve Sandra for the first time in a long time.

"This isn't what we agreed upon."

She attempted to discourage him, but his brooding look stopped her.

"I've just changed my mind. Do you have a problem with that?"

"No, of course not," she assured him, taking a long sip from her drink, hoping it would calm her nerves.

"Make it happen, and I will make sure you get that account you pestered me about." He was silent for a moment, deep in thought. When he glanced up at her, he stated, "On second thought, leave it to me. I want to do this." He rose to his full height, making an impressive figure in his formal slacks and dress shirt. He had put in some effort to look after himself, and it had paid off, Sandra noted.

"I want to court her." He blushed again.

Dumbstruck, she looked at him, her eyes huge; she couldn't understand the man. He was acting like an infatuated teenager. Court her? He couldn't be serious. Fool! But she kept it to herself.

"What flowers does she like?"

Sandra was taken aback with that question. She didn't know. She had to admit that she hardly knew her daughter, and couldn't remember the last time she'd had to think so much about her. What flowers Anabella would like, she really had no idea. She diverted her eyes to sweep through the living area looking for any clue, but none came.

"Very well," he said, after a moment of waiting. "I will start with something simple, two dozen red roses. That should do it."

"Yes, I guess it will," she agreed.

He grinned sheepishly, running his thick fingers through his gray hair. "I need to go."

Sandra couldn't believe it. The man was actually planning on leaving. Impossible. "Excuse me, André, but could you repeat what you've just said?" She had to make sure that her hearing was not playing games with her.

"I said it is time to leave. I will see you Sunday afternoon for her party."

"Yes, of course, André," she conceded, stunned once again as he walked out the door. She followed him, flabbergasted at the act. This was the first time André had left without as much as touching the couple they had invited tonight. She shook her head as she watched him pull out of the driveway.

Closing the door, her well-manicured hand flicked a wisp of sandy blond hair from her shoulder on her way to join the other three, still deep in thought.

It was 5:30am when Anabella woke from a deep sleep and stretched herself to her full length. Her body was stiff from long hours of sitting in an unnatural position with no exercise during the twenty hour flight.

She looked around her room, still shaded in dawn, familiar with all her posters and photos covering the walls. Displayed on nooks, her medals shone in the early morning sun; a testimony of all the competitions she had taken part in for the last four years. Her rosewood dresser was home to bottles of perfume and creams, and a carved jewelry box her grandmother had given her when she was ten. Since then, she had filled it to the brim with all her favorite jewelry. Her CD player, along with her stack of CDs, stood untouched on the TV unit, just as she had left it three months ago.

Everything was still the same, but it felt different, as if it was a stranger's room. Nothing had been moved, the light, green drapes smelled clean as they played in the breeze; they had to have been washed recently, but she still got the impression that someone had been there and used her room. A strange, uncomfortable feeling enveloped her. She hadn't noticed it the previous night as a result of her tiredness, but now that she felt refreshed she could sense it.

Someone had lived there. For a moment she lay in her bed, bewildered at the thought, but her senses went into overdrive and she shot up. She was uncomfortable in her own bed. She quickly removed the light, green cotton sheet from her body in one smooth motion, getting out as if something was chasing her. Stepping on paper the moment her bare feet hit the carpeted floor, she looked down and noticed the envelope once again. She frowned, puzzled, and bent down to pick it up. Again, she turned it around searching for any clues, but there were none.

She opened the flap, pulling out a sheet of white paper. Her eyes were wide with shock as she read the message. Letters, cut from a children's book, had been pasted on to it. The kind that had shapes of various animals in different colors. It formed an uneven line, but the sentence was clear, and to the point.

Leave Aldrich alone. He is mine!

*Who is this from,* she wondered, outraged at the audacity of the person. She peeked into the envelope to look for any more clues, but none were forthcoming. There was no name, where it had come from, or anything else to indicate the source. Just that one line.

The absurdity of the statement was too ridiculous to comprehend. Aldrich—the man she loved with all her heart—why would she give him up? There was just no way that that would happen. Not now that she knew he loved her, that he was committed to her. She smiled, her eyes brimming with delight as she remembered the previous night. She was now engaged to her love. Her heart skipped a few beats, accelerating with the thought of them being together, always.

Crunching the paper into a ball, she rejected the notion that someone else would want him enough to scare her. It wouldn't work. *Who could this crazy person be?* The crunched up paper fell to the ground, and she rubbed her eyes in disbelief, willing it to go away.

"I will deal with this later," she murmured to herself, and with one final sweep of her room, she hastily put on her swimming suit. She couldn't stand to be in her room any longer. She had to leave. Besides, she had enough to keep her busy, and having a lunatic disrupt her plans was not on.

With a full itinerary, her day was already packed. First, to the swimming pool to get some much needed exercise. Then, she and the team had to go to the Olympic Board's office to meet with the board. Right after that was a meeting with the press, a photo shoot for You magazine, and one for Sports Illustrated. That would be followed by a late lunch with them. Finally, she could relax with Aldrich on the beach, and have that late night picnic he said he would pack.

"Hi, Dad," Aldrich greeted his father at their favorite restaurant. This had been a tradition with them since he started working, getting together on a Saturday morning, have breakfast and talk about their week.

"Hello, Son." They gave each other a hug before sitting down. The place was jammed-packed this morning, Aldrich noticed. The bustling waiters ran around attending to the customers, which created a fast tempo. Customers' soft mummers joined the fast-paced trend, becoming a symphony of diverse sounds all around them. A child's displeasure filtered through the air, followed by a father's stern voice. Children's voices floated from outside as they played on the jungle gym, while their parents followed them around. Everyone was relaxed, just out to enjoy the early morning coolness before the heat would descend with its fierceness, making everyone scamper back indoors. It was only the very brave who would venture out to the beach during this time. It was unusually hot, the temperature gage in his car read 36° Celsius at 8am; the weather report said it would increase to 43° Celsius by mid-afternoon, but everyone seemed to discard it. However, the humid air was a tell-tale sign; they were covered in a sheen of perspiration.

"How are you, Son?" Thomas asked when they placed their orders for drinks, the waiter walking away in a mad rush.

"I'm well, busy as always." He grinned. "I am finally done with Ms. Etsibeth's case," he informed his father cheerfully.

His father gave him a lopsided grin. "That is good; do you think she will leave you alone now?"

Aldrich had told him all about the clinging woman. One night, during a gala event for business people, Thomas met the young woman hanging on to Aldrich's arm. The woman was relentless in her pursuit. Draped on his arm, she had held on to him steadfastly, almost like a lifeline, and Thomas had

had to admit that although she was lovely to look at, she was just not Aldrich's type of woman.

"How is our little swimmer?" he asked, effectively changing the conversation. He knew his son didn't like to talk about Ms. Etsibeth.

"She is doing great, Dad. Had a bad episode in the States, but otherwise she's doing fine." He smiled crookedly, looking at his dad with sparkling eyes.

Thomas returned his smile. His son was smitten with her, all right. He never thought he would see him. Not even with Pauline had he been this much in love, and they had been close in the years they were together. It had taken him years to get over the shock, the loneliness, and ultimately the loss.

"I asked her to be my wife last night." Aldrich's whole body was shaking with excitement.

"That serious, hey?" Thomas studied his son's features, pleased with what he saw.

Aldrich nodded, the smile spreading over his face, touching his eyes in sparkling sapphires.

"It is."

Just then the waiter brought their coffees, and they then ordered their favorite breakfast. Omelets filled with bacon, tomato, cheese, and mushrooms accompanied by toast. Promptly, the waiter wrote their order down, repeated it and when they were satisfied, left.

"Anabella is just the right woman for me. I want no one else, and she feels the same, Dad." He paused to take a sip from his cup before he continued. "From the moment I saw her she captured my heart; she draws out the playful, energetic side from within me out. I enjoy life when I'm with her. My life is meaningful with her in it. She is talented, beautiful, humble and innocent." He blushed sheepishly, grinning under his father's watchful stare. "I want to be the one who introduces her to her passionate side."

Thomas chuckled at his son's coy way of stating it. From early on in their lives, they had been open with each other, even with the things that were always uncomfortable to talk about in most father and son relationships.

"I understand that, Aldrich. There is nothing in this world that can compare to a union with the right woman." For a brief second, he thought of his own wife; even after all the years—they had been separated by her death—he still loved her, and no other woman could, or had replaced her.

Aldrich told his father about what happened to Anabella in America. For a while, they talked about Aldrich's concerns and the effects it could have on her, and how he appreciated her willingness to share what took place with him, while it could have been easy to hide it away and deal with it on her own. The trust she displayed toward him had only made him want her more. He told his father what she had conveyed to him about her parents, the lifestyle they lived, and their uncaring attitude toward their children.

It made sense to Thomas that what she'd experienced in America would be a magnet toward her attracting the same kind of attention, like bees to a honey pot. She was wide open to that kind of attention, as she'd grown up with it. Something this serious would make her choices in life harder than normal. He believed that the only way that she could get free was to break away from that life, finding refuge in the love of the Almighty, and a loving husband. She had shown Aldrich that she was willing to do that, but at what price? What would it mean for them in the long run?

Just then, a man he had only known through business dealings stepped up to them. André Herbst. He didn't like the man. His cunning rudeness in business deals had made him an unsavory fellow, and Thomas couldn't stomach that.

"Funny meeting you here," the man bolstered, causing several heads to turn in their direction before they continued with their own conversations.

"André, how are you?" he asked as politely as he possibly could. He had heard so many stories about his man; not only was he ruthless, but his behavior toward women kept them away, or drew them closer like flies. He was a real womanizer.

"I am well."

"Let me introduce you to my son, Aldrich Hagin. Aldrich, André Herbst."

"Pleased to meet you, sir," Aldrich greeted, extending his hand while studying the man.

"Thank you, young man," André replied, briefly watching Aldrich with more than a healthy interest, before he turned his gaze back to Thomas.

Thomas frowned at the man's audacity. Was nothing sacred to him? He had heard the rumors about his tastes in both women and men. Obviously, it had to be true from what he'd just witnessed.

Aldrich couldn't explain it, but he felt dirty from the look he received, uncomfortable with the stranger's close proximity.

"Would you like to join us?" Thomas asked.

"No, not today," he said.

Relieved that his offer had been declined, he sighed inwardly and glanced at Aldrich's frowning face.

"I have another appointment, but I will come and see you. I have a business partner I want to introduce you to. I know your company would benefit greatly from their expertise."

This wasn't the first time André mentioned this business. Frankly, the first time he had mentioned it, his gut had been in knots the entire time. The exact same feeling he'd experienced just now. His gut said to stay away, as far away as possible.

"Will Monday do?" André insisted with glaring eyes, his posture demanding only one answer. Yes.

This riled Thomas, but he kept his peaceful demeanor, asking instead, "In connection with?"

"I mentioned it to you a while back. The partnership could benefit both companies tremendously, and I promised I would link you up. It would be very lucrative for both parties involved."

"Who are they?" Aldrich asked, having observed his father's reluctance to give in to the man's demanding attitude.

"Synergy Import and Export," he replied. "I know them quite well. It is a family business, run by the father, Jason Anthony."

Aldrich frowned, the company name did sound familiar, but he knew he'd never dealt with them at business level. But, and this was the puzzle that disturbed him greatly, the owner had the same surname as Anabella.

"In what capacity will they do business with Hagin Contractors?" Aldrich asked the pressing question, which was on Thomas' mind as well. His father's business didn't need anything to be imported or exported. He knew a great deal about his dad's dealings, had handled all the legal contracts for him in the past, and knew they had nothing in common.

Aggravated, André answered abruptly, "I will discuss it with your father on Monday."

Aldrich and Thomas raised a brow respectively in question. Thomas knew he would have to give the man an answer, but before he could, the man continued.

"This has to do with moving large equipment, and I believe your company could help them in this."

Thomas watched him closely; he appeared determined to have his way. "All right."

Just then, the LCD screen lit up with swimmers, in particular, Anabella. Thomas drew Aldrich's attention to it as he'd sat with his back to the screen. With a beaming smile, his son turned around and watched the TV with an appraising gaze.

Thomas smiled at his son's openly smitten stare. He couldn't fault him; she was beautiful, standing there in her Olympic uniform among the other swimmers as they spoke to the reporter with confidence and poise. The group was in a good mood, it was evident on the youthful faces as they joked into the camera. He hadn't met her yet, but already he was very proud of the young woman who would be his daughter-in-law soon. A fine young woman, he could understand his son's infatuation with her.

He turned his attention back to André in order to reply, and was shocked at the man's expression. He saw a look he didn't foresee. The man was looking at Anabella with loving admiration. Could it be? André's gaze swept hungrily over her body, devouring her, making Thomas frown.

Glancing back at his son, he saw how riveted his attention was, noticing nothing else. Was the woman double-crossing his son? It couldn't be, not according to what he'd understood from Aldrich. He knew nothing about her, really, other than what Aldrich had told him. Besides, this man was much older than she was, so there was no way it could be a match. He tried to be rational about his thought, trying to not jump to any conclusions. He would hate to see his son losing his heart because of a woman's deception. Unsettled, he watched the two men, neither aware of the other's reaction. He frowned and drew both of their attentions back to him.

"I will see you at eleven, André," he confirmed, hoping that this would cause the man to go before Aldrich saw anything.

André looked at him sheepishly, as if he'd been caught with his hand in the cookie jar.

His eyes glimmered with delight as he nodded and walked away.

The man was clearly distracted. André Herbst had never acted this way, and Thomas knew enough about him to know that he would always get the last word in. Now, he'd simply walked away. Strange. He was known for his shrewd dealings, and nothing ever distracted him, however, the young woman had definitely unsettled his typically cool appearance. Thomas would love to know why. He knew his son was truly into her, and he trusted that she was being honest with Aldrich. He couldn't picture the young girl with the much older man, who was visibly interested in her. Things just didn't add up.

Thomas watched his son who was still fixated on the screen, and only when the presenter came back after some footage was shown did he have his full attention once again. The glimmer of delight and love he saw in the blue depths told him his son was head over heels in love with Anabella Anthony. Thomas frowned, the surname; it was the second time in one day he heard the same surname. Coincidence?

Thomas and Aldrich visited for another hour, enjoying their breakfast, and after paying the bill went their separate ways. When Thomas got home, he went straight to his study, closing the door in order to spend the afternoon in prayer. Seeking answers from the one who knew everything. God.

"This is a beautiful night," Anabella sighed in contentment. They'd met an hour ago on a secluded beach spot, and had eaten the delightful picnic Aldrich packed for them. She was pleasantly surprised at his selection of food, eating every morsel of the feast he'd chosen. Now they lay on the blanket, her head on his chest where she could hear the soft pounding of his heart in sync with her own, enjoying the starry sky, and the moon filled ocean. The small waves were tranquil, crashing with a peaceful rhythm as they broke onto the shore not too far from them.

"Yes it is. A beautiful night and stunning company," Aldrich complimented her as he stroked her back gently. Their love had brought them closer as a couple; they were relaxed in each other's company. They hadn't spoken much since they'd arrived, but rather allowed their lips their own conversation during the picnic.

She smiled, squeezing his hip in appreciation. She lifted herself on to her elbow, and when she looked down at him, her hair fell, curtaining them in their own private space. The moonlight caressed his handsome features.

Anabella trailed his face with one finger, appreciating every part of its rugged surface. "I have missed you," she said.

"Me, too. I watched you on TV this morning."

"You did?"

"I am so proud of you, sweetheart."

"Thank you, Aldrich. Coming from you, it means a great deal," she admitted with a shy smile.

He cupped her head, his fingers spreading in her hair, bringing her closer to him for another kiss. He wanted her all the time; his body had craved her touch. The closest he allowed himself was to let their mouths melt together. Their lips were speaking their desire.

"You are everything to me," he murmured.

"I love you, Aldrich Hagin."

This time he captured her lips with greater hunger, a bigger demand. Her words were echoing his heart's message. He needed her. Aldrich had a hard time controlling himself with the young pliable woman in his arms, her sweet taste intoxicating to his hungry soul. Soon, he flipped her over on to her back, and rested his full length upon her, pressing into her, as his mouth possessed her.

Her hands were in his hair, keeping his head in position. Soft words of love mingled with her moans created their own language of love, longing and adoration. Both were eager to show the other how much they cared, reacquainting themselves after such a long separation, and confirming their heart's desire. When their hands started to roam over each other's bodies, they let go, the temptation too great to ignore, yet both knowing it was for the best. They were breathless. They stared at each other, the outside world forgotten as they panted for breath, not breaking eye contact.

When he touched her cheek, Anabella could feel the tremor in his hands as he held back, and she moaned softly under his touch. She lifted her head and met his lips once again, whispering, "I need you." She could feel his body reacting with the invitation before he relaxed pushing her back onto the blanket. The slight breeze was playing in his hair, and she again tangled her fingers in the soft tresses. Love shone through every pore on her body for this man.

He captured her hands, kissing each fingertip slowly before he answered her, "I need you, too, sweetheart, but not like this. When we come together, I want us to be married."

She groaned her displeasure, but smiled anyway. "You are so old-fashioned," she teased, her mouth drawn in a disappointing pout.

"Maybe, but you are worth the effort. I love you, and want to do this the right way. I want to show you the pleasures of the pure bond between a man and a woman." Aldrich had to admit that saying the words hadn't come easy. His body reacted to hers fervently. He wanted her more than he could think, but he wanted her to experience life without any complications. To bring sex into the picture now would just create problems. He would rather take it slow, even if it killed him. His body was demanding release within her, wanted to enjoy what she was offering. She was enticing, and vibrant with a passion that matched his.

There was nothing to stop him from having her right there, right then, but he made a silent vow that he would take it slow. He had to show her what it meant to love someone in a wholesome way. She had to learn the difference. It didn't stop him from enjoying her, and he did enjoy her. He grinned when he saw the pout on her lips, and kissed her once again.

"You are an amazing woman." He followed his words with yet more kisses on her eyes, which he trailed to her lips.

She smiled ruefully when he moved away.

"I brought dessert," he said huskily, his voice betraying his inner struggle to hold it together.

She ginned teasingly. "Let me guess, strawberries and cream?"

Aldrich chuckled wholeheartedly, sitting up straight. He had to put some distance between them. She looked positively ravished just by his kisses alone. His body was painfully aware of her proximity, but he wanted their first time to be perfect and unique for her. He wanted her to cherish it for the rest of her life.

"What are your plans for tomorrow?" he asked as he took out the dessert, and searching for the spoons he handed her one once he found them.

"Mother is holding a welcoming celebration for me." She took in huge breaths of air, ashamed of her parents' reactions toward Aldrich. She looked down as she sat up straight, avoiding his eyes.

Ever since her mother had told her about it that morning, she had her doubts. She wished she could invite Aldrich. It would give her the courage to go through with it. Then common sense had filtered through, and she knew she didn't want him there. Their behavior made her edgy. Her mother had talked to her about it, demanding she attend, because many people were expecting her. Anabella had originally refused. Even her father had come to the kitchen, speaking in an authoritive tone for the first time, giving her no leeway.

After that confrontation, when she had been in her room, Roy's visit startled her, because until now she hadn't understood the meaning behind his weary words. He had warned her to be careful, but had given no indication as what he meant exactly. However, she couldn't ignore the seriousness in his entire posture. When she questioned him about it, he had said, "Be careful." And then left. She tried not to think about it too much, but it did scare her. Just like the letter she received. She didn't want to mention it tonight, fearful that it would destroy the peaceful evening.

She'd been separated from Aldrich for three months, and it had almost killed her. If he left her, it would destroy her. She needed this time with him. She didn't want to think of the negative things which tried to separate them. She knew he would be upset, but what could he do? He couldn't protect her while she was at her house. He wasn't welcomed.

She took the spoon from him and watched him. He was relaxed, enjoying this time just as much as she was. The moonlight accentuated the square, masculine jaw, which was highlighted with stubble. Bathed in silver, it gave him a serene expression.

Although she couldn't tell him how she felt about her parents, she wondered about the note. She'd read it again before meeting him tonight. It had been on her mind the entire day. She narrowed it down to one conclusion. It had to be a woman, but who? If she were honest with herself after hearing his confession last night, she was jealous.

This woman liked him and wasn't hiding her feelings for him, either. He'd gone out with her a couple of times during the period she'd been away. Could he, in all honesty, say that he felt nothing for her? Could this woman be the one? Maybe she should go ahead and ask him, see what he had to say, watch how he acted. There was only one way to find out the truth.

"Aldrich, is there anything I must be aware of?" she queried, taking a bite of a strawberry dipped in sweetened cream to hide her discomfort.

He looked at her, astonished at first, swallowing as confusion set in, which became apparent in his expressive eyes. "What do you mean?"

"Girlfriends. I need to know about your previous girlfriends, the ones you aren't telling me about," she clarified, carefully watching him, as she took another bite of the sweetness.

Surprise played over his face, and a hard line edged his jaw. "I am not quite sure where this is leading." His gaze hovered over her

She swallowed, meeting his dark gaze. "I received a warning letter, stating that I must stay away from you."

He gasped out loud, his breath blowing over her as he exhaled. "From who?" He placed the bowl on the blanket and shifted to look at her directly.

"I don't know, there was no name on it," she said softly, seeing the shock displayed on his face. She knew he was being honest with her. The realization helped her to relax, but she had to see it through.

"I want to see this letter," he said as he wrapped her in his arms, asking, "Are you okay?"

"Yes, I am, but I was stunned. Who could it be?" She relaxed into him, her dessert forgotten.

*I was silly to think that there was someone else,* she thought. *He is just as shocked as I was. How could I have ever doubted him?* She pressed herself more firmly against him, seeking his warmth. Lifting her head, she met his gaze. "I will give it to you when I see you again."

"Maybe it is nothing," he said, his mind racing, sifting through all the women he had known over the years. Since Pauline's death, he'd never had any relationships. Occasionally, he had ventured out, but had kept it platonic, never given any woman any indication that he was interested in her. Then a thought struck him, could it be Giselle? She'd clung to him, hadn't accepted no for an answer, and she had made it clear that she wanted him. If it was her, he would have to nip it in the bud and make it perfectly clear that he wasn't interested in her. To send Anabella a warning letter. The mere thought of it angered him as he held her tighter. The bloody nerve of the woman!

Aldrich kept his thoughts to himself. He could sense Anabella's hesitation, but also her willingness to believe him as she relaxed against him. Something he was grateful for.

"Maybe you're right, but I was scared."

"I know, sweetheart, and I am sorry. You don't need this on top of everything else." He kissed her forehead tenderly. "Let's forget about that for now, all right?" he said, lifting her chin and smiling at her. "This is our night, and I won't allow anyone to spoil it."

"Okay," was the last word she said, before he claimed her lips.

"Is everything still going according to plan for tomorrow afternoon?" André asked, out of breath after their marathon. He held Sandra in his arms, watching Jason still buried within the new girl.

Jason had met her at a party they attended four weeks ago, immediately mesmerized by the young woman's beauty and energy. That very night, he had his first taste of her, bringing her home afterward. They had shared her that night. She'd shown no hesitation when Sandra joined in, eagerly accommodating her. Her willingness to share and discover with them had held their attention since then. Jason could not get enough of her. She had been in their bed almost every night, even André found her bubbliness enticing, and she managed to keep up with his demands, which impressed him. Her young body was pliable to every act they introduced, willing to learn all the tricks they knew.

What Sandra loved the most was watching her husband enjoying himself. His passion for the feminine body had never dwindled since she met him. He had been an excellent lover since then, a friend and a confidant whom she loved dearly. He had never slowed down due to his age, and in fact their lovemaking had intensified with each day. He would never miss an opportunity to have sex wherever or whenever with her. Women loved him, and he in turn loved women. Every part of them had to be explored. He was a modern Marco Polo of the feminine body. Over the years, there had been several who stuck around for a time until they found someone new. Still, this hadn't prevented them from coming back on several occasions just for the thrill. By now she was used to it and shared his love for the body, any body. Their openness in marriage was the reason they were still married.

"Yes, of course. She insisted on bringing a friend, but we put a stop to that notion quickly," she added, carefully.

He raised a brow; irritation laced his tone as he asked, "Who is this friend?"

"We have never met him, but I understand from the boys that she loves him very much."

Abruptly he sat up looking at her with annoyance, his sudden movement made Jason stop and look at him quizzically. "No, this has to stop! How can she love someone else? I forbid it!" His voice was laced with anger as he swung his legs from the bed.

Sandra looked at him in disbelief. "André, she doesn't know about you, yet."

"It does not matter, she is mine." He walked to the bathroom, his gait rigid.

She watched him with a mixture of foreboding and enjoyment. He was the ideal man for Anabella, but this friend could be a problem. If he was not willing to join in their lifestyle, he could take Anabella away. They could not afford to aggravate André Herbst. He was a powerful client, one that could make life very unpleasant for them.

Jason's brow furrowed, sensing her unease. "What is up, love?"

The young woman tried to get his attention back by turning his face, but he shrugged her hand away, kissing the fingertips as he gave her a bright smile.

Sandra grinned at the woman's displeasure, her body glowing all over; she was in the throws of an orgasm.

"André is angry about Anabella."

"Why?" He kissed the young woman to silence her whimpering.

"Anabella's friend."

"So what is the problem?"

"He does not want to share her." She gave an ugly snort. Roy had told her about the young lawyer who was madly in love with Anabella. They'd confronted her about it. That was where she was this evening, with him. Sandra knew she had to do something to stop it. She had plans for her daughter, plans that involved André, not this lawyer. After tomorrow night, she would make sure the man wouldn't be interested in her any longer.

"André doesn't like it at all. You know how he is. When he wants something, nothing will stop him, and he wants Anabella."

"Tomorrow night we will make sure she not only likes André, but is willing to share that perfect body of hers," Jason concluded, bowing his head to kiss the woman in his arms. He knew several of his friends who would love to have her. He had watched his daughter grow up into a fine specimen, had shown her off often enough that men couldn't help enquiring about her. His wife wasn't the only one who had plans for her. He smiled crookedly down at the young woman sprawled open before him and whispered endearing words in her ear when she captured him between her legs, forcing him to enter her, grinning as he hit home. Her eagerness was intoxicating.

Sandra watched as her husband impaled the blond's aroused body, reveling in the sounds that they both made. She crawled from the bed to where the two had been in the throes of the lustful act and kissed her husband on his soft spot—on the collarbone, where bone and flesh met. He groaned with pleasure, knowing the effect it would have on him, which caused the young woman to squeal with delight.

"Have you decided to join me?" he uttered between grunts.

All she did was smile as she continued to enjoy him.

Jason had been a sex addict from the age of sixteen, when a much older woman had introduced him to sex. She had been the mother of a school friend and had taught him how to please a woman expertly. Since that introduction, it became his favorite playtime. He loved a woman in his arms and the pleasure of bringing her to orgasm as she opened to him. The thrill and excitement that coursed through him was like a drug to his system, he couldn't get enough. He had married Sandra, because she loved and shared this passion with him. Jason had been her first lover, and still after twenty-six years of marriage, he couldn't get enough of her, or any other woman.

He had mistresses all over the city, and in other cities all over the world. She never complained as he allowed her to have her own lovers, and just like now, would rather join in to the pleasure he experienced. He loved sharing this with her.

André was in a huff as he showered in the luxurious bathroom situated in Sandra and Jason Anthony's bedroom. He didn't care for the Italian marble displayed in the richly decorated bathroom.

Normally, he would enjoy the exquisite taste of his friends, but tonight wasn't one of those nights.

He really liked the couple. They had been friends for a long time, so he'd seen the children grow into adults, and the moment the boys had come of age, he had had his first taste of their chiseled perfections. Between himself and other members of their exclusive club, they'd taught them everything they knew. He loved running his hands over their bodies, loved to feel the ripples of their hard, muscular frames under him. He had driven them hard since the day they could take it. He was more careful with women, and used a softer approach. Except for their mother, of course, she was a wildcat, one that could handle him.

Her daughter had the same qualities; her fiery character had turned him on from the moment she had shuffled him out of her way three months ago. His member reacted just with the thought of having her, and he grinned.

Anabella.

Her name alone had enticed him to cum on several occasions. When buried deep within someone, her name would be on his lips, his mind and his heart.

He smacked his lips appreciatively as he played with himself vigorously. When he ejaculated, he gasped with pleasure, but then the grin faded. Up until now, he'd never been able to have her, and he was growing impatient with both Anabella and Sandra. To learn that she loved someone else angered him. It wasn't acceptable.

He liked her. Her youthful body tempted every nerve in his body. He had watched her on TV a few times, made a point not to miss anything concerning her; studied the slender body meticulously, every curve, every muscle defined by her training, and had had a few hard-ons. He'd never had a woman like her, and admitted to himself that he was obsessed with the young woman, more than with any other woman. She had captured his imagination from the moment he grabbed her firm breast. And he dreamed of the time they would finally be together. He couldn't wait any longer, and now she had a 'friend'. He slammed his fist against the tiles, pain shot into his knuckles and up to his shoulder making him wince

"Damn it, she is mine!" he fumed, "Mine!" He turned off the taps, and glanced at his physique in the mirror. He smiled, satisfied with the new body he had worked hard on the last few months, had sacrificed a lot to have her. Wrapping a sheet around himself, he returned to the room. His shameless eyes glanced at the three people on the floor. Grinning sardonically, he decided to join in. His body demanded attention, and the enticing butt of the young woman was just in the right position for him to take her.

She wiggled her hips invitingly at him. She was gorgeous.

He dropped the sheet, his skin still wet, but he didn't mind as he braced himself to enter her, knowing that she was ready. He entered the blond quickly, his thoughts with the young woman whose picture was in his wallet.

Anabella Anthony.

# Chapter Ten

"It is time to let you go, Bella," Aldrich whispered in her ear. More goose bumps appeared where his lips had caressed her skin. Both were unwilling to end the closeness they shared. For the past hour, he had fed her dessert as they talked, laughed and kissed, forgetting the obstacles in their path. They reveled in their love.

Aldrich could not get enough of the young woman in his arms. Her sweet innocence so different from the women he knew. She was refreshing, intoxicating and full of life.

"Mmm," she murmured, dozy and incredibly lazy in his arms.

"It is late." He chuckled, seeing her slow reluctance to move away from him. He was pleased with her total abandonment, letting go of her guard when she was with him.

"Yes, I am tired." For emphasis, she hid a yawn behind her hand and looked up at him with a lazy stare. "This was nice," she whispered, "thank you." And with that, leaned over to kiss him on the cheek.

"It was my pleasure, we will do it again soon."

"I would love that."

They packed the basket, folded the blanket after they had given it a thorough shake, and hand in hand walked to their cars on top of the cliff. Reluctantly, they parted, driving away, each their separate ways.

It was already after one when Anabella walked into the house. The house was quiet, but she could see the light coming from her parents' bedroom. She knew they were not alone, the two cars parked outside said as much, and she sighed.

After taking a cool shower, she got into bed as her phone buzzed with a text message. It was from Aldrich, whishing her a good night's rest; she smiled at the small cell phone.

"Goodnight, Aldi." She lay her head on the pillow. When she turned to turn off the bedside lamp, she heard a crackling sound from under her head. Lifting her pillow, she could make out another envelope in the dim light. With apprehension, she looked at it dumbfounded, not sure what to do with it. With trembling hands, she opened the brown envelope, and pulled out a sheet of paper. The words immediately screamed at her. This one, too, was written in the same fashion as the first letter.

*Leave Aldrich alone! He is mine!*
*You are promised to another!*

Anabella shot up in the bed. *Now what does that mean?* Shocked, outraged, and stunned into silence, she could only look at the paper, the words danced before her as tears formed in her eyes. Without hesitation she grabbed her phone and dialed Aldrich's number. On the second ring, he answered with a pleased smile in his voice.

"Sweetheart?"

"I have another letter!" she all but yelled, holding her fingers before her lips, her voice shaky.

Silence fell between them before he asked, "What does it say?"

She read it out to him, repeating the dreadful words, gasping for air as the meaning settled in her mind. "What does it mean, Aldi?"

"I don't know." Silence followed yet again. Aldrich, too, was shocked. He shook his head trying to make sense of it before he continued, "Put it back in the envelope. I will get it from you tomorrow morning and take it to the police. I have friends who can help."

"Aldrich, but why? And to whom am I promised?" A sob shuddered through her. "I only want you, no one else," she whispered, fearful of the implication.

"I know, sweetheart, I feel the same." He sighed, his tiredness gone. How could he sleep knowing that Anabella was being threatened? Who was this deranged person? She was scared, he could hear that, and he had to admit that he was just as anxious. However, he had to calm her as best he could.

"No one will take you away from me, Bella." Aldrich clenched his fists, punching the duvet in anger. "Settle down and try to sleep. You have practice early tomorrow morning, and tomorrow night I will take you to a movie."

She swallowed as the sobs forced their way through her lips. With a hiccup, she relaxed into his calming voice. She had never really been scared of anything before, but the letters were making her afraid. How had they ended up in her room, with no postage stamp, or even her name? Where had they come from, and who had put them there?

"Sweetheart, I want to make a call. I will speak to you soon, meanwhile sleep."

"Okay, Aldi. I love you."

"I love you too, sweetheart, now get some rest."

"I will. Goodnight." Reluctantly, she shut down the phone and placed the sheet of paper back in the envelope, to fall into a restless sleep.

*"You are mine!" The words played over in her head, repeatedly. It was a different voice, one unknown to her. It sounded possessive and demanding. A hand grabbed her legs, pushing them apart, and she kicked and yelled against the hold. Frantic with fear, she screamed, demanding that they must release her. Tangled and out of breath, she nevertheless continued to struggle, exhausted from the fight, but refused to stop. They shook her persistently, until she heard a second voice. A familiar voice.*

"Honey, wake up," a gruff voice called to her. "It's only a dream."

Startled, she opened her eyes and found Derek hovering over her, concern etched on his sleepy face. "Honey, are you okay?" He sat down on the bed next to her, his eyes never leaving her. He touched her arm, soothing her as she slumped back into the softness of the mattress, and nodded yes.

"Here, have some water," he offered her a glass. She took it from him with shaky hands. After she pushed herself up, she took a long gulp from the glass, allowing the cool, refreshing liquid to run down her dry throat. She tried to concentrate on its revitalizing taste, hoping to forget the dream. But it was difficult.

"What time is it?" she asked him, the moment she handed the glass back to him.

His steady watchful gaze studied her face; he didn't answer her, but asked instead, "How many times does this happen?"

She looked down at the covers. "Not many."

"You are lying, Anabella." His blue eyes searched her face.

She wanted to hide in shame because she wasn't willing to admit to him her struggles.

"You need to get out of this house," he finally said with conviction, when she didn't want to answer him.

Stunned, she looked up at him, meeting his serious gaze.

"This house is not good for us," he admitted, "and the sooner we can leave, the better."

"What do you mean?" she asked, now wide awake from his statement. Something in his posture alarmed her.

"This is not a normal house." He sighed, as if he carried a heavy weight on his shoulders. "I would love to have a normal house," he murmured.

She reached for him, offering comfort. Her thoughts were in a jumble, shocked at the declaration her brother just made. She always thought he'd been okay with all of this, but it seems he wasn't. They lived so far apart from each other, each in their own little world. On the occasions they did get together, they had spent those days on fun things, anything at all but the issues at hand. They never really talked about their feelings, or the lifestyle within the house. Hearing him speak from the heart startled her.

"I know what you mean."

"We are tired of this life," he said, a tear running down his face.

Her heart ached for him. She could hear his struggles just in those few words, spoken with so much pain, it hurt to hear them.

"I can believe that." She sighed as she brushed his hand.

"I have found someone," he admitted sheepishly, a soft grin appearing on his face.

"You have?" She raised a brow in question, a soft smile on her lips.

"I love him."

"Derek!" she gasped.

He placed a finger on her lips. "I know it comes as a shock, but please be happy for me." His face was cloaked in shadow, but yet she could sense the anguish in him as he waited for her answer.

"Of course I am. When can I meet him?" Questions raced through her mind, but this wasn't the time to ask them. Not now while he was sharing his heart openly with her. Many things fell into its particular slots, things that were so obvious now that she thought about it. Who was she to judge him? He was her brother, her protector, and friend.

"Soon, I promise." He pressed a kiss to her forehead.

"I love you, sis." He got up and walked out of her room.

She flopped back onto the pillow, staring at the white ceiling. The thought of her brother in a relationship with a man shocked her, but then she could understand the choice. In the end, it was his choice, not hers to make. She couldn't blame him, nor turn her back on him.

It was true what he'd said, though. They had to get out of this house, but how, she was still a minor. She had no money to buy a house, or even rent an apartment. All the money she had earned so far went to her studies and swimming fees. She was still dependant on her parents for her daily care. The monthly allowance that she received from them wouldn't be enough to live on her own. She stretched out on the bed, and scrunched herself up into a fetus position. There were so many things to consider, but she was tired.

Her eyes fell on the envelope she had tossed on the floor last night, and the threatening words returned. She shivered and pulled the cotton sheet over herself, her body cold with fear. Who was she promised to? She'd made no promises to anyone except Aldrich. He was the only man she cared about.

The woman remained a mystery.

Early the next morning, Aldrich phoned Giselle Etsibeth's number. He needed answers. Quickly.

He hoped that his hunch was correct where this woman was concerned. He hadn't slept last night, his mind had kept going through all the women who had shown any interest in him in the last two years since he'd met Anabella. Few people knew about the relationship, or even that they were serious for that matter. The people who did know were trusted, and wouldn't do something like this, not to Anabella.

It disturbed him that he hadn't met her parents, but Anabella was adamant in this regard, although he'd met her brothers. He doubted her parents even knew about him. Therefore, the letter couldn't have come from them. What disturbed him the most was that it had to be someone who had access to their house. That would explain how the letter got into her room without a postage stamp. It had to be someone they both knew, and to accomplish what they had, it had to be someone who shared the lifestyle the parents lived. But who?

He knew no one who shared their lifestyle; there was no common threat that could connect them. Most of his friends were married with children, and they had a deep sense of family values and respect for the marriage bond they shared.

Except for Monica, Anabella had no friends other than her teammates, and he knew that they had never been to her house. So who could it be?

On the third ring, Giselle finally answered. Still sleepy and sounding annoyed, she growled, "Who is this?"

"Giselle, it's Aldrich," he said in a clipped voice. He wanted to make it plain that this was not a social call.

"Oh, darling," she replied huskily, her tone softer than a moment ago. "I was wondering when I would hear from you again. I have missed you." Without giving him a chance to explain his reason for calling, she went on about the party she'd had the previous night, and how angry she was at him for not attending.

Finally, he had had enough of her whining and interrupted her, "Do you know someone by the name of Anabella Anthony?" He couldn't accuse the woman outright, so he had to ask subtly. That is, if his temperament would hold.

"The name sounds familiar, darling, but I cannot say that I do. Why?" she purred into the phone.

Someone had to have told her once that it was sexy, because she continued to talk in that manner. It always aggravated him no end.

"She is a swimmer, with the South African Olympic team." He was abrupt.

"No, darling. I don't watch sports. But forget about it. I want to see you today."

"Not going to happen," he growled softly, but instead asked, "Are you sure you don't know her, or her father, Jason Anthony?"

"What is going on, darling, why all the questions? These names mean nothing to me," she whined in his ear.

He sighed in relief. He knew her well enough to know that she couldn't fabricate something like this; her selfish and self-centered ways had no room for anyone else, so he said his goodbye and disconnected the call.

Just then, his phone buzzed again and he answered it quickly. "Hi, Dad," he greeted tiredly, brushing his hair back in frustration. The problem with it all was he still had no idea who was responsible for placing the letter in her room.

"Hi, Son. Listen, I need to see you today, as soon as possible."

"Why, Dad?"

"It is in connection with Anabella."

Aldrich frowned. "I can be at your place in half an hour."

"Great. See you soon."

They disconnected, and Aldrich jumped into the shower.

Twenty minutes later, he was on his way to his father's house in Constantia, fifteen minutes drive from where he lived. He simply put his foot on the accelerator, and made it in ten. As it was Sunday morning, many people were still home, so it went quicker than the average morning traffic. As soon as he stopped, his father opened the door and welcomed him in. They hugged and walked straight to the kitchen where a prepared breakfast had been laid out at the kitchen table.

Aldrich could see the seriousness portrayed on his father's face, had seen it since he'd arrived. He knew his father. Knew the relationship his father had with the Lord. When he acted and talked like this, it had to be important.

They ate in silence, and when they were done, Aldrich sat back and thanked his father for the pleasant meal. His father kept his rigid stance as he looked at him with concern etched on his face.

"Son, how serious are you about Anabella?"

"Very much. I asked her to be my wife, Dad, you know this." He couldn't help but feel cautious at his dad's strange behavior. But nevertheless, he waited for him to explain.

"There is another man who's interested in her, but his intent isn't pure, and I feel she is in danger."

Aldrich sat up straight and watched his father. Absolute shock was written all over his handsome features, his usually tanned skin, pale.

"Dad!"

His father held up his hand, stopping the flow of words he knew were about to rush out of him. "Money was exchanged, and I am afraid her parents might be a part of it."

Shocked, he rose to his full height, the chair tipping halfway over before it returned to all four legs, but neither noticed it.

"Dad, I need to tell you about the threatening letters she's received two days in a row."

"What threatening letters?" Thomas asked, his face also a sickening pale color. It was always upsetting when he received word from the Lord, when it was confirmed, and the accuracy of it. He never knew if he should be happy, or fall on his face in pure humbleness. Since the time the Lord equipped him to listen to His voice, he'd been amazed—sometimes startled—when the facts and promptings concurred. Like right now. He gaped at his son in astonishment.

Aldrich told his father about the letters Anabella had received, and the wording the person used. His voice trembled under the strain. He had to hold himself together for Anabella's sake and be strong, although it rattled him more than he let on, but with his father, he could relax and let go of the bottled-up emotions. "Who would want to hurt her?" he asked when he was done, looking at his father with tear-filled eyes. "She's an innocent, made a decision to turn her life around, and now this."

"Tests are never easy, my son," he said as he approached Aldrich, squeezing his shoulder. "You could have expected it. The law of attraction is working greatly to draw her into the lifestyle her parents live, and all of this just proves that she is under tremendous pressure. We need to pray for her safety, Son." He smiled reassuringly at Aldrich; well he hoped he was as he felt shaky himself. Aldrich needed him now. He looked so vulnerable at that moment. His strong and in control son had lost it for a few seconds, but this was why he was here. To hold him up, and he couldn't thank the Father enough for giving the timely word.

"Let us pray for protection for her and for you, and that these people will see the light."

"Yes, Dad, thank you," he said softly as he wiped the tears from his eyes, doing his best to be in control once again.

They prayed for the better part of the morning, and when Aldrich left he felt better. Relieved that whatever this was, it wouldn't come to its fulfillment. He would see her tonight, and they would have a serious talk.

He had an urgency to get married as soon as possible, because then he could protect her. This only confirmed that they belonged together. He couldn't forget the words Roy had uttered at the airport. He had to keep her safe, and the only way would be to take her out of that house and provide a safe haven.

Anabella was getting ready for the party when her mother knocked on the door and walked into her room smiling.

"Honey, are you ready, the guests are here."

Anabella couldn't help feeling uneasy about her mother's sudden change since her return, and tried hard to dismiss the uncomfortable feelings she experienced when her mother ventured close. She wasn't looking forward to the afternoon's party, and had no idea what to expect. The last time any birthday party had been given to one of them was when she was eight years old. Since then, nothing.

Her mother looked very classy in a pair of black slacks, and white lace top. Her long hair was pinned up on her head, except for a few wisps hanging around her face; she looked younger and beautiful to Anabella. Her mother had always been an attractive woman, but time had left its mark on her. Her once flawless skin was now hard from all the makeovers and unnecessary thick makeup.

"Yes, Mother." She looked at herself in the full-length mirror. Her makeup was done to perfection, highlighting her green eyes and high cheekbones. She planned to make an early exit so that she could meet Aldrich at his place. He was taking her to watch a new movie at the mall. The black pants suited her tall, slender frame, and the red tank top she had chosen showed just enough cleavage not to be shameful. Her long hair sat high on her head in a ponytail, her favorite style. It swept behind her as she turned around. With it, she chose silver jewelry to compliment the outfit. The small hoops in her ears moved slightly as she followed her mother out of the room.

"You look beautiful, honey," Sandra said as they walked to the stairs, which spiraled down to the guests she could clearly hear. Lively chatter filtered through the air. A man's deep laugh was floating upstairs. A woman's shrill voice sounded excited as she stifled a laugh.

"Thank you, Mother." she replied, and looked down at the people standing around in the foyer. Her father was the centre of attention, and the man she'd met when she got home from the airport stood at the bottom of the stairs looking up, watching her as she and her mother descended. Briefly, their eyes met before she looked away, aware of the man's eyes raking over her body, and a smile of approval playing over his face.

The moment she stepped onto the tiled floor, she greeted him. He nodded with a huge grin on his face. The smile on his face told her that she was on the menu and a shiver ran down her spine. The idea flustered her, but she had no time to think about it too much. Her father, Roy, and Derek came to meet her, all looking handsome in their semi-casual clothing. For some reason all five in the family had chosen black pants, the only difference being their shirts. She welcomed the effort they had all made.

"Ah, here is my stunning daughter," her father announced to no one in particular.

Everyone looked at her with mixed emotions on their faces; men with interest, and women with jealousy hidden behind make-believe smiles. One woman, especially, drew her attention. She was shorter than most women there and very blond, and the glare she gave Anabella was one of disdain and hate. Stunned, she looked at her. She knew for a fact she didn't know the woman, but the woman's animosity was apparent toward her as she clutched her father's arm.

"Honey, this is Chaney," her father introduced, and the woman smiled sweetly up at Anabella.

All, of course, a show, and in an even sweeter voice she said, "She is beautiful, Jason."

Her father grinned as she trailed a finger down his arm, latching her fingers in his.

With absolute self-control, Anabella watched the woman, annoyed at her clutching behavior. She wanted to rip her hands away, but thought better of it. If her mother said nothing and her father was okay with it, who was she to say anything?

"Hi, Chaney," she greeted, her smile forced, but the woman's attention was again with her father. She sighed.

"Come, darling," her mother called, pushing her subtly in the direction of the dining room.

They walked in, where more unfamiliar people were already seated. André held out a chair for her, smiling, and when he helped her to sit down, he promptly sat down next to her. His thigh brushed against hers, but she moved slightly away from him. He unnerved her completely. She couldn't understand the man's interest in her. His constant attention had been creepy from the start, now it had intensified and she wished she could get out of there. His face was familiar, yet she couldn't place him.

His burning, lustful eyes were fixed on her, undressing her and with a grin on his face, as if he had a plate of food in front of him, he spoke to her.

"You look beautiful, Anabella."

"Thank you, sir," she replied.

His voice was familiar. She raked her brain, tried desperately to remember the man who obviously knew her very well. She took every detail in, his smell, which wasn't too bad considering, and his appearance. Nothing rang a bell except for his behavior.

Her eyes met her brothers', who were mostly obscured by the arrangement of red roses in front of her; they had a strange look on their faces. Their bodies were tense, and their eyes wide. They were trying to get her attention, eyes darting between her and the man next to her while they mouthed something in her direction. For a fleeting moment, it looked like warning signs, but she couldn't be sure. *Are they trying to warn me?*

Her mother appeared between them just before she could react. She was making sure that Anabella didn't give them her attention. Maybe she was being over-sensitive. After the phone call, she had been very distracted, struggling to concentrate on one conversation. Aldrich had said that she had to be alert at all times, but there were so many things to watch for at the same time. He had demanded that she not go anywhere alone throughout the course of the evening. Once again, he'd offered to come, but she stopped him and said it was unnecessary. She couldn't tell him that her parents didn't want him there, something she was still riled up about it.

She'd been shocked at her mother's boldness that morning. After her practice, she had stepped into the kitchen where Sandra cornered her about her friend. She told Anabella that the relationship was unacceptable to them, and that she had to forget about him.

Her mother knew nothing about Aldrich, and yet condemned him as her friend. She loved him, he was everything she'd ever wanted in a man. Not being able to see him again would shatter her. She tried to defend him, but her mother had shut her down every time she said something. Afterward, she'd had a long cry in her room.

Catering staff carried food in, delicious smells filled the spacious dining room, and she looked around the table at every one who was invited. Not knowing them, she watched with interest as they talked amongst themselves. They were all in good spirits, the tone animated and filled with an energy she enjoyed. This was the first time she was really meeting her parents' friends, that she was dining with them even, and she found it fascinating. She could have enjoyed it entirely except for the man next to her, whose hand brushed up her shoulder every time he spoke to the person on the other side of her. He could have spoken to the woman next to him, who had tried very hard to capture his attention, but no, he had chosen to speak with the man to her left. This caused the proximity of their bodies to be too close for comfort. The closeness unsettled her and put her on edge.

She met Roy's eyes again, and he rolled them to one side, as if he wanted her to move away, but her mother expertly caught his gesture once again. They had a few words under their breaths, and Anabella frowned at the unusual behavior between her mother and brother.

Even if she wanted to, she couldn't move to the side, the chairs were too close for her to shift. If she wanted to move, it would have to be backward, but that would not suffice, either.

They immediately started to eat, the big man's eyes still on her, making her uncomfortable. She noticed that Derek had moved, trying to get around the flowers to talk to her, but André stared him down with hateful eyes, which was strange and frightened her. That something troubled her brothers was a fact. Again, she felt compelled to move away completely, the feeling so strong that she moved her chair but the leg was stuck. She struggled for a bit, but the two men placed their hands on her arms respectively. She knew she had to let this feeling go and focused on the meal that was by now lukewarm.

Her mother and father talked as if nothing were wrong, keeping the conversation light between them and the guests. Confused with the whole scenario, she recognized that she had to get out as soon as possible. The growing unease hadn't left her. Stay alert at all times, she reminded herself.

When supper was done, they made a big announcement in her honor and then rolled out the cake, the one her father and brothers supposedly baked, but she doubted it. Her mother had made a big show about it that morning. They had never baked anything in that house, not as long as she had lived there. Everyone stood up and congratulated her to loud cheers and clapping.

She caught Chaney's ice-cold stare, yet she smiled brightly.

Perplexed, Anabella looked at her; she couldn't believe the hate vibes she was receiving from this woman she hardly knew.

Finally, the two men moved so that she could stand but still kept her boxed in, barely allowing her any movement. She felt uneasy with the whole scenario. The men became very adamant as they showered her with hugs and kisses. André made a big show and congratulated her as he pressed himself firmly against her body. He allowed her no time to move away, or even stop him as he grabbed her arms and held them in a vice-like grip. He came down on her hard and kissed her, crushing her lips underneath his. She could feel the sting of blood as her teeth cut her lip. She fought him. She pushed him, but his chest rumbled with pleasure as he pressed his thick, wet lips deeper onto hers, hurting her.

"Come on, wildcat, open that juicy mouth so that I can taste," he mumbled.

She heard people laughing. Her discomfort didn't bother them. Shocked at the realization, she felt abandoned. She was pinned against the table so that she couldn't leave. An ugly sound followed. The sound of ripped material reached her ears, and she realized it was her top. She desperately tried to clutch the material together, but it was no use.

"No, please let me go!" Anabella felt hysteria bubbling up her throat and screamed out her desperation. She couldn't believe this was happening, not here in her own house. She tried desperately to hold on to her sanity; this wouldn't be the time to lose control.

The moment he took a breath, she pleaded to the group, hoping to find someone who would listen. Desperately, she looked around for help, but everyone laughed, enjoying the show at her expense. By now, she had been moved as her body pressed into another person's body, someone who was holding her close to him.

Her father's voice reached her ears, and in a soothing manner told her to relax.

"Dad, please help me," she whimpered in distress.

She saw him smile. All he said was, "Just relax honey. André is very fond of you. Isn't that right, André?" But the man didn't reply, his hands were all over her.

"Dad, please, not like this," she pleaded, but he ignored her as André continued with the assault, her body aching from his firm grip. She couldn't believe her father would do this to her. Horrified, she released a sob from deep down. Frantically, she searched until she found her brothers; they were being held back, struggling against the hold, tears running down their cheeks as they called to her.

Her face was forced back to look at André, squeezed in his meaty paw as he growled, "Mine! Wildcat, you are mine tonight, to do with as I please." An ugly grin on his face flashed his sickening desire, and her heart slumped before it quickened its beat.

Terrified, she kicked him, but he just held on tighter, kissing her face and neck, his hands grabbing her breasts.

"You will love André, he is a wonderful lover. Relax, honey."

She heard her mother next to her, and she screamed at her. "How dare you! You are my mother!"

The grin on her mother's face was evil as she watched them with growing interest.

Tears ran down her face as fear gripped her, her body immobile. She had no idea what to do and desperately cried out, "Oh God, please help me!" She looked for a way to escape, kept on pushing, but he was too big for her, too strong. More hands joined in, holding her captive. Sweat formed on her face as she fought with all her strength. "Dad!" she screamed again, sending him a frantic look in the hope that he would help her, but he was too far back now with Chaney in his arms keeping him busy, a satisfied grin on her face.

"Come on, wildcat, I want to see your sexy body." And with wet lips he started to kiss further down her body, biting away the lacy bra that was no match for his teeth. She felt the sting on her skin. His warm breath sickened her and she wanted to gag. His rough, big claws forced her pants down. She could hear the material tearing as he swiftly got rid of it. A hand moved between her legs, while another pair of equally rough hands helped him get rid of her clothing. Her shoes had been removed from her feet as someone knelt at her legs kissing and licking, forcing them apart. She felt helpless and terribly alone as she scratched the air. She fleetingly made contact and scratched someone, but hands grabbed hers firmly holding her in position for the brute's onslaught. It felt just like in her dreams, only now it was real and even worse.

"Please, no, stop!" By now she was crying, terrified with the knowledge of what was about to happen. She looked up hoping help would descend from the ceiling. She heard her brothers call her name and a calmness came over her. In the midst of all the turmoil, she felt at peace. It happened suddenly; her mind acted as if it knew what to do and snapped into calm control.

She became quiet, looked at the man still busy with her breasts, pulled up his head with her one free hand and kissed him back, exploring his lips with her tongue. She could feel the grip on her other hand being released and she cupped André's face. It took all of her willpower to do so, absolutely nauseated by this man's lips against hers, his breath smelling like garlic. The smell triggered her memories and flashed through her. She knew the man! It was him. The fat, ugly guy on the stairs. *God, no!*

"That is more like it," her mother said next to her excitedly, clapping hands as she kissed him.

He growled with pleasure.

She felt naked and utterly alone. Her brain cut out the people she trusted the most as they had deserted her. She refused to think about it at that point. She had to make it through this. Her choice was made. This was not for her.

She couldn't believe that this was happening to her, knew she had to act, now, before it was too late. She pushed him down to her breast, crushing his face into her body, and he groaned in delight. And then, with one knee free, she kicked him hard. She connected with his privates, making him scream as pain shot through him, his body collapsing against hers. She felt the restraining hands falling away, and it gave her the strength to act. Affording herself no time to celebrate the faint release, she made her move. Shoving him hard, she unbalanced him, and the moment he released her, she rushed past him.

She could feel hands trying to grab her as he shouted, "You bitch!" And promptly fell to his knees.

Chairs tumbled over as she knocked them in her haste to get away. She turned to where her mother stood in stunned silence. Their eyes met, and all the hate she felt toward her poured from her and without thought, Anabella slapped her with all the power she had and moved away. Her mother yelped in pain, but all she could hear were her brothers screaming at her, "Run, Anabella, run!"

Her father was pressed deeper in the corner as André's body pinned him against the wall, desperate in his attempt to reach her.

"You bitch, come back, you owe me!" she heard the man scream. "I want her, get her! You bitch!"

Her mother shouted something as well, but she didn't hear her or her father, who called her back. She ran for the door, past the people who looked at her, perplexed at the commotion. Anabella was shocked they didn't try to stop her. With her brothers' voices ringing in her head, she ran to the open door, and she did exactly that.

She ran. Her feet took to the road and she ran as fast as possible, taking her away from the horrible house. She passed the manicured gardens, she passed the decorated iron gates, neighbors' houses hidden behind huge walls and into the twilight. The fading sun was touching everything with a brush of yellow gold. The harsh heat of the day was still evident, but Anabella didn't notice any of it.

Her body hurt all over, but her feet weren't complaining as yet. They just allowed her to run on them. They would heal when she was gone from that place. Fear surged through her painful body, her skin bare, cold and shivering, but she kept on running. Cars passed her, and the honk of a horn filled the quiet evening air—but still she didn't stop. She just kept on, not realizing how it must all look.

The raging anger of the man screaming still surged through her, her mother's laugh echoed in her mind. It motivated her to continue on the asphalt. Sobs wracked through her body, tears ran down her face, her father a distant memory. Only her brothers' voices encouraging her to run are what kept her going. Her feet slammed hard against the warm asphalt as she hit it with every stride, running, taking her further from that place, that horrible place.

Raggedly, her breath circulated through her lungs. Detestable, bloody bile filled her mouth with each inhale she took. But at that moment it wasn't really registering, hardly even entered her mind. All she knew was that she had to get away, far away.

# Chapter Eleven

She finally stopped at the Richter house, a haven in the shadowy night, the only place she recognized through the haze of tears. The waving curtains welcomed her home. She had no recollection of how she got there. Should she even knock? If anyone were to ask her at some point, she would not have been able to tell them. All she knew after she saw Mr. Richter was that she was home.

When Mr. Richter opened the door, she fell into his arms, shaking, her face contorted in pain as tears streamed down her cheeks.

*Safe. I am safe. They will protect me!* It was the last coherent thought running through her as sobs wracked her body, forcing her into his waiting arms. Before he could say anything, she was there, clinging to him in desperate need of security and comfort.

Almost naked, she was in a terrible state, her bra torn to expose her to all within range. Her clothes were shredded, revealing even more, and her body was covered in red, swollen bruises, especially between her legs.

With one look of utter shock, Mrs. Richter ran upstairs to find a blanket. Her swift movement went undetected by the men.

Mr. Richter stood at the door astonished and shocked at the sight of her, it was the last thing he expected when answering the doorbell. His eyes raked over her young body and he squeezed his eyes shut, willing the image to disappear, but he knew it would stay with him for a long time. As she fell into his arms, he held her cold body to his and froze on the spot, unsure of what to do. Just to hold her was uncomfortable enough and the state that she was in just made it worse. The force of her sudden movement caused him to take two steps back before he regained his balance.

Tim—who had stopped for a visit—stood just inside the door. He watched as the whole scene played out before him, as if in slow motion. He moved to close the door to any curious onlookers. Alarmed at Anabella's disheveled look, it took him seconds to do the only thing he knew he had to do. Grabbing his phone from the coffee table, he immediately speed dialed the person he needed to speak to as a matter of urgency, waiting but a few beats before his call was answered; no exchange of pleasantries took place.

"Aldrich, you'd better come. It's Anabella." He somehow forced his voice to stay calm, but Aldrich heard the tremble nonetheless and tried hard to keep it together.

"What's wrong?" Aldrich clenched the phone tightly, his mind racing a mile a minute. Something was wrong, and Tim sounded distressed. "Is she at your mum's place?"

"Yes, she is. Just come quickly."

"On my way." Aldrich's own voice had become unsteady. His friend's tone unnerved him. Thinking of Anabella, one thought stuck. *Has something happened to her?* Tim wasn't prepared to talk over the phone, he could hear it in his voice. They knew each other well enough not to question the abruptness of the call.

"See you soon." Tim made another call, this one to the family doctor, knowing he would come without hesitation. Not only was he their doctor, but he was also a family friend, one that could be trusted in a situation such as they found themselves in. He was sure Anabella wouldn't like it if the newshounds got a hold of this; it would tarnish her name and reputation.

His mother returned with a blanket, which was now covering Anabella's shivering body. She continued to clutch his father, not willing to leave the safety of his arms.

Mr. Richter felt every tremor as it rippled through her every time she exhaled. His arms were around her like a shield, his heart aching for this sweet girl. With a sad expression, he looked at his wife whose features mirrored what he felt; tears spilled over her cheeks unhindered for the younger woman.

Finding a chair to sit down, he held her like a baby. Which was an accomplishment, seeing that she was as tall as he was; his old and frail body no match for the youthful strength, but for now he was the pillar she needed.

"I will switch on the kettle." Mrs. Richter excused herself, turning her tear-stained face away as she disappeared into the kitchen.

The only sounds in the quiet house came from within Mr. Richter's arms.

Placing the phone in his pocket, Aldrich grabbed his keys, trembling in distress. His friend's voice had sounded distressed. What could have happened? Tim's behavior was out of character as opposed to his cool persona—an effective tool in the courtroom.

He shot up a quick prayer as he hurried to the elevator, his body tense as his fingers rapped against the steel wall, waiting for the doors to open. His concern caused him to charge through the doors, trying to silence his thoughts as all kinds of scenarios played through his head.

He moved as if in autopilot as he drove toward their house, his heart thudding in his chest while he maneuvered through the evening traffic. He had to believe that she was okay.

Fifteen minutes passed in silence as the Richter family waited in the living room, sipping the aromatic coffees that tasted more like plastic at that moment. When they heard a car pull into the driveway, slamming on the breaks with a loud screech, Tim moved to the door.

Aldrich ran up to the porch. Tim let him in and they both just stood there assessing each other. No words were exchanged between them, but Aldrich saw on his friend's pale face that whatever had taken place was not good.

*Oh dear God, please*, Aldrich prayed silently as he entered the house. Walking past his friend, he found Anabella in Mr. Richter's arms. She was hanging on for dear life. He took in the whole scenario with one swift glance when alarm bells went off in his head. The picture didn't bode well. The blanket covering her had not prepared him for what lay beneath. Her feet were dangling from underneath the blanket, and realizing the state they were in, he swallowed the bile rising from his gut.

They were swollen, crusted with blood, and covered in dust.

No one had noticed until Aldrich pointed it out unsteadily. "What happened to her feet?"

Tim looked at them, only then registering their condition, cursing under his breath while walking to the bathroom to find a cloth. He couldn't believe he'd missed that. His desperate attempt to erase the image of her bruised body from his mind was futile; it continued to linger there as he simply shut out the rest, which was unacceptable to him.

When Aldrich's and Mr. Richter's eyes met, the older man released his hold on her. He knew she would be in his safe hands.

Aldrich nodded appreciatively, grateful to this man who had been there in her hour of need. He crouched down beside them and slowly loosened Anabella's hands from around Mr. Richter's neck. He didn't want to frighten her anymore than she already was. Her face was covered by her hair, which he gently pulled back. Keeping his face expressionless, he studied hers. She looked terrified. Her normally smooth skin was covered in red smudges and dust, her eyes puffy and red. All signs of the pain she was in. His heart clenched as he took her into his arms, speaking to her in a soft voice, all the while holding her like a child. She collapsed into his arms without as much as a flinch once she recognized him.

"What happened?" he asked, when he saw her face.

"We don't know. She hasn't said a word since she arrived," Tim answered him, instead. "We've tried to speak to her several times, but she just cries."

Aldrich nodded in understanding and cradling her, he sat down on the couch. His mind was in turmoil as he sorted through the information he'd received. Then a thought struck him. "Where is her car?" He was trying to make sense of her condition, how she'd gotten there, and where exactly she'd been.

"I don't know, but it's beginning to look like she ran here."

By now, she had calmed down but continued to hold Aldrich as he comforted her in a soft voice. Her breath quivered against his neck and was interspersed by the deep breaths she took. When he attempted to get answers by asking her where she had been, she didn't respond.

*Whoever has caused this, will pay,* Aldrich vowed to himself, trying hard to control his emotions. It just didn't make sense, none of this did, and finding an explanation from her at this point in time was non-existent.

Minutes later, the doctor arrived, taking charge of the situation. "Please, allow her lie down on the couch," he demanded sternly, once he'd greeted every one and had placed his doctor's bag on the table.

And then Mr. Richter spoke for the first time, clearing his throat before he managed to get anything out. "No, she is exposed." Again, he cleared his throat and rubbed his eyes, exhausted.

Horror filled Aldrich's face. "Oh, Lord. Please don't say that!" A cry escaped his mouth, and shock vibrated through every pore. He squashed her against him, her hands clasping around him as if she wanted to comfort him, forgetting the pain she was in. Although dazed, Anabella knew he needed the assurance from her.

"Is there a place where I can examine her?" the doctor asked, waiting on Mr. Richter for an indication, who in turn, snapped out of his silent stupor.

"Yes, upstairs. Aldrich, could you carry her to Monica's room?" No reply was needed.

"Follow me. I will show you the way," said Tim, who until then had said nothing.

Slowly, they went up the stairs. Aldrich carrying his beloved in his arms, Tim leading them; a silent procession as each man pondered over the situation.

Tears filled Aldrich's eyes. *Please, Lord, not this. Let it not be rape!* In desperation, his thoughts raced to the one who could give him strength as he placed her on the bed, delicately.

Her cries had quietened down as she held on tight to him, eyes wide open, watching every move he made, yet not a sound escaped her. In her silence, she gave no indication of how much she had suffered, her own turmoil too explicit as she watched and listened to everyone—too tired to respond.

With a kiss to her forehead he straightened, brushing away the tendrils from her face and neck. The sweep of his hand caused the blanket to open, exposing her just enough for him to notice some of the bruises on her chest. He gasped, dismayed as he stared for the longest second directly at her body before he turned his gaze back to her.

In return, her eyes were lifeless and withdrawn; shielding herself from the rejection she thought she saw in his eyes, not sure if she could handle that from him.

Aldrich had no idea how to react to what he was witnessing, he didn't even have enough time to shield the awfulness, so when the doctor passed him, he stepped back in disbelief.

"Please, leave us, let me examine her. It will be best to call the police in this situation," the doctor informed them, after one quick glance at her.

Anabella moved for the first time, waving her hand in protest and shaking her head fiercely, as if to say no. She was too tired to utter one word, but they understood her perfectly.

Aldrich wanted to argue with her but knowing her, it would be futile. She was in no state to put up a fight, and he didn't have the heart to rebuke her decision.

"All right, then, please close the door," said the doctor.

Tim led Aldrich away, supporting his friend with a hand on his shoulder. "Come, Aldrich, she will be fine." He didn't dare look at his friend's face. The sorrow and questions were clearly evident. It was too painful to watch, and he turned away so that he wouldn't see his distress.

Reluctantly, Aldrich walked backward out of the room. Numb, but still fixated on her.

"It's all right," the doctor assured Aldrich in a gentle tone. "I will examine her and give her something for the shock. When I am done, you can sit with her. Not that she will remember much as she will fall asleep immediately after the injection." Replaced by sympathetic concern, the doctor lost his professional tone.

A deadening silence filled the room and the hallway. The two friends stood outside the door waiting, leaning against the wall for much needed support.

Aldrich pulled out his phone and dialed a well-known number. It was answered in seconds.

"Dad, please come. I am at Tim's parents' house." Not willing to say anything further he ended the call, visibly shaking as he swallowed at the lump in his throat. He knew his dad would understand. What could he say in any case? Until the doctor confirmed or denied his suspicions, he had no news. However, he wanted his father's quiet strength there. Unbidden flashbacks of a previous time entered his mind, and he crumbled to pieces, sobbing, not caring that Tim was witnessing his meltdown.

It'd felt like hours before the doctor finally opened the door.

"Well, doctor?" Aldrich almost screamed out, his nerves on end. The air electrified with anticipation as both stared at him.

"She was not raped." Relief was visible on the older man's face.

Thankful, Aldrich kneeled as if he were praying, the pressure too great. He trembled from the sudden release.

"Thank you, thank you," he murmured in gratitude as he stared up at the physician. Tears were running down his face unhindered and through the stubble that had already formed on his face.

"She was definitely attacked, but she fought back. She has skin under her fingernails. Her body is bruised, but no broken or fractured bones. I gave her a mild sedative. She will sleep now."

Without any prompting, Aldrich rose fluidly from the floor, pushed the doctor aside and went straight to her. At her bedside, he knelt down to be close to her. He grasped her hand in his own, kissing every digit with the utmost care. It felt cold and unresponsive in his. Hands that could cleave through water were now numb and lifeless.

When he looked at her, he felt immense love for her; small and fragile she lay in that bed, dried tears had streaked her cheeks. Tiredness covered her body in a pale shade, devoid of any life. She looked at him and gave him a weary smile before she fell asleep.

Mrs. Richter followed soon after, speaking softly to him so as not to disturb Anabella, but she needed to be cleaned. At first he shook his head but she assured him that she would be quick about it. She explained that the doctor said it would help Anabella's healing and reluctantly he left, waiting outside the door. When she opened it minutes later, he was back in. There was no stopping him this time, and everyone else left them alone.

He just sat next to her for the rest of the night. Much later, his father and Monica found him still holding her hand. He'd fallen asleep right next to her, his arm wrapped around her protectively. They thought it best to leave him, even if his body would ache in the morning due to the unnatural position.

"We didn't sign up for this," John spoke the moment Anabella ran out of the house. No one had chased after her, and John was upset about the sick scenario. He couldn't believe what he'd witnessed. He held his wife's hand in a frantic attempt to hold it together. With a feverish anger, he looked at those laughing, who upon seeing John's face quickly stopped. Some were ashamed with their behavior, avoiding his eyes, shuffling away.

He couldn't believe that he'd brought his wife into this set-up, wanting to bed them. It had been a long time fantasy for him, and when they both turned forty, Martie had been willing to explore. She'd read a few novels about the subject and had been intrigued from the start. He made contact with a group on the Internet, which had led him to this gathering tonight. It would have been their first time, but after what he'd just witnessed, he wasn't sure anymore.

"What kind of people are you? You are her mother!" Venom dripped from each word as he spoke, disgusted with Sandra while he continued to pin her with a heated look. "And you allowed this? It is sick! You are sick." He waved his hands around the room, taking in everyone gathered there. Seething, he watched the older woman just stand there with anger and disdain written on her face, as if she were the one who'd suffered.

*God Almighty, what mother does things like this,* he thought.

André—a man whom he'd had the highest respect for due to a business connection—was in the middle of it all. During the introduction, John had been surprised to see him there; never once thinking he would meet the man under these circumstances. Now he was venting his own anger on the sons as they watched him with mock arrogance. At least they had been more than willing to help their sister.

The father, Jason, whom he'd met a week ago, he really liked. The man was a real gentleman toward his wife. Martie had been giddy as a schoolgirl with all the attention he'd flourished on her. He had been satisfied that it would be a great adventure to them both. Now here was the father in the arms of a blond, while his daughter was being molested. She'd managed to get away, running down the road practically naked in the dark. *What kind of man does this to his only daughter?*

"Come, Martie, I want nothing to do with this." He walked away, his wife following his lead, both utterly outraged with what they'd seen.

"Mustn't we call the cops?" she asked John as he drove away, his car spinning down the road in the opposite direction to where Anabella had ran.

"And tell them what?" he fumed. He just wanted to distance himself from those people. A case would be harmful to him if word got out that they had attended such a party. They both fell silent.

More people left, the 'joke' had turned sour and they thought it in their best interests to go, now showing disgust toward both the parents and André. Soon it was only Sandra, Jason, Roy, Derek, André, and Chaney left in the dining room.

"So, does this mean the party is over?" Chaney asked, her voice trembling with bottled-up anger. She'd thought that this night would be the turning point for her, but no, Anabella had messed it up. Big time! She hated that girl.

"Yes, darling, I think you need to go home," Jason said somberly. He never turned a woman away, but the forlorn look on his face said he was done for tonight.

"I don't want to leave, I want to stay with you," she insisted, and pressed her curvaceous body against his.

He smiled ruefully at her and slapped her on her bottom. "You are a tease, darling, but not tonight. I will call you soon."

"You promise?" she pouted up at him, and he nodded as he kissed her gently. She walked to André, who appeared calmer now than minutes ago, staring into nothing. "Are you okay?" She leaned into him, trying to draw his attention toward her, but he just growled something incoherent.

Feeling all alone, she looked one last time at Jason before she walked away. She left the house contemplating her next move.

"André, I am sorry," Sandra began, slumping down on the chair next to him. She couldn't believe how disastrous the night had ended. She had waited a long time for this, and was sure that Anabella would join in the party she had planned. She'd seen the curious looks Anabella gave the group of late, and she was convinced that she'd still have been persuaded to embrace it. She looked around her dining room; the cake was untouched and still in the same spot, now a mocking reminder of the failed night.

Sandra knew they'd lost many friends tonight, and she couldn't help but feel a little guilty. They could have handled it differently. Maybe if they had taken her to her room she would have changed her mind. It wasn't supposed to have turned out the way it had. *How could Anabella have done this? Where did I go wrong with her?*

That the problem lay at her doorstep didn't enter her mind. Neither did the fact that Anabella had the right to refuse and could decide what would be the right choice for her. None of these thoughts ever entered her mind, so preoccupied was she with her own life and wants.

Anabella was her only daughter, and she wanted her to experience the joy she'd had on many occasions; the thrilling experience of opening oneself up to a man so that he could have his way. The power a woman has when a man loses himself. Now her dreams were shattered. She looked at him; he was visibly shaken after the ordeal. Would their relationship change after this?

"It wasn't your fault," he exclaimed softly as he got to his feet. He looked ten years older than he really was. The angry scratch on his face was a silent reminder of what had taken place. She watched as he walked out of the house without another word, his shoulders slumped under the heavy weight of his worries.

Moments later, she heard his Land Cruiser start up, then growing faint as he reversed out of the driveway and onto the street, and with a soft purr the engine roared away. A stillness she'd never experienced before covered the house, not even the night critters made a sound. She shivered, because at that moment, it felt ominous and dangerous.

Her husband stood quietly across the table as he watched her. Their eyes met. He opened his arms and she rushed toward him, crying softly into his chest. Sandra couldn't understand her own emotions. She was a person who'd never given in to such frivolous things, life was too short. This was all a first for her. She had no idea that what she felt was the emptiness of a relationship she'd lost with her only daughter. She had no idea of the devastation she had caused Anabella, and how she would feel about them now. Severed deep into its roots, a life long relationship had been destroyed, with no opportunity of repairing the damage. They would never speak again.

"I would think that tears are a little too late," Roy's sneering voice broke the silence and her sobs.

Both turned to their eldest and listened to his rebuking words.

"You should've thought about what you were doing a long time ago, but as always, you didn't. It is all about your own wants and needs. Neither of you knows your daughter, and yet you thought she would be okay with all of this." Waving his hand in the air he indicated everything, his face showing a sour and disgusted look. "Good for her that she managed to get away."

Both Roy and Derek stood there, their rigid stances clearly marking their disapproval and disdain toward the two people who called themselves parents.

"I am leaving this house and I will never return. Don't call me," he clipped, and marched out of the dining room.

"Me, too," Derek said, his face swollen where he'd received the brunt of André's anger. "I've had enough. I thank you for the things you taught me not to be." With a sneer on his youthful face, he left.

They could hear their sons run up the stairs, slamming doors and drawers in their haste to pack and then again, minutes later, as they came down in a flurry and walked out of the door. Slamming it behind them with finality.

An ominous cloud of silence loomed over them, willing the life out of everything. Sandra and Jason looked at each other, stunned at the turn of events. In one night, they'd managed to lose not only their friends but their children as well. In one night, their life had come to a halt.

He captured her hand in his and walked to the stairs.

"What now?" she asked softly.

"Now I am going to make love to my wife." He kissed her cheek, allowing his lips to trail down her neck and end with a kiss on the swell of her breast.

She giggled with excitement. "I will love that," she purred and followed him to their room.

The disastrous night was history. This was what they lived for, the present, the next climax in bliss, forgetting everything else in the ecstasy of arousal. It was a drug to them, so deeply embedded that they couldn't function without it, and at that moment they needed it urgently.

"Where do you want to go?" Roy asked as they stood outside the house. A dead silence encompassed them as they stared emotionlessly at the vacant driveway covered in darkness. The garden and fountain offered nothing but emptiness as they searched for something, both knowing they wouldn't find it—not there in any case. There was nothing to say, really. Both had seen the end coming fast, like a derailed freight train, it was inevitable.

"You can drop me at Frank's townhouse."

"Okay, but first we must take Anabella's car to Monica's place."

"Why?"

"I think she will be there, they are like a family to her." His own confession left a bitter taste in his mouth. If he'd done a better job being the older brother, this would never have happened. Right there and then, he vowed to be a better man, friend, brother, and lover.

"Yes, you're right. I will follow in her car." Derek nodded approvingly.

"Okay."

They drove away from the house. Each busy with their own thoughts of the disastrous night. Both trying to stop the guilt that wanted to devour them, and both knowing that they hadn't done enough for Anabella. It was something they'd have to deal with for a long time, and only then would they find peace.

When they stopped at the Richter house, all the lights were on, cars parked haphazardly in the driveway. Aldrich's black BMW was an indication that he was inside. Walking up to the door, they didn't have long to wait. Tim opened up for them, strict and rigid he stood sentinel as he looked at them both with loathing. They couldn't blame him.

Mr. Richter invited them in, rebuking his son softly.

Tim left them standing at the door without any hospitality, or apology.

They inquired if she was there. Mr. Richter assured them that she was, but she was sleeping. He informed them that the doctor had examined her and had given her a sedative for the shock. A stranger stepped closer, inviting them to sit, which they accepted gladly. The group gathered around them listening as Roy told them what had happened earlier, leaving nothing out.

Roy could see why Anabella felt welcome at the house, she'd mentioned the Richter's a few times during their odd conversations. Her well-founded trust was evident as he relayed the story, without the Richters once showing any judgment toward them. They knew who the real culprits were.

Satisfied she was in good hands, they left for Frank's house where Roy dropped Derek off with a goodbye, turning the car toward Camps Bay. He watched his brother walk into Frank's house and the door closed behind him. A final gesture that his brother, too, was ready to move on with his own life.

Wanda, already expecting him, grinned with excitement when he arrived. Having a family with her was the right choice for him. He tried not to think about his sister's frail body when he'd gone to check up on her. Aldrich was by her side, sleeping, not stirring at all. Roy had then left. He was happy about the relationship. Aldrich was a good man, one who loved his sister dearly. Anyone with half a brain could see it except, of course, their parents. He couldn't believe that he'd endured it for so long, bearing witness to the damage they'd caused to both his siblings. His own guilt laid heavy on his conscience. He was the oldest, was supposed to have protected them, and it had almost destroyed Anabella. He hated his parents for what they'd done.

They were sick in the true sense of the word. To sell her for a night, promising her to a brute who cared only about one thing. He just couldn't continue like this. Eventually, the day that the dam would break its banks had to come, and tonight had definitely been it. If his parents ever saw it that way was another matter altogether.

However, he highly doubted it.

Aldrich slept through the night, albeit in an uncomfortable position—he slept soundly. Knowing that Bella was with him made a world of difference. When he woke, he felt the heaviness of a blanket draped around his shoulders and let it fell onto the bed. The sun was streaming into the room, highlighting the furniture. Not that he noticed it as he stood and stretched his numb limbs, all the while never breaking eye contact with Anabella's sleeping face. She looked peaceful, taking in deep breaths, her arms spread above her head, her hair covering the pillow. She was a picture of relaxation. Smiling, he bent down and kissed her.

She whimpered and gave him a glorious smile without opening her eyes, then rolled onto her side.

He smiled and placed another kiss on her forehead, inhaling her sweet essence and then straightened himself to his full height. He needed to walk the numbness off, so he left the room and made his way downstairs. Everyone was seated at the dining table, each with a cup of coffee. The soft, animated buzz ensured him that all was well.

"How is she?" they asked in choir form, the moment they noticed him.

"She is still sleeping."

"Doc said we must leave her. She will only start to wake around noon, and then he will be here to check up on her," Tim explained.

Aldrich nodded as he pulled out a chair and sat down next to his father.

"Coffee, Aldrich?" Mrs. Richter placed a cup in his hand without waiting for a response. He thanked her, noticing the older couple's tiredness with a grateful smile. *This could not have been easy for them.*

"We need to talk to you," his father said carefully, his heart aching for his only son.

"All right," he answered. His father's attentiveness alerted him to the fact that this wouldn't be good news.

Once they were all comfortable, Mr. Richter began to speak. "Her brother, Roy, came just after you went upstairs with her. He was extremely worried about her, and it took some time for him to calm down and tell us what happened. They had a party at their house for Anabella."

"I know," said Aldrich, "she talked about it two days ago. She was upset because she couldn't invite me." Awareness filled him. "Now we know why." He breathed out and continued as realization dawned on him. "Her parents... they did this to her." Abruptly, he scraped back the chair to stand, but a hand appeared and held him back, calming him enough to stay in his seat.

"Well, her mother arranged a party all right, with Anabella as the cake." The sarcasm was not lost on anyone when Mr. Richter spoke.

"What do you mean she was the cake?" He was dumbfounded at the harsh reality, his brain having trouble with the news. First, he looked at his father who smiled at him before he returned his gaze to Mr. Richter, listening to every word intensely.

"A man, a friend of her parents, paid them R10 000.00 to have a night with her."

Aldrich gasped; nothing could have prepared him for this information. His face paled and his hands trembled as he balled them into fists.

"He was the one who attacked her while her mother looked on. It was her initiation night into her parents' lifestyle."

Aldrich smirked in disgust. He hated this woman. He'd never met her and hoped he never would, afraid of what he might do.

"Roy and Derek also left the house. They said they were finished with that lifestyle, and with them. Trapped while this happened, they felt guilty because they couldn't help her. They'd tried to convince their mother not to continue with her plans, but she didn't listen. It seems their father showed no interest in any of it either, just said they must support their mother. When she broke free, they screamed at her to run, and she ran all the way from their house to ours." Silence met them.

"That's fifteen blocks," Aldrich muttered, and no one said anything. "In. The. Dark!" he added for emphasis.

Guilt etched on his face as comprehension of her night struck him anew. Aldrich put his head in his hands. "I simply cannot believe this. What kind of people are they!" he spat angrily as a fist connected with the tabletop.

Everyone present jumped at the sudden sound, then slumped back in their chairs.

Throughout the night they'd discussed what had taken place, became angry and vented at the people who did this. Therefore, they understood Aldrich's turmoil.

His father placed one arm around him reassuringly. "She is safe, Son, that is what counts."

"Yes."

"God helped her; He gave her strength to fight them."

Aldrich nodded, but rebellion grew in his heart. "It was still unnecessary for her to have experienced this."

"Yes, it was, but now she can move forward."

"Let's hope." Aldrich was devastated. "How is it possible for parents to do this? She is sweet, innocent, and full of life. I don't understand." His words rang true as everyone had asked the same question.

"A lot of questions have definitely been answered, though," said Tim after a long break in the conversation.

"Yes, now I understand why she was with us so much," said Mrs. Richter. Her grief was tangible as she stared at them with red-rimmed eyes.

Once again, silence fell over them, all busy with their own thoughts.

Monica was also hard hit with it all. Her best friend was in so much pain and it was hard for her to watch. She listened as the grown-ups talked, without uttering so much as a word. Tim had phoned her last night, and it had taken her a while to calm down enough to go over to her parents' house. Shocked, she heard the story they had just told Aldrich. She had always known what her parents did, but never thought they would sink as low as to sell her. It sounded like a storyline from a book, not real life. How was it possible for parents to be like this? No wonder Anabella refused to take part in it.

*Will she ever heal as a person? After last night's traumatic experience, will she ever be the same?*

She knew enough about her home life—that it was bad—but what happened to her was the extreme; her friend had paid the price. Raped or not, she had still paid the price. Anger welled up within as tears streamed down her face unhindered, her heart aching for her best friend.

Aldrich slowly came to life thinking of something, he removed his cell phone from his pocket. Once he located and dialed the number, he spoke swiftly with Mrs. Smit.

As he ended the call, Monica asked him about the woman. "Who is Mrs. Smit? Is this the lady that Anabella is seeing for counseling?"

"Yes, she's Bella's counselor."

"Then it's good that you phoned her."

"It is." He stood and left the dining room, and made his way out through the patio doors. He wanted to be alone, he needed to make sense of it all. He remembered her condition the previous night, the devastation on her youthful face, and now this. No wonder she didn't speak, the betrayal had sent her into shock, and now she was struggling to work it out on her own. Damm them to hell!

The news still stunned him; parents who arranged for their only daughter—for quite a substantial amount—to be a common whore. Unheard of.

Revulsion rose with bile up his throat and he had to swallow hard for it to stay down, taking deep breaths to calm himself. *Was this their family business, the one Mr. Richter had referred to?* He simply couldn't believe it.

When his thoughts wandered back to Bella, love soared through him for her braveness, her strong will as she persevered, her sweet innocence and her determination not to give in to the lifestyle her parents were clearly living.

He loved her. The thought rushed through him and left a trail of sweetness in its wake. His heart was beating a strong rhythm as all obstacles fell away in an instant. He knew he was right, she was his. She'd shown it in every choice she'd made. He could never doubt her love for him. It was clearly identifiable, her heart belonged to him and he would treasure it for as long as he lived. Standing on the patio with the sun radiating from the sky, he felt contentment with this knowledge, and for the first time since he had arrived, he smiled. It was the golden lining around a dark cloud and he knew all would be well with them.

# Chapter Twelve

An hour had passed since they'd talked. Both women were now preparing lunch in the kitchen. Mr. Richter and Mr. Hagin sat discussing the future of sport and the effects of politics within it. Both deeply concerned about the negative influence it had on the athletes and the country.

Tim and Aldrich were standing in the shade of the patio, discussing a case they were working on. Not that Aldrich was concentrating much on it anyway, but at least it kept his mind busy. He'd had to restrain himself from checking up on Anabella every few minutes, but it was difficult. She needed the rest, still, he couldn't help wondering how this would affect her in the long run. Her reaction the previous night had him worried; although the doctor had told them that it was normal. Normal or not, he had to be certain she would be fine.

Now, he stood in the heat of the day contemplating a case while his fiancée was struggling, which in turn made him feel helpless. He wanted to do more than stand around. A few times now he'd thought about Roy's warning at the airport, and resentment built within him. Not once did they think that she would be in danger from her parents. If he'd known, he could have done more to prevent it.

A few times he'd walked away as anger and bitterness tried to overshadow the immediate concern. He wanted to go over there and tell them exactly how he felt. But then sanity prevailed and he stopped himself.

Anabella had to get up. The incident was crashing down on her with a weight she couldn't fathom, still shocked at the evil she had encountered at the hands of her parents. The sickening feeling of betrayal that she had experienced in her home had broken her to pieces, leaving a gap in her heart. She wanted to sink into oblivion and sleep forever, but knew it would only extend the inevitable. She had to face this day and move on, could not allow them to have the upper hand. Not after all her hard work.

When she'd looked at herself in the tall mirror, the stranger looking back had eyes as big as sources, glaring at her from an emotionless pale face. She'd never thought of herself as fragile, but at that moment she realized how delicate she really was. How easy it was for people to break someone with absolutely no regard.

She'd broken down and cried until only dry sobs wracked her body. Exhausted, she went to the bathroom and showered, inspecting herself as an observer would. Cold and detached, she moved her fingers over every inch of her body. She noticed the bluish marks left from the fingers that had grabbed her fiercely, and purple marks on her breasts where the man had bitten her. Although she wasn't in pain, it was sensitive to the touch.

Calming herself down enough, she left the bathroom, the pair of long pajamas she'd borrowed from Monica covered her from head to toe, giving her some confidence when she approached the stairs. Muffled voices trailed up as she ventured down, holding on to the railing for support, her feet awkwardly tilted to the sides so as not to rest on her raw and bruised soles.

As she approached the living room, conscious of how she must look, she could see Mr. Richter in conversation with a visitor. This man looked familiar in so many ways, but she knew she had never met him before. He smiled at her, his eyes soft and welcoming, and she returned the smile without hesitation.

"You are awake!" said Mr. Richter excitedly, calling everyone. "She's awake!"

Immediately, they rose to greet her.

Aldrich made like lightning.

Tim had no idea that his friend could move that fast, but it seemed that he could. And he grinned. He was already around the corner, throwing the door open and running toward Anabella in seconds. From the time he'd met the young woman, Aldrich had been distracted and on several occasions, his mind had wandered resulting in Tim having to remind him of where he was. He envied his friend, seeing as he was still searching for the elusive perfect woman.

"Bella. My love!" Joy was displayed on his face. He couldn't conceal his emotions anymore. By now, it was obvious that he loved her. With one sweep, he took her in his arms and held her close, enjoying every part of her against him, his heart overflowing with the sight of her.

*He's still here. He didn't reject me,* Anabella thought in amazement, her heart pounding as she bathed in his appraisal. These lines of thought had plagued her the most the moment she'd opened her eyes. Would she see him again after last night? Would he still be interested in her?

Now, seeing him still very much present soothed her sensitive heart and she chased away all the doubts she had anticipated. She giggled as she wrapped her arms around him, hugging him fiercely. Burying her face in the softness of his neckline, she inhaled his closeness, his strong arms barricading her from anyone else. Relaxing in his contact, she absorbed his love as it filled her with strength and hope. She loved him so much. Her heart felt bigger than before knowing he was with her. However, they were not alone, and this became even more obvious when someone cleared their throat.

"Please put me down, Aldrich," she asked, giving him a peck on the lips, feeling shy with all the attention as chuckles filled the air and knowing that the room full of people was looking at her curiously. As she pulled away from him she smiled, seeing the joy and relief in his handsome face. His eyes were reflecting his heart, and all she could see was love in the blue depths shining down on her.

When he put her down, she flinched with pain. Realizing his mistake, he cringed, lifting her quickly as he muttered an apology to her. She forgave him instantly as she wrapped her arms around him. She knew it wasn't intentional; not like anything her parents had done. He placed a kiss on her cheek and walked to the couch. Not to be the cause of any more pain, he sat her down and took a seat next to her, holding her hand as he watched her intently.

"Thanks, love."

His eyes sparkled when he heard her repeat the tender words. He placed a kiss on her forehead. "Are you all right, Bella?"

"I'm fine," she assured him.

He studied her for a few seconds more before he turned away and waved the unknown man closer while he rose.

"Dad, I want you to meet someone." Pleasure filled his voice as his dad walked to them. He gleamed with pride as he watched her.

*Dad.* She felt faint. She couldn't believe she was meeting his father. She swallowed hard. Aldrich spoke often about his father, and she had always wanted to meet him, but not like this. He was a man that Aldrich admired. What would his thoughts be regarding her? She wanted to hide away in shame, but the man's reassuring smile convinced her that it was all right.

"Anabella, this is my dad, Thomas Hagin." Finally, his father and Bella were meeting each other for the first time. Aldrich knew his father would love her, and he was not disappointed.

"Pleased to meet you, young lady." A smile adorned the older man's face, so very like Aldrich's smile.

She returned his greeting with genuine friendliness.

"So, this is the young woman who holds my son's heart captive in her hands." He took her hands into his larger ones and held them close to him, crouching before her. His milky-blue eyes radiated affectionate care; she detected no falsehood within them.

*How on earth was I so lucky to find not only one but two men who look at me with wonder, as if I'm the best thing that has ever happened to them? How is it possible?*

"How are you, little one?" His sincerity was genuine, something Anabella couldn't miss, and she loved him immediately. He was everything she had wanted in a father—she'd observed this with just one glance. He was honorable, kind, and filled with tenderness, yet powerful and strong as if nothing could touch him. An older replica of Aldrich with more gray in his dark hair; it simply distinguished him from the rest. Now that they stood side by side, the similarities were so obvious she couldn't help but smile brightly up at them.

"Mr. Hagin, I am pleased to meet you. Please accept my apologies as I haven't made much effort to look presentable. What kind of an impression will you have of me? In my pajamas at..." she paused and looked pointedly at Aldrich. "What time is it exactly?" A twinkle of delight played over her face.

Aldrich smiled. "11:30am."

"In my pajamas this late in the morning," she continued, eyes filled with amazement as she looked at him.

They chuckled at her playfulness.

"Yes, it is a crying shame. Don't let it happen again," he teased playfully, already liking her tremendously.

"I'll do my best not to." She grinned.

But all playfulness disappeared as he asked with watchful intention, "Are you okay, dear?"

"Yes, sir. Now that I am safe, I'm just fine." She beamed brightly up at him. Even to her own ears her response sounded truthful; something she hadn't felt for a long time.

Everyone swallowed at the lump forming in the throats. Her youthful vibrancy and honesty touched them, although her body said something differently.

Aldrich couldn't believe he was looking at the same woman from last night, her capacity to recover was one of the reasons he loved her. Admiration for this woman flooded him once again.

Happy to see her out of bed, Mrs. Richter and Monica joined them, with Tim just behind his mother. Hugs and kisses rained down on her as each took a turn to greet her, all the while Anabella laughed and joked with them to ease the discomfort she could sense emanating from them.

Mrs. Richter asked her what she wanted to drink, and then brought her a warm cup of coffee. By now, Aldrich was sitting next to her allowing her to lean against him, while supporting and comforting her at the same time.

Seated around her, the small group fell silent and Thomas cleared his throat.

"I have to ask, Anabella, how did you get away?"

When she looked at him the sparkle in her eyes dimmed as fear and distress replaced her cheerfulness; the wounds still raw and open.

They all realized at that moment that the road to recovery would be a long and difficult one for her.

She grew silent for a moment, swallowing at the tears that threatened to erupt. "It was the strangest thing," she said, her voice steady as she glanced from one to the other. "I fought like crazy against the man's onslaught and tried desperately to escape. But the man was too strong for me." Her voice hitched and she took a gulp of air.

Aldrich squeezed her hand supportively and she continued, blinking away the tears. "I remember looking up to the ceiling asking for help. Just before that, I noticed that my brothers were being held down. My father stood to the side, a blond in his arms, while my mother was next to me telling me to relax. I couldn't do it and continued to struggle with all my strength. A calm and peace I never experienced before captured my thoughts. It was a fleeting feeling—like a clean breeze that filtered through the stench—and all the fear was gone. That's what helped me to act quickly. I knew I had to relax in his arms. It was a natural reaction, and the moment he thought I'd played along, I kneed him and ran as fast as I could."

Silence fell in the living room as a sob left her lips. She wrapped her arms around Aldrich, and he buried her in his allowing her to cry. Tears streamed down his face, his throat dry from unshed emotions. He held her trembling body and rocked them both to calmness. Words of endearment left his lips as he spoke to her softly; he could feel her relax into him.

After a few minutes, a shiver ran down her spine and she grew quiet, just resting in his arms. He could feel her breathing had returned to normal as she placed a tender kiss on his open neck. "Thank you for being here," she said softly.

"There is no other place I'd rather be," he replied. "You are my life, Bella."

She smiled at him, the people around them momentarily forgotten.

With a clearing of the throat, Tim bid them farewell and went to work.

Monica also excused herself, said goodbye, and held her friend in a tight grip.

Mr. Hagin followed suit and in a gentle voice said, "When you feel better, you need to come for a visit, all right? Be strong dear. If you need a father figure and you will let me, I will be honored to fill that role." Sincerity was written on his face.

Anabella looked at him and knew why she'd immediately fallen in love with this man; not because he was Aldrich's father, but because he accepted her as his daughter, unconditionally. Tears filled her eyes, and when she reached out to him he bent to hold her firmly to him, like a father would hold a daughter; secure and warm, and full of love toward her.

Anabella removed her arms and replied honestly, "I will come as soon as I'm able to."

"That makes me happy. I will eagerly await your visit." He rose, wished them both a good night and left.

"Thanks, Dad." At that moment, Aldrich's heart felt too big for his chest.

"André, please sit down." Thomas offered him one of the office chairs. He had arranged with the man to come in later because he wouldn't have made it for ten. Surprisingly, he had accommodated Thomas without any demands. For some reason, the man wasn't his boisterous self today. The scar on his face looked painful, and wondering what had happened he shifted his focus to the man himself. "Can I offer you any refreshments?" he asked when the silence continued between them.

André nodded. "Coffee would be fine."

Thomas asked his assistant to organize it and sat back waiting for him to carry on.

He stared at some remote place in his office, distant, unsure, even uncomfortable.

*Does he even know where he is,* Thomas wondered. The silence stretched out, and when Patricia placed the tray on the table, he lifted his head in surprise and shifted in his chair. When she left with a final glance toward him, Thomas asked, "André is there something I can help you with?" On a personal level he didn't know the man well, had never said two civilized words to him, yet there he was, sitting in a state of bewilderment.

"I…" And he fell silent, a blush appearing on his face. He cleared his throat before trying again. "I did something foolish last night." He looked down in shame.

Thomas studied his face, now devoid of the usual stern malicious look on the once chubby face.

André had lost weight, but since Saturday he looked like a ghost. Dark rings had formed under the usual cold, steel-grey eyes, now shadowed by his black lashes, as if he were hiding.

*Something has rattled him pretty good,* Thomas contemplated. "Do you want to talk about it?" Sincerity caused him to sit forward, arms resting on his desk, sending a quick prayer for the necessary guidance and wisdom.

The man lifted his eyes, and Thomas could have sworn he'd seen a tear forming before he blinked and got up.

"I'd prefer to take this up again tomorrow."

Before Thomas could answer, the man left.

He raised a brow in question, bowed his head and brought the distressed man before the Lord.

The moment André Herbst stepped out of Thomas Hagin's office, he had to blink against the overwhelming glare reflecting directly into his eyes from a car's window. In the process, he bumped against a person who muttered a *sorry* and walked away. André fumbled around for his sunglasses and covered his eyes. The scowl on his face grew with every second that ticked by, irritated with himself, mostly.

He couldn't believe his reaction whilst in Thomas' office. He'd never reacted that out of control in his life, but the previous night's incident was becoming his undoing. His obsession with the young woman had left him unbalanced, uncertain, but mostly scared. He wanted her like a desperate man seeking a rare gift, a gift he almost destroyed in a crazed moment of lust. He had been distracted since the incident, and could hardly form a coherent sentence. The fear on the young girl's face and the fact that he was the cause of it, kept him awake all night. It played repeatedly in his mind's eye. Not even the bottle of whiskey he'd taken with him could stop the visual movie in his head. He had never sunk so low in all of his dealings with women, always believing in mutual respect and agreement to whatever was agreed between them. But last night, he'd been totally out of control and lost it with Anabella Anthony. *How could I have been so stupid? No, scrap that, a damn FOOL! With big, black capital letters.*

He wanted her like no other. For the past three months, his dreams had been saturated by her, filled with every lewd act he wanted to carry out on Anabella, and he hadn't been able to wait any longer. No getting to know her first, he just grabbed what he had considered his and now he loathed himself for the very act.

Sandra had phoned a few times throughout the evening and that morning, but he wasn't in the right frame of mind to speak to her. He avoided her as much as possible, wanting no reminders. He'd chastised himself enough and couldn't believe he had stooped so low. *I bought an unwilling woman for a night of pleasure, and for what? What have I become?*

Again, he bumped into someone and a soft voice spoke with concern, "Excuse me, sir, but are you okay?"

"Yes," he muttered, looking at the young woman, somewhere in her late thirties if he'd had to guess. The expression on her face told him she didn't believe him, not that he cared anyway.

Big, smoky-brown eyes stared at him from a delicate face framed with long blond hair, neatly cut in the latest fashion. Her pouty lips colored in a shade of soft pink; all inviting features on a woman, usually, but this one was different. She had a realness about her that caused him to stop and take note, a directness—but without the tease, as if she knew him and was interested in him, and not as a lover but a man. He growled, not meaning to, really. When was the last time anyone had shown him any real concern, like this woman, and Thomas? He was not worthy of their attention, not today, not with the knowledge of last night.

He was a beast.

He walked away just as she was about to speak, cutting her off, and Annie Blignaut shook her head. She continued walking to the salon just next door from Thomas Hagin Contractors.

For the rest of the day, he was very present on both Annie's and Thomas' mind. The burden to pray for him never left them.

At 1pm, Mrs. Smit arrived and took Anabella aside to a corner of the living room where they could have more privacy. She had insisted Aldrich stay with her, and reluctantly Mrs. Smit agreed.

From the moment they met, Anabella had liked the older woman, her hair was white as snow, and soft wrinkles adorned the edges of her mouth and eyes. Her smile revealed one dimple just under her left eye, and bright green eyes returned her stare. With her short stature she barely reached Aldrich's chest, but that didn't mean she was a pushover.

Gently, she talked to them both, but with an authority of years of experience. With the softest hands Anabella had ever felt, she held her hand, assuring her that she was there for her.

Hesitant to meet her at first, Anabella hadn't been sure she could deal with the subject just yet, but Aldrich was insistent that it would be good to speak about it. Now, they talked a few minutes with Mrs. Richter before she left them. When they were seated in the cooler corner of the living room, Mrs. Smit asked her to tell her what had taken place the previous night. Like a small little girl, she bundled up, shame overtaking her in waves. The older woman assured her there was absolutely nothing to be ashamed of, that she should jut relax and tell her whatever she could remember.

Aldrich couldn't bear the pain and in tears he watched as she relived the trauma once again. He couldn't help but feel bitter once more, ready to strangle them with his bare hands. He soon calmed down, sat back, and continued to support her.

She was shaken up. All of her defenses were down.

"You don't want to report this to the authorities?" Mrs. Smit asked carefully, after she concluded her story.

"No, it wouldn't be good for my public profile, nor for my brothers." Anabella didn't say it out loud, but her parents had stolen enough from her and she wouldn't allow them the luxury of taking what she had built, turning it into a circus. Giving her brothers a clean slate would help to move on. "If it can be helped, I don't want anyone to know, not including the people that were here last night."

"Okay, I had to ask, but I do understand."

"Thank you."

Mrs. Smit started with the hard questions, asking her how she felt about her parents, and Anabella disclosed that she felt rejected and betrayed by them. She emphasized that she wouldn't return to the house and that she never wanted to see them again. Bitterness was thick in her voice, adamant that she was finished with them. She wanted to run as far as she could, because it felt like her heart had been ripped into thousands of little pieces; she felt small and helpless.

Aldrich stopped her. He knew she didn't want to face this, but he managed to convince her that it was for her own good. Once she calmed down enough, they dealt with the rage and bitterness she felt toward her parents. Mrs. Smit assured her that it was normal to feel these things but that she must not allow it to fester within her. This was hard to do as she had no idea how to get past it. She could still hear her mother's voice, still feel the man's hands on her. She wanted to scream her hate toward them, confront them and ask them why, but in the end she sunk into Mrs. Smit's soft arms who in return embraced her.

The counselor led her to a place of calmness where she openly talked about forgiveness. As hard as it sounded, she listened as Mrs. Smit pointed out the advantages of forgiveness, that it would be necessary to give them no place to control her mind, or her thoughts. That she had to sever the connection in order to heal properly.

Even her relationship with Aldrich had been touched, and she had to admit that her parents' reaction left her astounded when they learned she was serious about him.

Aldrich smiled throughout, not letting on how those words had hurt him.

With tear-filled eyes, Anabella listened as she prayed with her, sobs wracked her body as the pain filtered through her. However, reliving the ugliness once again brought some peace as well.

Aldrich wrapped her in his arms as she cried, giving her the assurance that he was there. The whole ordeal had shattered her, but she knew she had to move on—she couldn't allow them to win.

Shortly after, Aldrich received counseling to deal with his shock and rage upon receiving the news. He was also dealing with the guilt of not being able to protect her, for not giving heed to the warning Roy have given him at the airport.

They talked about the threatening letters and Anabella was silent for a moment. There was something she had to remember, something very important, but what? Deep grooves formed on her forehead and when Aldrich asked her about it, she said that she couldn't remember.

Mrs. Smit placed her hands on both of them and prayed for them individually, but also as a couple;

that they may be granted the wisdom to face this in the best way possible.

When the session came to an end, Anabella promised the counselor that she would see her more as her schedule allowed. The issue of forgiveness was a hard pill to swallow.

Mrs. Smit excused herself and left, leaving the two alone.

For a while, they just sat there staring out the huge windows that framed the manicured gardens, holding hands as each worked through the episode in order to find closure, their thoughts in turmoil.

Anabella watched Aldrich. He was bent over, staring at the carpet. She knew this had affected him deeply. His face betrayed his guilt, and she kissed him softly on the cheek. "This was not you fault, Aldi."

He looked at her, his blue eyes dark with emotion playing behind them.

She gave him a reassuring smile. "You aren't to blame. My parents were the culprits. They knew what they were doing, so they are the ones who must carry the blame. I think I even expected what happened from them, although I didn't want to think about it at the time." She shuddered as years of memories flooded her mind. They hadn't once had any consideration for her or her brothers, or what this could do to them. They must account for their actions, after all, this was their doing. She refused to allow Aldrich to be dragged into it, refused to allow him to feel guilty for things he couldn't prevent and were out of his control.

"This was not your fault," she whispered again, closer this time, leaning in to assure him of her own feelings.

He hugged her fiercely. "Bella, I have never been as scared in my life as I was last night. Maybe it isn't something a man should admit, but the ordeal shook me into reality. I cannot understand what your parents were thinking. I was never brought up in that manner, but I want to assure you that I love you very much, and that I will protect you no matter what. You know this, yes?"

"Yes, love, I know this. I have no doubts about us. I love you so much, you are my whole life," she declared.

Holding her hands he asked, "When do classes start?"

"I think the twenty-fifth of February, why?"

"And you don't want to go home, right?"

"No, never," she replied shaking her head.

"And your next meet?"

"The beginning of February, the Midmar mile," she answered, still in the dark.

"I'd like you to come to my home, all right? Tomorrow, when you are up to it, I will take you to my beach house. There is an Olympic size pool you can practice in. We will have to get you some clothes as well." He gave her the most beautiful of smiles.

"Oh, Aldi, you are so good to me."

"That's because I care." He placed a delicate kiss on her forehead.

At first, it used to frustrate her when he did that, but now she accepted it as a sign of his affection and devotion to her.

"You are really okay with all of this?"

"None of this was your fault, sweetheart, so of course I am. Don't ever doubt my feelings for you." He cupped her face in his hands. "I love you, you are my life, and I am not planning on going anywhere."

She nodded, and he kissed her briefly on the lips, letting it linger. Slowly, she parted her lips inviting him to deepen the kiss.

When he finally let go, he smiled at her still closed eyes. She was living in the kiss' moment, savoring it. He cleared his throat while enjoying the sight, knowing that if he didn't stop now they could be seriously embarrassed. As if in slow motion, she opened her eyes and then smiled dazzlingly.

"There you are, my sunshine," his gentle voice filled with love, and dimples appeared on her cheeks.

"Hi."

They both chuckled as he let her go.

"Your brothers brought your car back, it's parked in Mr. Richter's garage."

"My brothers?"

"Yes, they told us what happened last night; they were really concerned about you and the mess your parents created. They also told us that they moved out of the house last night."

"Really?" Again her eyes flooded with tears thinking about her brothers, because just like her they had a lot of scars, too. They had been sucked into that world, and had been a part of it for a long time. She believed they had enjoyed it at first. What young teenage boy wouldn't love to have the opportunities they had? Having inhibited sex with your parents' blessing was a dream come true, but it had affected them nevertheless. The things they had learned and done would always be with them. She wondered if they'd continue to partake in the lifestyle they grew up with and participated in. She had no idea. But the mere fact that they were finally away from the oppressive hold was a major breakthrough, and now they could make their own choices and move forward.

"Yes, they did."

"I will call them tomorrow and talk to them. Can we go now, Aldi? I am so tired," she said, trying to stifle a yawn.

"Yes. The doctor has given you a prescription. I have it with me. We can pick it up on our way. Let's say goodbye to Mr. and Mrs. Richter. Seeing as they haven't slept, they could surely enjoy a quiet evening."

With that, they stood and walked to the kitchen leisurely with Aldrich supporting her every step of the way. They found the older couple reading the newspaper while the late afternoon sun streamed in.

Anabella walked to them where they were seated at the table, and when they noticed her, stood up. She couldn't help herself as a lump formed in her throat, her admiration for them both reflected in her eyes as she held their hands and said softly, "You are the parents I never had. I learned to be responsible just by watching you. The influence you have had on my life is something I can never repay. I love you both so much. Thank you for everything. Thank you for being there for me, for being the people I could run to when I needed love, when I needed to be cared for, and for the being the people who always made me feel safe." Anabella held them close, crying and kissing them both on their cheeks. The moment was filled with appreciation and gratefulness.

Aldrich stood back, allowing them this time, knowing he would do all to help this couple with whatever they might need.

Mr. and Mrs. Richter were speechless by her words as unhindered tears rolled down their faces. This acknowledgment from her meant much to them. They each returned her kiss before they released her, walking with her to the door.

"You and Aldrich are always welcome in our home, Anabella, never forget that," the older man finally said.

She couldn't help but give them one last quick hug before they left.

The Richter's watched as Aldrich picked her up and placed her in his car, the tenderness he showed toward her comforting to their own hearts.

With one last wave, the BMW sped away toward the city. Afterward, Mr. Richter held his wife in his arms and comforted her as she allowed the tears to roll down her face. Anabella's words had buried themselves deep in their hearts.

When they arrived at his house, he accompanied her to the spare bedroom, helped her to get comfortable on the bed, made sure the curtains were drawn, and gave her something for the pain. Gently kissing her, he moved away when she stopped him.

"Don't leave me, please." Fear was visible in the emerald depths as she stared at him, only now showing how she really felt. She was badly shaken and until now had covered it with smiles. Now that they were alone, however, it just wasn't possible. She needed his assurance and his comfort.

"I'm not leaving you, Bella, but I do need to make a quick phone call, take a shower, and then I promise I will return as soon as I'm done, all right?"

She nodded and relaxed against the soft mattress, dozing off almost instantly, yet still aware of his movements in the apartment. Until, that is, she fell into a deep sleep.

The minute André stepped into the sports club he frequently visited—already unsteady on his feet—he saw a young woman sitting at a table with a few people he knew. The woman was familiar, but he couldn't place her. Sure that this was something he could rectify, he stumbled on, greeting the many familiar faces. There wasn't a woman in the club he hadn't had a fling with over the years, he usually tried them all.

This blond was new to the club and maybe he could forget his sorrows between her ample breasts.

"Come join us!" the young man called the moment he noticed him, waving for him to come to the same table where the blond sat.

"Hi, Leon!" he called out in a slurred voice and staggered to the table, and upon losing his balance he landed on top of the blond.

She frowned in displeasure over this unknown klutz and then something about him registered. It was the man who had been on her mind constantly since they'd bumped into each other that morning.

"André, meet my sister, Annie. She is visiting from Gauteng."

"Please to meet you, Annie," he said, and then frowned. Why did she seem so familiar? His mind was in a fog after his failed meeting with Thomas, after which he'd gone back to his office where he calmed himself down by drinking the rest of day away.

"Come, let me help you," Leon suggested, pulling a chair closer.

He plopped into the plush seat.

Everyone started talking at the same time, ordering more drinks. He couldn't help but notice that the young woman watched him warily before she said, "You don't remember me, do you?"

"No, sorry, but I don't," he answered coyly, his eyes raking over her body, taking in every detail with appreciation. "But we can remedy that," he said lewdly.

"I'm not that kind of woman, Mr. Herbst." Annoyance painted her voice in irritation.

"Oh, really?" He raised a brow with a smug smirk. He was not used to women who refused him. "What kind are you, then?"

"The kind you aren't used to," she emphasized very clearly, and then turned to answer a question someone else asked her.

He had just been dismissed, as if he were a young kid. André had to admit that he was intrigued. Not many women resisted him, excluding Anabella Anthony, and his face paled. Uncomfortably, he cleared his throat. Phasing out the rest of the conversation, he shifted in his chair and took a gulp of the golden liquid from the glass before him, placed there by the waiter only moments ago.

"How are you feeling?" she asked, her attention now back on him.

Her eyes were filled with intelligence and care, the third time he'd seen that from someone that day. The crease on his forehead deepened and then it hit him; she was the woman he had bumped into in front of Hagin Construction. He took another sip and stared at her, suddenly agitated with all of this. "Are you following me?"

"No, Mr. Herbst, you bumped into me, remember?"

"Yes, of course, how rude of me. Did I apologize?"

"You did." She took a sip from her sweating glass.

It had to be a soft drink, because he didn't smell alcohol on her breath as they were seated right next to each other. He grinned as she continued.

"But, I see you are not yourself."

"Stop interrogating the man, Annie," Leon interrupted.

"Of course," she said and sat back, a soft smile playing on her youthful face.

She was a beauty all right, and he leaned forward, intrigued. "So, what would it cost me to make you the kind of woman I like?"

She flushed with anger. "Excuse me, Mr. Herbst, but I think your remark is way out of line." She picked up her glass and left the table. He chuckled softly, taking another sip as he watched her swaying hips in the white pants.

"Mmm..." he groaned.

"You must excuse my sister, but she is correct, she isn't the kind of woman you are used to," Leon said.

André raised his brow in question. "And how would you describe my taste in women?"

"Slutty and cheap," he replied with a playful grin. "My sister is neither a slut or cheap."

André chuckled. Yes, that pinpointed it; slutty and cheap.

He sank back into his seat and looked at the glass, which was still half full, the ice dancing around in the confined space—his thoughts still bothering him. *Don't you think it's about time you find someone other than the slutty and cheap variety? Look at what you did last night.* His conscience spoke as it had all day, leaving him filled with guilt and remorse. He tried to drown his sorrows as much as possible, but so far it hadn't worked one damn bit. Again he looked at his glass, then at his shaky hands now resting on his knees. No matter what he tried, his thoughts couldn't get away from what had taken place last night. He was miserable and felt downright angry with himself. He had messed up, big time. He rose from the table and walked away, bumping into a few chairs and people without a second glance toward the group, or his drink.

"Where is he going?" Annie asked the moment she joined them again, watching the back of the retreating man.

"Don't know," Leon replied, turning his attention back to the current conversation.

"God has an appointment with you, Mr. Herbst,' she muttered softly, then told her brother she was leaving.

# Chapter Thirteen

Early the next morning, Aldrich cleared his schedule for the day and informed his assistant when he would be back. Afterward, he took Anabella to the Canal Walk Mall to buy some much needed clothing. Because she refused to return to her house, she had nothing to wear apart from the clothes Monica had borrowed her.

At first she protested, but he refused to listen and dragged her from shop to shop indulging her with dresses and accessories she had no idea when she would wear. Then, he went on to buy her casual clothing, piling the heap that included lingerie—holding the scraps of material in front of her—on to the counter while she smiled throughout. His eyes totally betrayed how much he loved buying these particular items for her, never once asking if she even approved of some of the colors he had chosen. With him, the whole shopping experience became an adventure as they lingered at shop windows, admiring the many offers on display.

Lastly, he took her to buy swimwear and yet again she protested, explaining that many of her things were stored at the dorm and it was unnecessary to buy more, but he turned a deaf ear as he piled more things on the counter. With each purchase, his credit card worked overtime. She couldn't thank him enough, and couldn't help but feel guilty at the unfortunate expenses, until he finally reprimanded her.

"Stop thanking me, Bella. I do it because I want to. If I want to buy my fiancée dresses and the like, she should just accept it with a smile. Okay?" He lifted a dark brow, his body language brooking no resistance from her, but she still caught a glimpse of a lopsided grin he was trying to contain.

"But… still, this is too much," she protested, even if it was poorly.

"Nope, it isn't, sweetheart." His stance softened as he brushed her jaw with a thumb. He stared into her very soul with those blue eyes. She couldn't miss his sincerity. His compassion touched her and with watery eyes she looked back at him.

"I love doing this for you, it makes me feel needed, because finally there *is* something I can do for you; so please let me enjoy this."

*Well, if he puts it that way, how can I resist him,* she thought, nodding as her face slowly turned up a bright smile.

"Let's get out of here," he said, placing a kiss on her forehead.

Both their hands held packages that were bulging to its limits. All proof of the marathon shopping spree they'd had.

"Finally," she quipped with a heavy sigh when they got to the car, her feet aching in the slip-ons she'd worn.

Aldrich gave her a lopsided grin as he pulled out of the parking lot.

Upon arriving at his house, he gave her two suitcases, and after careful consideration she packed many of the clothing away—the ones more fitting for the beach—and hung the rest in a cupboard. Just after 3:00pm, they left the city behind and were on the road. They passed Blouberg beach with its marble-white sand and luxurious apartments overlooking the ocean, and on to his house down the west coast toward Paternoster.

Before leaving, she had had another hour long counseling session with Mrs. Smit, and for the most part she'd felt vulnerable and exhausted, not willing to let go of the anger and bitterness toward her parents. How could she forgive them? It was hard, and she told her counselor as much. She just couldn't do it. Animosity and rage filled her with bile each time the subject was mentioned, giving her acid burn, which she drowned with gulps of water. The betrayal hardened her to understand any reasoning.

In the end, comprehension dawned on her as Aldrich explained once again the benefit of forgiveness. To walk away meant that she had to put this behind her and move forward, and she couldn't do it shackled to them. She had to cut the cord, and for a while she remained quiet, pacing the floor as she contemplated it, finally accepting the truth. She forgave them, releasing herself from the bond that connected her to them and accepted the redeeming love of Christ in her life. The wonder of it all pushed tears over the edge, and for the first time in many years, her mind wasn't clouded with her past. Every muscle in her body responded as she relaxed, relenting to the power of the Cross. With that, a new perspective filled her. She was more determined to accomplish her goals.

As they drove, they spoke about her plans and agreed that she should continue with her swimming career. In order to continue, she had to send a message to her parents informing them that after everything they'd done to her and put her through, they hadn't won, that she and only she controlled her destiny.

Although her training schedule would be more demanding this year, she felt only peace in the discipline it brought into her life. Mr. Clark always demanded her full attention and agreed that she could train at the pool after Aldrich explained what had taken place. They'd given him a few details, and he'd agreed that she needed time to heal properly. One lesson she'd learned through all of this was that more people cared about her than she had previously assumed.

Thinking of her studies and the funds needed due to the sudden changes since Saturday night, Aldrich brought up the subject first; varsity. It seemed that the Hagin men were determined to have their way in this part of her life, and Aldrich informed her that his father had paid for all her classes in advance that morning. When she prepared to argue the point, Aldrich silenced her with a mouth-watering kiss. Now who could argue with that? Although they almost drove off the road in the process, but both chuckled as he got the car under control, speeding away on the long stretch.

She loved this man dearly, couldn't think what she would do without him. He'd turned her whole world around, making it possible for her to be the person she wanted to be. After Saturday night, she had felt helpless for the first time in her adult life but with everything falling into place, it gave her the safety and independence to move forward. This in turn placed her more in control over doing what she loved.

Anabella enjoyed varsity life. She was constantly surrounded by energetic students, the frantic rush to complete her assignments and even the late nights. To give it up would strip her from something important, something she knew she would regret for the rest of her life. Her life had changed much since she returned from the States, finding friends who supported her, with the added bonus of older couples she trusted as they added their insight and wisdom. Aldrich gave her safety and comfort and encouraged her with positive words. For the first time, she felt she belonged—not looking in but as part of a group. It was a great feeling.

Watching him as he steered the powerful machine, she couldn't help but admire the gorgeous man sitting next to her. Her love for him shone from her green eyes.

When she asked about the beach house, he said it was a two hour drive, giving her no details of what she could expect. He had seemed distracted while he packed the trunk; a sadness emitted from him and when she asked about it, he just gave her another kiss on the forehead. His silence became more apparent the closer they came to their destination. She knew he'd talk when he was ready, but clearly, he had to work it out himself first.

The silence gave her the opportunity to watch the scenery around her. His hand stayed glued to her thigh, while one of her fingers traced the muscle on his hand in an attempt to lift the tension with comfort.

"I am so glad you talked to Mrs. Smit this morning," he finally said with a smile, breaking the silence between them.

"She is a wonderful person and I'm glad you introduced us. I could talk about my past freely without any judgment from her. She said she would phone me daily while I'm on vacation." With a sweep of her eyes over the lush fields, she said thoughtfully, "I never thought I needed the Lord as much as I did. I have a peace within me I never experienced before."

Their eyes met briefly before she continued. "I didn't grow up with any spiritual guidance in my life; no one ever talked to me about the Lord. When she spoke about Him, I could feel the love she has for the Lord. Her conduct is different than that of Christians I have observed, and her unconditional love for all people left me surprised. It emanates from her."

Her eyes moistened, and he squeezed her hand.

"She has become a pillar I can now lean on. Just as you have become irreplaceable in my life, I cannot imagine getting through this without her, either."

Aldrich was pleased that she enjoyed her sessions with Mrs. Smit, and was happy that he had introduced them. He remembered while Anabella had been in America that when he had phoned the counselor, she'd said, "You're her motivation, Aldrich. She loves you very much and this isn't a fleeting emotion, or a school girl crush. She genuinely loves you." When he'd heard this, he was filled with great joy.

Now a plan had already started to form in his mind about his next move, and he hoped that he could do it soon. He could sense the changes in her, the manner in which she now spoke was relaxed and easy. Prior to these sessions, her acceptance had been hesitant, not sure of herself in many areas. Of course, her parents had done a fine job in breaking her down. He could hear a new determination, an energy radiated from her that changed her perspective. Her parents would never win this battle for her soul because she'd made her choice. Now all he could do was to stand with her and help her to grow in this newfound security. When she tapped on his leg to gain his attention, he glanced her way; a tentativeness marked her features.

"If I may ask, how do you know her, Aldrich?" Anabella had wanted to ask him, but could never find the right time and now that they were talking about Mrs. Smit, it was the perfect opportunity.

"She once helped me through a traumatic time in my life," he replied, shielding himself from her inquisitive stare.

Again, the sadness became apparent. Anabella sensed it immediately. And again, his mind drifted to a place she wasn't invited, his eyes fixed on the horizon.

"Will you tell me about it one day?"

"Yes… one day."

He seemed almost distant, and she left it at that.

"From time to time, I still go and see her, and over the years we have become good friends. Her home is always open to me," he said as an after thought.

He wanted Anabella to heal first before he would talk about his own past. However, going back to the house wasn't easy as it held so many good memories for him, memories he'd shared with Pauline before it had all come crashing down around him. To take Bella there would not only rekindle those memories, but would also create new ones. Although he would deal with all his emotions as and when they surfaced, this was having an effect on him. He felt strange in taking another woman into that sanctuary, but yet it was filled with new possibilities. When he'd built the place, he'd had so many dreams that were never accomplished and for a long time he'd felt cheated, even betrayed. But it was time to move forward and create new dreams with this young woman beside him. A woman who had changed his world the very moment she'd stepped into his.

Respectful silence filled the car as they watched the scenery pass in a green blur; vineyards lined the land, their branches heavy with clusters of ripe grapes. Workers were scattered between the vineyards, harvesting them. The countryside itself looked beautiful, colored in different shades of greens with patches of wild flowers in between. From time to time, the scenery would change, and Anabella could make out the white sand that emerged from areas of field flowers and tall grass. The sky was painted in shades of light blue, sparkling without any filthy smoke choking the sky as in the mother city. The tranquility outside streamed inside the vehicle and filled them with contented peacefulness.

Eventually, they slowed down, and at the next turn-off Aldrich turned left on to a gravel road. A large, white board was erected in the field and read, **PARADISE RESORT**, in big, bold, black letters confirming that they had reached their destination. With a keen interest, Anabella watched as Aldrich drove slower on this road that stretched before them like a big, white snake baking in the sun. The road was well maintained with extensive marshes edging it on both sides, hiding the ocean just behind the hills.

Approximately twenty minutes later, they descended a hill and the clear, blue waters of the ocean stretched out in front them as far as the eye could see. Water lapped on to the beach in soft whispers, and seagulls played just above its watery line. Peace cloaked the area in soft colors, inviting all to be one with it. It was breathtaking. Anabella noticed a large, log house further down from where they were. Nearby, a few trees framed it with pointing fingers toward the sky, enhancing the white sand and the house naturally.

The car came to a complete stop. Impatiently, Anabella was the first one out with an excited yelp, her sandals left inside in order to appreciate the warm sand. A dreadful mistake she soon learned. The white sand was deceitful in hiding the scorching heat within its bosom, and before long it became too much forcing her to search for the nearest covering for her feet.

Looking around for Aldrich, she noticed he was still inside the vehicle, his attention riveted on the house. When she waved at him, he slowly opened his door and got out, and when he joined her in front of the car, their fingers connected immediately, intertwining in a tight clasp. Standing there, they fixed their gaze on the panoramic view. It was truly breathtaking. A soft breeze was present and it carried the smell of the sea toward them.

Taking deep breaths, Anabella filled her lungs with the salty freshness, enjoying the exquisite atmosphere. White seagulls floated lazily with the breeze only to dive into the water, playing with childlike energy just above the water line. It was a lovely warm day, the sun still high in the sky, although it was already 5:30pm. She returned her gaze to the house that had captured her from the first moment she saw it nestled against the slope. It promised her a welcoming peace. She noticed the big porch in front, which probably offered the perfect view to its natural surroundings.

"Is that your house?" With appreciative curiosity, she looked at Aldrich.

"It is," he replied.

Giddiness fluttered through her, and she could envision herself on that porch as she enjoyed the sight and sounds of all that was glorious. She was so looking forward to her time there and was glad she'd accepted his invitation to spend the last days of her holiday at his vacation home.

Aldrich had been almost abrupt in answering, but in truth his mind was far from the present. This would be the first time in seven years that he would walk into his house, that he would be at this beach. He'd never been able to return before, the memories too painful up until now.

"It is beautiful."

"Thank you."

"Thanks for inviting me to stay here, Aldi."

"It's a pleasure." He smiled, holding her tight, not wanting her to see the turmoil he was in. It took all his strength to gather enough courage to face this place once again. He had to let go of the past.

"Come, it is time for you to see the house," he finally said, releasing her with a swift kiss on the cheek.

This time, when she returned to the car, she was careful to step on grass and not the scorching sand. Her feet were still sensitive after her ordeal, even more so with the gruff surface of nature.

Once inside, he started the engine and slowly moved forward toward the house, the dirt road leading up to it was hard and well maintained. Up close, the house was magnificent; it was truly a sight to behold. She was used to wealth and all it could offer, but she hadn't expected a beach house to look so outstandingly beautiful. From outside, she could see no expense had been spared. That was how she knew it was his, he didn't do anything half-heartedly.

Once parked under the shade of a tree, he led her up the stairs and onto the wooden covered porch, the coolness welcoming after the bright sun. She couldn't help but turn to enjoy the view she would have for the next few weeks.

Entering through its double, wooden front doors interlaced with smoky colored glass, she enjoyed the coolness that the house offered. It was a beautiful, yellow oak log that gleamed in the late sun, with wooden furniture in a darker shade of oak; the staircase was delicately crafted and spiraled up toward the second floor. Everywhere, little nooks were created to sit and enjoy the scene.

"Did your sisters also decorate this place?" A woman's touch was undoubtedly visible in the big living space. The smell of lemon polish hung in the air; someone had cleaned the house prior to their arrival. Some windows had been left open to allow fresh air into the spacious area.

"No, Pauline did," came the soft reply.

She watched him closely. Once again the melancholy was back, this time more perceptible. She gave his hand a squeeze. *Who is Pauline, and why did she cause such sadness in him?*

He walked to the large patio doors, pulled them open and stood there, deep in thought. His jaw was tightly pressed together as he struggled to get a hold on his emotions.

She'd never seen him like that, but she knew that she had to give him the space he obviously needed, so she continued on to investigate the house alone.

The top floor housed the bedrooms and bathrooms. Three rooms were sparsely furnished; each only with a bed and dresser. The large, main bedroom had more furniture, an indication it had been used often. The huge en suite bathroom startled her, the view absolutely stunning, but the huge shower, bath tub and basin stopped her in her tracks. White marble gleamed in the sun, and potted plants framed the corners with a small couch overlooking the vista. She just knew she would have a wonderful time in this room. The walls were decorated in creamy damask, and adorning the floor lay a rich cream and coral rug. The same coral was visible throughout the room, contrasting beautifully with the cream, creating a serene look.

The second bathroom was spacious, its shower hiding behind smoky glass doors. Cabinets lined one wall, but were empty of any contents. The mirrors sparkled, showing her how disheveled her hair was, which she had no choice but to comb through with her fingers.

When she returned to the living room, Aldrich was still standing in the same spot. She walked up to him and wrapped her arms around his waist, at the same time resting her head on his back; he was trembling. She felt immense love for this man who was fighting against unknown memories and squeezed him tight, placing gentle kisses on his back to remind him that he wasn't alone. He turned to face her, his face shining with love for her. He drew her into his embrace and kissed her with such passion, her defenses crumbled. His hunger met her own, their bodies melting together as one.

When he finally lifted his head, she smiled up at him. "This is perfect, Aldi," she exclaimed. Her heart filled with gladness and joy. He'd done so much for her, giving her everything she could ever have wished for, but mostly, she loved him because he gave of himself without hesitation. His love shone like a strong beacon withstanding every onslaught to be her anchor.

"I am glad you like it," he said softly, staring at her as he cupped her face in his strong, able hands. "You are perfect," he sighed, "and there is nothing I wouldn't do for you. Everything I have is yours, Bella. Everything."

"You're too kind, Aldi, but thank you for that." Something told her that this moment was a turning point in their lives and she took his seriousness to heart as their lips melted together once again, silencing everything around them. Time stood still as they sealed unspoken promises to each other in the most basic of lovers' rituals, allowing their lips to talk for them in passionate exclamations. Long shadows formed on the glistening floor showing only one person as the moment stretched out into ages before he let go, leading her to the kitchen.

"I'm in the mood for coffee," he finally broke the silence, "want some?" he asked, so natural, as if this moment was an every day occurrence, but both recognized the changes it brought within them, capturing this time in their hearts that would last for an eternity.

"Thanks, but I would rather have something cold if you don't mind, Aldi."

"Don't you drink coffee?"

"Only on the rarest of occasions," she grinned, "besides, it is not good for me while I am training."

They sat at the kitchen counter drinking their beverage of choice.

Anabella's mind spun with all the questions she would love to ask. She went with a safe one. "Who built this house?"

"I did."

"You mean… you built it with your own hands?"

"Yes, the house and the furniture."

"Gorgeous and talented. I like." She chuckled.

His big, blue eyes sparkled like diamonds as a smile spread over his face. "I'm a man of many talents."

"I noticed," she agreed with a grin.

"Let's get the bags. We'll unpack, then go for a walk. I will show you where the swimming pool is. Oh, how early would you like to start with practice? I want to arrange all the details with the resort owner before I leave."

"As early as possible, say, around six?"

"I don't think it will be a problem."

"Let's get going, then."

After rinsing their glass and cup, they rushed out of the house into the sunlight to unpack their bags and groceries. He'd stopped at the nearest store to make sure she was well stocked with food to entertain a small army.

Aldrich couldn't help but smile as he watched her dancing through the place. This was exactly what this house needed—new life, and exactly what Anabella represented. He wasn't the only who'd been neglected, but this house had been, too, and it was high time that they both returned to their former glory.

They unpacked their bags, each in their own room respectively. He had insisted that she must take the main bedroom as it was better equipped and spacious with a beautiful view over the azure sea. His—one of the smaller rooms—had a beautiful view of the green covered hill.

"You don't mind that you'll be alone for so long?"

"I'm used to being on my own. Mr. Clark gave me the strictest routine, which will cover most of my day. So, during the quiet times, I will take long walks and think about how much I'm missing you."

She gave him a radiant smile, and he couldn't help but chuckle; her playfulness was intoxicating. "The Olympics are only eighteen months away, so there really won't be any time to sit around idly," she reminded him matter-of-factly.

"I will be able to get back by the end of the week, but I'll keep you informed of any changes." He would miss her, but this was necessary. He could in no way send her back to that home. Monica had also promised that she would visit before the new semester started, and would return to the dorm with her, unless his plans worked out and she stayed with him, forever. He grinned at the prospect.

"When will you leave?" she queried.

"I need to be back tomorrow, so will leave when you start your day." He winked. "Everything you will need is here. The resort is not far so you'll be able to have many of your meals there and you won't feel so lonely. I'll also know that you are well taken care of."

She nodded, reassured once again that this was the best place for her to be. She trusted him completely.

"Okay, let's take a walk so that I can show you where everything is." With that, he took her hand, placed a chaste kiss on her mouth, and hand in hand made their way out to the patio and onto the paved footpath. The rich flora lined the back of the path forming a natural wall of greenery, shielding them in. It was already 6:30pm, a pleasant time to take a stroll, the sun low in the sky basking the earth in soft pastels.

After strolling easily for about 10 minutes they reached the underbrush, which was a bit further from the house than she had originally thought. Bending, Aldrich led her through the path, taking her into the dense plants that caused the canopy to shield the sun for a few moments. She shrieked at one point when her face met a spider web, quickly brushing it away.

Aldrich laughed at her annoyed shriek and still holding her hand, pulled them forward. A few steps further and they were back in the sun. A large opening appeared in front of them with an unobstructed view of the white beach, and the sea to their right. To her left, about fifty meters away, the swimming pool shone brightly in the late afternoon sun and when they approached, the cool aqua invited her to dive in. A few guests played in the water with a beach ball as cries and laughter filled the air.

*Tomorrow, I will accept your invitation and swim, that is a promise.* She smiled at the guests' antiques when they stopped for a few moments to appreciate the entire area, one big enough to accommodate large groups at a time. They followed the path around the pool to the offices directly behind it and met the owner, Mr. Copeland, who was just locking the door.

Aldrich greeted him as if they knew each other well, then turned to her and made the introduction.

Mr. Copeland recognized Anabella immediately.

"Miss Anthony," he extended his hand to her. "It is an honor."

He was an elderly man, about her father's age, his head crowned with thick, gray hair, and his gray eyes twinkled with delight. He was shorter than they were, so stretched out fully and tilted his head to meet her gaze.

"Miss Anthony, it is such a privilege to meet you," he said in a deep voice.

She in turn greeted him with enthusiasm. "Great to meet you as well, Mr. Copeland."

Aldrich got right to the point by stating, "She will be staying at my house during the summer holiday, but needs to practice every day, if that will be acceptable to you?"

"As if you should ask, of course she may." His face lit up with excitement. "At what time would you prefer to train?"

"Every morning, as I said, at six," Aldrich informed him.

"No problem, no problem at all," he said with a bright smile. "I will make sure that she is well looked after while she is here."

Mr. Copeland was a talker and he explained everything in detail to both Aldrich and Anabella, and both listened intently. He was very proud of the district and the resort, sharing stories of how it had all come about. She knew she would love it here; the calm surroundings were a perfect place to train and help her forget the last few days.

"Let's speak about the fee in your office, Mr. Copeland." Aldrich stopped the flow of chatter after a few minutes.

"All right, then. Please follow me." With that, he turned and unlocked the door.

After much debate over Mr. Copeland not willing to take any payment at first, in the end Aldrich got his way, adamant that he would pay for the use of the pool. More words were exchanged between the two men as Anabella listened, trusting Aldrich to make all the arrangements. They said their goodbyes and left.

Aldrich directed her onto a different path as they left the swimming area, and walked until they reached the beach, which looked like white lace stretching as far as the eye could see, dividing land and sea. Up close, the marble-white sand shimmered in the late afternoon sun, warm and soft, and when pushed down under the weight of one's feet, flowed away, leaving their footprints to trail behind them. The water was bitterly cold as was expected from the Atlantic Ocean, and only the very brave would venture in and then only with protective clothing.

As they walked along the beach, he pulled her closer, putting his arm around her shoulders. They fitted well together, he thought, enjoying the closeness they shared. Stopping, he kissed her hungrily, needing more of her after the kiss they had shared earlier. With the rolling sea lapping against their legs and the receding sun making its disappearance into the water—that's what it always looked like—they were lost in their little world. With each brush of his tongue it became more intense, he demanded more as his hand wandered over her body, more daring. He knew he wanted her with all the desire he'd kept hidden, wanting to release the passion he had denied himself for far too long. Throughout their time together, Aldrich had kept his distance, and other than a kiss on the forehead or a quick hug, he hadn't explored it further. But after the incident, all he had wanted to do was claim her fully as his.

There were too many men who wanted to take that right away from him and he was becoming impatient with it all, not that he would admit it to Anabella. Through it all, her body remained pure, but he knew in her mind she wanted what they offered, and he would be dammed if that would happen. His kisses grew in intensity as he held her, consumed by her mouth and body—which was only too willing as it pressed up against him. She drove him to the point of no return. He wanted her, of that there was no doubt.

"I want you so much," he murmured softly in her ear so that the sea breeze couldn't carry it away. His mouth trailed down her jaw, his heart racing with the desire to be one with her. He could feel her heart rate pulsing against his lips as he enjoyed the soft skin; it drove him crazy. It would be so easy to take her, here, now.

The proximity of his body, the warmth, and Aldrich's accelerated breathing ignited a fire in Anabella with a new desire. She burrowed closer to him, feeling his well-built body pressed hard against hers and kept on drawing him closer, needing him as his words echoed within her. She wanted to give herself to him completely, but wondered if it would be wrong. Lost in the sensations his mouth and hands drew from her, she relaxed, her own hands roaming over the broad shoulders and the length of his strong back. He was beautiful, and he was all hers.

"I want you more," she mumbled, her mind clouded with all that was him.

His groan trembled against her skin. "Oh, sweetheart," he barely managed to get out, the intensity of their love taking them on a gust of air that was instilled with their hearts desire. But in the back of their minds, they knew it wasn't the right time. Reluctantly, they parted, but continued to stare at one another, knowing they both wanted more than just these stolen moments. They continued with their walk, his arm still around her, her head on his shoulder.

His cologne, when mixed with the smell of the sea, complemented the other, creating a unique aroma she would always associate with him. She wanted to stay in that moment for as long as possible. Tomorrow morning he would leave, and she would only have those moments to remember him by. For the rest of the evening during the barbeque, the supper, and cleaning of the kitchen they stayed close. The light conversation was filled with laughter and cheerfulness as they sat out on the patio enjoying the starry night sky. They enjoyed each other's company and the closeness it brought.

It was getting late and it was time to get some rest. With a final kiss, they went to bed, aware of one another's proximity. It was a long night, one of tossing and turning as each struggled with their thoughts and wants, but both finally managed to fall asleep sometime in the early hours of the new day as they relaxed in the knowledge of a binding love.

Early that morning, he kissed her goodbye, got in his car and left. Glancing at his rearview mirror, he saw her standing on the porch, waving at him, full of vibrant life.

"I will be back, Bella," he promised out loud. "Thank you, Lord, for keeping her safe."

"Aldrich, Mr. Dorflinger wants to see you," Chaney informed him the moment he stepped into the office.

He nodded and briskly walked past her to the senior partner's office without as much as a glance in her direction.

She pouted her usually ruby-red lips, and crossed her arms as she followed him with smoldering eyes.

"And now, Chaney, why so glum?" Betty, another secretary, asked with a grin.

"Men," she replied, "one moment you are everything to them, and then they walk right past as if you don't exist," she ended huffily.

"Yes, some do." Her eyes followed in the direction Chaney was looking. She frowned, but didn't comment further.

"Why does he do this to me?" Chaney seethed as she sat down at her desk. "Why does he ignore me all the time? I love him, doesn't he realize that?" Wheels turned in her head. She picked up her cell phone and went straight to the number she wanted and dialed. "Soon, you will be mine," she muttered under her breath, speaking the moment her call was answered.

With a steady stride, Aldrich passed her desk minutes later and she smiled once again, forgetting her momentary anger, and then followed him. *You're such a handsome thing, you're good to eat,* she thought, chuckling to herself as she appreciated his posterior with pleasure, her lewd thoughts running rampant with what she wanted to do to him. Her confidence and boldness had grown since she'd met a group of people willing to explore all manner of hedonistic pleasures. She couldn't wait to have him in the same way. That magnificent body of his belonged in her bed and attached to her body. She sighed.

Briefly, she looked around when she was convinced everyone was occupied. She followed him into his office and closed the door with a low thud. She walked to the desk, her hips swaying seductively in the short, black skirt she wore, one chosen with him in mind. She knew she was the perfect example of a seductress in her low-cut, silver blouse, showing enough cleavage to make it sinful. After all, that was what she aimed for, to be sinful with him.

Aldrich had already made himself comfortable behind his desk, waiting for his computer to start up, when he noticed her. Annoyed, he watched the show from a woman he'd once thought beautiful. She swayed her hips provocatively and he had to admit there was a time he would have been influenced to succumb to her spell, but not today. Not after tasting Bella yesterday. No one else compared.

She leaned over the desk showing off her ample cleavage, and again he had to admit that she had beautiful breasts. She knew that every part of her was on display and had practiced it perfectly. Normally it worked, because she was that confident in her abilities. She purred softly as she reached for him, "I have missed you." She trailed a long, black fingernail down his arm.

Aldrich raised a brow and then snapped, "For goodness sake, please go away, Chaney, I have work to do."

"Just one kiss," she purred once again, ignoring him as she stalked around the table.

"Not happening, Chaney, please leave." He didn't hide his annoyance and merely turned away from her, stood up, determinedly walked to the door, opened it and waited for her to leave with a bored stare.

Fury burned through her soul and her body shook, irritated with another rejecting brush off. She couldn't believe that he was being so cold toward her while other men couldn't get enough. Hatred filled her as she sneered, "I bet you don't say that to Anabella Anthony." She straightened her body in defiance.

"That is none of your business."

"Where have you been these last few days?"

"That, too, is none of your business." He looked at her like a father would an undisciplined child.

She stomped her foot in rage, balling her small fists in frustration. She was not a child! She was a grown, gorgeous woman. *Why can't he see that?* "Please, Aldrich. I love you."

"Leave, Chaney. You're imagining things."

"How dare you!" With a last hiss, she stomped out of his office.

He slammed the door shut, smirking at her arrogance. But then he paused. What had she just said? *How does she know Bella?* As far as he knew, they hadn't met and he certainly hadn't mentioned Bella in front of her. Deeply concerned, he thought about this tidbit before he was distracted by a phone call.

# Chapter Fourteen

The first week passed quickly with Anabella spending most of her time in the pool. She concentrated on her events with energetic tenacity as she prepared for the Midmar Mile in early February, which was part of her training.

When Mr. Copeland wanted to talk during her practices she kept the conversations short, hoping he would understand that she needed this time alone. However, during both her lunch break and supper he would seek her out and engage her in conversation, and she would listen to his stories quipped with laughing moments; he was a proud swimming supporter with a vast knowledge of the sport.

Word quickly spread that she was practicing at the pool and a few youngsters challenged her to a race which, of course, they lost. She took it all in stride and as part of her training, but she allowed these brief moments to relax and connect with people. Curiosity would lure them to the pool as they watched her cleaving through the water in record speed. It went without saying that a few wanted her signature; she accommodated them during supper time.

At night, she would read what Mrs. Smit had given her for that day and spend time in prayer. The whole experience was new to her and caused a few awkward silences. When she was unsure about something, she would scribble it down to discuss during their phone conversations. Her dreams were filled with peace and tranquility, focusing on the things that really mattered.

However, there were times that the memory of that day had her in tears, times that she curled up into a ball and sobbed bitterly. The betrayal was too enormous to comprehend and her heart was broken. She could still see her mother's face, contorted in a hellish laugh. The man's face still real when she closed her eyes; the madness behind his eyes driving him to harm her. At times, she found herself showering twice just to rid her body from the brutal attack, her body still sensitive, her skin still telling the tale.

During these times, she would phone Mrs. Smit, bitter, angry and unforgiving, but then the counselor would soothe her racing thoughts, calm the storms in her heart so that she could be at ease in order to concentrate on her practices with renewed energy.

Derek had phoned and they chatted for a few minutes. He sounded pleased with his life, even considered enrolling for computer classes at the local college in the city when it opened.

Roy had sent her a few messages, which included a photo of him and Wanda rock climbing. Anabella knew that he was deeply in love with her, and he'd hinted at asking the big question. She supported this entirely, knowing that the marriage bond was the only place safe for them. He was adamant to change his life around, and at the age of twenty-six it was time to do so. Wanda was a wonderful woman, she understood him and loved him as he deserved.

From her mother and father she heard nothing, no text message, no email, not even a missed call. Not that she expected they would have bothered, but still they hadn't given her the time of day, not at all interested if she was safe. But what would she say to them anyway? That particular bridge had been severely damaged; going back was not an option. Not for her.

Aldrich phoned early every morning just before she was ready to start her day, and she could hear the longing in his voice echoing her own. She missed him, now more than ever. Being apart caused a void that intensified with each day that passed. Because of a case which was keeping him occupied, she heard the rising tension in his voice, although he tried very hard to hide it from her. She wished she was closer to him, because then she could make him some tea as it always seemed to calm him.

Anabella was expecting her friends over the weekend and with no idea when he would return, she would make the best of her time with them. She looked forward to this break. There was plenty for them to do and she knew that Moni, especially, would love it there. She was crazy about the sea and never missed an opportunity to sit on the beach with a good book. The resort catered for everyone's pleasures, which would make their stay that much more enjoyable.

She'd prepared the rooms, putting clean sheets on all the beds and added arrangements of flowers throughout the house, filling it with its sweet smell, all to let them feel welcome. With the help of Mr. Copeland, the fridge was well-stocked with all kinds of delicious ingredients that had her mouth watering already. She couldn't sit still, anxiously awaiting their arrival.

"Mr. Herbst, we meet again," Annie said, the moment she recognized the man coming from the same office as before.

Frowning, he looked at the beautiful woman, sure he had seen her somewhere before. I *must be getting old,* he thought, scolding himself. The face looked familiar, but he couldn't place exactly where they had met.

"Leon's sister, Annie Blignaut," she helped out, after a few seconds had passed.

"Oh yes, Annie, how could I forget such a beautiful lady?" He smiled his most charming smile, causing her to blush. André chuckled, enjoying her discomfort. The blush became her, highlighting the cheekbones and smoky eyes. His greedy eyes raked the youthful body with a lustful stare, his body responding by just looking at her; he really needed a woman. It'd been five days without any relief, and for him that was a record. *What I could do to her... if only I had the opportunity. Damn, I'm liking what I see.* Seeing that she was still waiting for him, he cleared his naughty thoughts instantly and asked, "What are you doing in this area?"

She looked at the salon to his left. "I bought this place the other day."

"Oh, I see. Charming." He glanced at the busy salon that advertised all their services in black, bold letters, and her name was elegantly displayed in gold lettering. **Welcome to Annie's**. Women entered the place, and each time the door opened he could hear the chatter resonating from inside.

Returning his attention to Annie, he said, "Since I bumped into you so rudely the other day, please let me make it up to you by inviting you to dinner tonight."

"I don't think so, Mr. Herbst."

"Please, call me, André. Mr. Herbst sounds so formal."

"I will stick with Mr. Herbst, if you don't mind." She took two steps away from him before he stopped her with a question.

"Does this mean you don't eat?"

She grinned. "I do, but, it won't be with you."

"And why is that, Annie?" He brushed a wayward strand of blond hair from her face, the innocent gesture stirring his body.

She, too, had the same idea and their hands met, which caused both to look at each other for a split second before she said, "Goodbye, Mr. Herbst." On that note, she entered the salon with quick strides.

He enjoyed looking at her shapely body so much he hadn't realized she'd left, leaving him on the curb. People walked around him, throwing annoyed glances his way but he could only grin, not giving a rat's ass about the pedestrians and the obstruction he was causing.

"Well, I never," he muttered with a glint of approval, his curiosity piqued for the woman who had just ignored him. Walking to his car—which was parked on the other side of the street—he didn't notice Thomas Hagin watching him from the window on the top floor.

It was an unusual visit he'd had with the developer, and mostly it had been about him personally. The man was in bad shape when he arrived, and Thomas had waited patiently for him to talk, not sure why he requested an appointment. But once he arrived, his actions confirmed it wasn't to talk business. It was clear by the way the man fiddled with the Bible on his desk, and then with the frame of his children, his shoulders slumped forward, contemplating.

Once again, he'd offered him coffee and he'd accepted, this time drinking the hot, strong brew without tasting it. His visit lasted for three hours and Thomas' emotions were mixed once he left, even sympathetic to his story, which had revealed much more about him as a person. He'd spoken about his somber teen years and his encounters with much older women who had shamelessly forced themselves on him from an early stage. This had led to his addiction. He recounted his countless affairs with men and women over the years, not willing to commit to one specific person, not believing the institution was meant for him. At one point, his tone changed, his mood grave as he criticized himself for what he'd done over the weekend, including the way he'd used people for his own desires and pleasures.

Thomas had been shocked at the things André revealed; especially about Saturday night. It took him some time to digest the information. His first instinct was to punch him in the face—hard—then chase him away, to reveal to him exactly what he'd done, but when he felt a tug at his heart he knew it wouldn't do. So he waited in silence, praying for forgiveness in his own heart.

Eventually, the man had grown silent, and it had given Thomas a few minutes to impart some wisdom into his life. Most came automatically from years of experience as his mind struggled with this news. André wasn't open to any spiritual guidance, yet listened as he explained to him about the redemptive power of the cross; how it would cleanse him from all sin, but he would have to take the first step by accepting what Christ did.

André had looked at him curiously with a deep crease on his forehead as he listened and processed the message. Finally, when a decision had to be made he rose, thanked Thomas for his time and left.

All Thomas could do was release him and prayed that God would do good work within him as he watched while André spoke with a woman down stairs.

"So, how about it, Annie Blignaut, do we have a date?" He waited for her to reply. The moment he'd stepped into his car he looked at the number clearly displayed on the salon window and dialed it. When the receptionist answered, he asked to speak to her. It had taken her a few seconds to respond to the call and now he sat waiting for an answer.

The woman intrigued him, there was no doubt. He had never made an effort with other women; if they were not interested, he'd walk away. But this one was different. He wanted to know her.

It was the first time he had to work to get a woman to agree, but he felt that if he didn't do this he would miss out on something bigger. He wanted to explore these new feelings. Since the incident with Anabella, he had changed, and only time would tell if it was for the best. Now he had this overwhelming sense of wanting to do the right thing for a change. With stunned astonishment it felt like it was natural, as if he'd done this a thousand times while in fact this would be his first. He grinned, liking the idea of courting a woman.

She chuckled into the phone, beginning with, "Mr. Herbst—"

He immediately stopped her with a correction.

She chuckled again and then relented. "Okay, then, André. I'm not the kind of woman you are used to."

"Let me be the judge of that, please, Annie. Just this once. Just a dinner at a very expensive restaurant. Nothing more."

Silence fell between them, the chatter of women in the background filling the airwaves as he waited. He couldn't believe he had just said that. *No sex? I must be insane!* He wanted her in the worst way, her backside residing in his mind. Then the blush came to mind, the wide innocent eyes looking back at him, and he realized that this was truly what he wanted.

"All right, André, just dinner, nothing else."

"Yes, thank you." He sighed with relief, the smile on his face grew and he brushed his hand through his hair as he rested his head on the headrest.

"Where do you stay?"

"I would prefer meeting you at the restaurant."

But with this, he was adamant. "No. Sorry, my mother raised me right. I will pick you up at your house." He heard her laugh in response. *What a beautiful sound,* he thought with a pleased grin.

"Okay, André. I will text my address to you. What is your number?"

"Thank you, Annie, this means a lot to me." Again he was met with silence. Not sure what to think, he proceed to recite his number.

She thanked him and said goodbye.

"Goodbye, Annie." The call was disconnected. He smiled brightly and drove away just as her text message came through.

At precisely 7pm, he knocked on her door—a town house in Brackenfell—and she immediately answered. She looked elegant in her black, off the shoulder dress which hugged her figure perfectly, the hem reaching just below her knees, and silver jewelry adorning her long neck and arms. Black sandals with silver studs complimented her long legs.

With appreciation, he said softly, "You look beautiful."

Annie blushed under his warm stare. Her blond hair fell in layers over her shoulders, framing her face stunningly. She was a vision.

"Do you want to go immediately?"

"No at all, we can have a drink first." She stepped to the side, allowing him access to the living area. It wasn't much bigger than a shoe box, but she was proud of her place.

"You have a lovely home," he complimented, looking dashing in a black suit, white shirt and matching black tie, his broad shoulders well-defined under the thin material. If there was one good thing that remained from the weekend, it was the fact that his body looked better and he'd kept it up, loving the newfound energy and agility he felt.

"Thanks, André," she replied as she directed him to a wingback chair in rich, earth colors.

"Wine?"

"Yes, that will be fine." He sat down in the offered chair and with a keen eye looked at the interior; well decorated with expensive furniture, which would have looked better in a bigger area, but she'd made the best of it by carefully placing them as focal points within the small sitting area. He then got up and followed her as she walked to the counter, selecting a glass from the cupboard to pour him wine. They shared a light conversation while he drank his wine, and when he was done they left for the restaurant nestled at the foot of Table Mountain. From their view point, they could see both the mountain and sea, and in the distance the Castle could be seen.

When they finally went home it was past 1am, and true to his word, he didn't try anything. This chivalry was a novelty to him but as he found her fascinating, he requested another date at her door and she agreed, this time without hesitation. Ecstatic, he gave her a small peck on the cheek before he returned to his car. The newness of it all was a fresh start for him, and he had to admit that he felt good about the latest turn of events. Deciding to take a stroll on the beach, he turned away from his normal route, taking the time to reflect over things and what it meant.

On Friday morning, Anabella saw Moni first. Her friend was looking wonderful in a short, denim skirt, and red tank top as she stepped from an unfamiliar vehicle. It'd been a while since they had last spoken, so this would be the perfect opportunity to catch up. *That's a new car,* Anabella thought. She hadn't seen it before. A tall, black-haired man emerged from the sedan and met her just before she reached the first step. Holding hands, they approached Anabella on the landing where she waited for them.

*He is new,* she pondered, smiling brightly at them.

"This is the most beautiful place," exclaimed Monica, splendidly surprised as she waved her hand over the whole scene.

Anabella knew what she meant, this place was unexpected.

"Look at the beach, I can't remember the last time I saw white sand like this; and the house…" she sighed in pure wonderment, "…it's beautiful!" Monica drew her friend closer, giving her a big hug and a kiss on each cheek. "It is good to see you my friend."

Her genuine words a smoothing balm to Anabella's ears. She had missed her friend as well and held her tightly, tears flowing from them both.

With a lopsided grin, she stepped away and brushed her hand over her face as she continued. "The kisses are from Mom and Dad," she explained with a chuckle, and turning to the good-looking man she made the introductions. "Sam Winters meet Anabella Anthony, my best friend." Her face glowed up at him, looking very petite against the long and lean man. "Anabella meet my boyfriend, Sam." Her possessiveness didn't go unnoticed by

Anabella and she returned the welcome as he gave her a white, toothy grin.

They greeted each other with a friendly shake; his genuine approach welcoming to her, so she could understand why Monica seemed positively smitten with him. His dark eyes gleamed with naughtiness, the kind that would make sure their visit would be filled with pleasantness and perhaps even mischief.

"Hi, Sam, nice to meet you."

"Anabella, I've heard a great deal about you. You are more beautiful than the photos give you credit for," he said in a deep voice, his flattering words honest.

She appreciated them for what they were, already liking him a great deal. "Thanks for the compliment, Sam."

"Pleasure, and thanks for accepting me without even knowing me. This sweet girl said you would be fine with me showing up unannounced."

"Think nothing of it, a friend of Moni's is a friend of mine. Were the directions easy to follow?"

"Absolutely," he replied, hugging Monica with a sweet smile.

"Come in and make yourselves at home. Would you like to unpack first before I give you something to drink?"

"Sounds like a plan. We have the whole weekend to catch up," said Monica.

"I'll go and get the bags," Sam offered, winking on his way out.

Anabella's gaze followed the young man; tall and lean with calf muscles bulging as he walked. She thought he might be a swimmer or cyclist; his suntanned skin and well-toned body a clear indication that he loved the outdoors. She watched as her friend's eyes followed him, too, with clear admiration. Out of curiosity, seeing as she couldn't keep it in anymore, she asked, "Come on, give, why haven't you mentioned him before?"

"We met at a friend's house two Saturdays ago. At first I wasn't sure about him. I mean look at him, totally out of my league."

"Nonsense, you compliment each other perfectly."

"You think?"

"I know. So, tell me more."

"The next day he invited me for coffee and never left, I like him. A lot." Her friend's eyes were sparkling. "I cannot get enough of him. He is brilliant, confident, and did I mention handsome?"

They both giggled as they watched the man closing the hood of the car.

"Well, he looks like a keeper," Anabella quipped.

"I hope you don't mind that I invited him."

"No, of course not, there is more than enough room for everyone." Anabella assured her.

"Let's go in. I want to see the rest of this stunning place," Monica suggested the moment Sam joined them, arms laden with luggage. Monica took the smaller bag from him and placed a kiss on his cheek.

*They look sweet on each other*, Anabella thought as she turned away.

"Where can I put these bags?"

"Follow me, please." She took them to two separate bedrooms on the first floor; both were impressed with the house and its fine detail. "These will be your rooms, and in there—she pointed to a closed door at the end of the hallway—"is the bathroom you'll share."

Monica giggled, blushing.

"Great," Sam concluded with a sly smile.

"I will leave you two to unpack, and when you're done join me downstairs. I will be waiting with something cold to drink."

"That sounds great. Thanks, Anabella," Monica gushed.

"Thank you for having a complete stranger in your house. I promise to behave," said Sam on another wink.

"You're welcome. When will the others be here?"

"They left about an hour after we did."

"Great, it gives us plenty of time to visit." With that, Anabella turned, leaving the couple standing in the room.

"Come here, you tasty little thing," Sam growled and kissed Monica fiercely, his hands already comfortable on her body as he explored her every curve. From the moment they'd met he had been unstoppable and was addicted to the small blond. Making her his in every possible way had been his motivation from the second he saw her. The instant she gave herself to him completely, he knew he would never leave her, she was his other half. In a short amount of time, he'd become enamored with her and everyone else paled against his sweet girl.

"Your friend seems nice," he said softly.

"Yes, she is. I told you, you will love her, and she is amiable."

"Not as much as I love you," he countered, pulling her closer to him.

Monica laughed. "Come on. We need to finish unpacking. Anabella is waiting for us."

"Not before you say it." He nudged her lips with his and she giggled into his hungry mouth.

"I love you, Sam," she finally relented, and on a groan he took her mouth like a starving man, kissing her until they were both out of breath.

Later, as they sat on the porch sipping their drinks, two cars pulled up with four people in each.

"Hi, there," shouted Monica as they stepped out, "here we are."

With a lot of welcoming laughter, they greeted each other

Anabella, who moved between them, was glad to see them all. "Hi, guys. Let me show you to your rooms. Hope you won't mind sharing."

"Nope. It will be fine, but I will sleep outside most of the time," said Herman, "that's if you don't mind?"

"Not at all."

He was a big man with fiery, red hair and big, brown eyes. His rugged face spoke of the outdoors; darkly tanned and his beard nicely trimmed, which gave him a chiseled look.

When Anabella met him at varsity, she had liked him immediately. They had a few classes together, and he always had a keen interest in her sport. She suspected he liked her, but she'd never given him the opportunity to follow up on it. Now, she noticed that there was something going on between him and Christel, and she was happy for him.

"It is beautiful here. You don't see this every day," he shared with a grin.

"Agreed! Count us in, we will join him outside," said the rest of the group in choir formation, except for Monica and Sam.

Anabella suspected that they would be mostly on their own. The man hadn't left her side since they had stepped out of the house, the electricity between them undoubtedly visible to all. Anabella was happy for her friend, because she deserved a good man in her life.

"As you wish. You can unpack in the rooms as there is enough closet space for all your things."

They moved off and quickly started to arrange the beds and luggage until every person was settled in. Mattresses lined the porch, ready to be laid upon and slept on.

"Come, I want to show you where the pool is and all the other activities before we light the fires. I believe you must be starving?"

"Starving? That is an understatement," boomed Hein, one of the men she only knew from friends; a quiet man who kept to himself mostly.

At his words, laughter broke out because everyone was in agreement.

"Let's go. We cannot keep starving people too long from food." Anabella laughed at their playful tone, enjoying the company of friends. She had really missed them and couldn't wait to return to her classes. She showed them around, walking at a leisurely pace as they took in the sights and sounds.

Mr. Copeland, of course, was delighted to see so many young people, and he introduced them to the resort and all its activities with flourish. "We have a well-known band playing tonight, you must join us," he informed them just before they left.

"That sounds good," Sam winked as he held Monica close, making her blush. "It's a reason to hold my heart close to me," he quipped whilst sneaking a kiss on to her rosy cheek.

Two hours later they were finally back home. The men started with the fires, and the women congregated inside to prepare the salads.

"When will Aldrich be here?" Monica asked curiously, while she added potatoes to a pot of water and flicked the gas burner on.

"He'll only be here in two weeks. He's busy with a big case that needs all of his attention," replied Anabella, chopping the cucumber into slices. She was already missing him tremendously.

"So, tell us about Sam," asked Christel, who stood and watched as they scurried around the spacious kitchen.

Monica proceeded to explain how they met with dreamy eyes, giggles bursting forth now and then with pure pleasure as she recalled the first two weeks of their relationship. It had happened so fast that Monica almost felt overwhelmed with the sudden turn of events in her life, but yet ecstatic that he was a part of it. She couldn't wait to join him again outside, already missing him.

The rest of the conversation was light while they busied themselves with the cutlery and plates, poured drinks for the men, and when all was done, joined them at the fire.

They had a nice dinner, joking continuously, the men teasing the women relentlessly until there wasn't a dry eye in the house as they laughed at the pranks played on them. It went on till late into the night, the band completely forgotten.

Just after dinner, Sam excused them both while pulling Monica along with him in the direction of the beach. He obviously wanted some alone time. He had thought of a better way to occupy their time and didn't hide the fact. Monica was shy at first, but with a nudge from Anabella, she left with him.

Anabella missed Aldrich even more, forcing herself to laugh along as she watched the couple disappear into the shadows of the night, wrapped in each others arms.

The three days passed quickly. She trained diligently and early every morning while they slept, and by the time she got back everyone was up and chattering away as they sipped their coffees, then became quiet as they enjoyed the view from the porch. This gave her the opportunity to clean the place and enjoy a peaceful few moments before the group joined her in the kitchen. The interaction between Sam and Monica made her aware of her own longing for her love, their last kiss still engraved on her lips.

They had a lot of fun throughout the weekend, finally joining the band for some dancing on the Saturday night. Anabella sat quietly outside enjoying the evening, not willing to dance with anyone. She ached for Aldrich and didn't want any other man touching her intimately.

They swam often with Sam going as far as daring Anabella to a friendly swimming contest, and she had to admit he was good. She'd had to really dig deep to win, but in the end he had had to admit to Monica that she was fast, very fast. However, it was good exercise for them both and she loved it.

Her friend's happiness was tangible, they blossomed as a couple and remained close, always doing things together. He really enjoyed Monica's company. Clearly, the man cared for her, and she could see her friend was head over heels in love. Her eyes sparkled when she looked at him, and as with her she knew that this would be her friend's first and last love.

During the time Anabella wasn't at varsity, the relationship between Herman and Christel blossomed, too, and soon they followed Sam and Monica on their moonlight walks, coming back later and later. It caused much teasing within the rest of the group, but the two men just laughed it away and the two women blushed, which Anabella thought was adorable.

Monday came too quickly. Everyone wanted to stay, but they all had other plans—the weekend was over. After a filling breakfast they packed the cars and were ready to leave.

"Thanks for the visit. I truly enjoyed having you guys here so much," said Anabella as they climbed into their cars.

"When will Aldrich be here?" Monica asked again, leaning against the window, already buckled up.

"I'm not sure. He wasn't certain when I spoke with him yesterday." Anabella shrugged with a faint smile.

"Don't miss us too much," Monica said ruefully. "I will try to come again. I know Mom and Dad planned a few things for the remaining few days. Let me see how it goes. Sam invited me to his parents' home before varsity starts as well, so I will phone and let you know, okay?"

"Great, Moni. Drive safe."

With that, they left, honking up the hill.

She slowly made her way up the steps, went inside and closed the door, refusing to feel sorry for herself. The silence was overwhelming, but she welcomed it after the weekend of constant noise. Never before had she had friends over, which made for a new experience altogether. An experience she would love to repeat when possible.

The house was in a mess, and although they had helped her clean it there were still a few things that needed her attention. She picked up magazines from the floor, put back chairs that were scattered around in their correct places, swept the floor, and ensured that the kitchen was in order. Her friends had already made sure that the sheets were in the washing machine before leaving.

When she heard soft footfall behind her, she turned around and right in front of her was Aldrich, his gorgeous face close to hers.

"Bella!" His eyes dark shinning with want for her.

"Aldi, my love!" Her heart thudded with the sudden intrusion, and what a welcoming intrusion it was.

They were in each other's space, and with one sweep of his arms their mouths melted together, doing all the talking for them.

"I've missed you so much," said Aldrich, close to her ear.

"You have no idea," Anabella murmured, her voice jingling with excitement.

"Are you happy to see me?"

"Oh, Aldi, what a question." A tear ran down her cheek.

He kissed her again, not missing her beautiful smile and the message in her eyes. "Let me look at you," he said, stepping back. "Can it be?"

"What?" she asked hesitantly, not sure how she looked. She hadn't made much effort when she'd gotten out of the pool that morning. *Surely, I can't look that bad. Monica would have said something.*

"You are more beautiful than ever."

She sighed with relief. "Have I ever told you that you talk too much, Aldrich?"

He chuckled, and with a strong pull she took his mouth into possession. He lifted her from her feet—which dangled in the air with the bliss of their union—while they enjoyed the pleasure of being together. Once he released her mouth, his eyes swept through the house; everything seemed in order. He could feel the house vibrating with energy, a feeling he appreciated. It had been built to entertain and relax, not stand as a ghostly reminder of the past. Taking Bella there was the best decision he could've made.

"How was the visit with Monica and your friends?"

"Wonderful, Aldi, thank you." She hugged him and he returned the gesture by kissing her lightly on the forehead.

He asked what they did, and she told him about Monica's new friend, Sam, as she dragged him to sit on the couch, tugging her feet beneath her as she divulged everything about the weekend.

He smiled as he watched her face light up with every story she shared, enjoying her body even more as she leaned against him, when his stomach growled announcing its presence.

She laughed. "Are you hungry?"

"Yes, I believe I am." He, too, laughed. "I left early this morning to surprise you, so there was no time for a quick bite."

"And surprised me you did! When do you have to go back?"

"I can stay for three days, and then I must return."

"Wonderful!" She kissed him on the cheek, inhaled his scent and snuggled deeper against him.

"You missed me?" he asked, grinning madly.

"You have no idea."

"I think I do." Their mouths melded together once again until it seemed their lungs lacked oxygen. Their hands explored as they reacquainted themselves with fine comb detail. The feel of her skin under his touch mesmerized him, and soon his hand explored every inch of her well-toned body, the material the only barrier that kept him in line.

He had missed her more than he was willing to admit to himself, while trying to focus on his work the past week. She was always on his mind, and at night he couldn't help himself as his body's want for her intensified. Now, having her back in his arms he could feel her body surrender to him and like chocolate he melted over her tucked snuggly beneath him. She was the loveliest woman he knew and he wanted her, every part of her. As his mouth started its own exploration, he could feel her reaction; she was ready. He couldn't wait anymore, he wanted her like plants needed water, his hands doing what they had wanted to do for a very long time.

When her body arched beneath his—inviting him in—he stopped, not having realized how far he'd gone until he lifted his head. She lay there, eyes revealing her own need for him, her breasts glistening from his wet kisses. Hard and pointed, they stood erect, inviting him to take more.

He groaned softly, "You're so beautiful, Bella. Just look at you, you're so ready for me." It was the first time he was seeing her naked, the first time he could savor more than just her smile or kisses.

She smiled, lifting herself closer to him, seeking to have his mouth on her again, but he had to stop. *Damn! I have to.* He'd promised himself he would wait, even if it killed him. His own body strained against his clothes, screaming its release. Her hands nestled in his hair; she was ready for him, he knew it and he took advantage of it, as if there were no limits. He couldn't believe his own indulgence where she was concerned that he lost himself so completely in her.

She was addictive.

With a body like that, who could blame him? With one final sweep over her exposed chest, he sat up straight and covered her. She made for an exquisite picture, her hair fanned out over the couch's material, legs apart that mere moments ago had been wrapped around his hips, her mouth wearing the telltale signs of his lust, before she moved as well. Disappointment was etched on her face as she sat upright, her quick puffs of breath the only sound she released, acknowledgement that she had been on the same rollercoaster ride with him as she righted her clothes without meeting his eyes.

*Have I taken it too far? Why is she so quiet?*

"Bella—"

She stopped him with her fingers, gently touching his lips, her eyes shining with love for him, forcing Aldrich to gulp away his own thoughts. Ever so softly, she said, "I want this just as much as you, Aldi. I love you."

"Oh, sweetheart, I love you so much." And with a gentle kiss on her soft lips, he helped her up from the couch and they walked together to the kitchen where they prepared a midday feast.

Sitting at the table, she told him about her practices, and he listened intently to everything she had to say, his eyes fixed mostly on her lips and chest; the picture of her naked breasts lingered in his mind, the taste of her skin lingering on his tongue, and he wanted her. He knew that the moment he had her he wouldn't be satisfied with only a little pleasure. He wanted it all. Her passionate reaction told him she felt the exact same way.

The reason he'd kept his distance all this time was because he knew that once he gave in to his own desires, there would be no turning back. But now, after experiencing her desire as he had these last few times, he vowed that before this week was over she would be his, convinced, more than ever, that this was the right time and that this was the right place.

Clearing his head, he looked around as memories rushed back, good memories of the past with Pauline in this same room, and for a few moments he relived them, enjoying the history they'd shared. It had been good while it lasted, but now there was no reason not to start over. He never thought it possible to love again, but the moment Anabella stepped into his life, he knew she was perfect for him. Pauline had been different in many ways and he'd loved her, but with Bella his life had turned around. She brought him new hope, life, and made him feel young again.

Anabella watched from the counter as his thoughts turned away from her. For a few moments, she gave him this opportunity in order to collect himself as different emotions played over his face, while she busied herself in the kitchen, but when he noticed her again that gorgeous face came alive with a beautiful smile. How she loved him, her heart constantly reminded her of this fact. She had never experienced what they'd just shared on the couch. His touch had been so gentle and tender as he explored her body. She craved him, wishing they could return to that place where they almost became one, because the promise of more was waiting for them. Her body ached for him. How she longed for that day to come. He had awakened desires within her that only he could quench, and she wanted it. Much more than the brief seconds spent on the couch.

Sensing that he was thinking about this Pauline he'd mentioned before, she wished he would share. Although she wasn't jealous about this ghost, she still wanted to know who she was. Where did this woman fit into his life? Anabella knew that he loved her—he wouldn't be there with her otherwise—his intentions were a matter of honor.

"Love?"

"Yes, Bella?"

"I made dessert, come." She beckoned him while holding two bowls in her hands.

"Great, that would be excellent." The playfulness was back in his voice. He stood and walked toward her, cupping her face in his much larger hands. "Have I told you that I love you?"

"It is a distant memory," she revealed smiling, lifting herself up on tiptoes to be nearer to him.

"Well, then, I will tell you again. I love you, Bella."

"And I love you, Aldi."

For a few moments they just stood in an embrace before she stepped back, the bowls held awkwardly between them.

"Come. I thought of sitting outside, it is a lovely day."

He followed her, appreciating her backside as she walked away, the gentle sway of those beautiful hips his hands had explored a short while ago. He could already envision his hands on those hips, doing what he wanted to do as he gripped them with his strength. *I really have it bad.* Putting the thought aside, he said, "Just give me a sec, I need to make a quick visit to the bathroom."

"Okay, don't be too long."

While she waited for him, she set the table on the patio where they could enjoy the view of the late sun bathing the ocean in its radiance while eating the dessert she had prepared. The man loved his sweet decadent desserts, but strawberries were his favorite. A tub of vanilla ice cream had been left after the wild weekend they'd had, and she filled two bowls with the creaminess. She'd found a can of strawberries and poured them over the ice cream, which formed a delicious sweetness that he would love. Wafers were stuck into the sweetness, inviting them to enjoy its tasty treat.

After dessert, he complimented her with a kiss, and they went for a walk along the beach, enjoying the view and each other's company. When they returned, the sun was already gone for the night, leaving the sky shadowed in black streaks interspersed with amber, embedding its peacefulness into them.

The light breeze stirred Anabella's hair and it flowed behind her as she walked beside him. Mesmerized, he watched her, her picture ingrained in his memory.

# Chapter Fifteen

Lounging on patio chairs, they enjoyed the lazy afternoon; their drinks on the table, while staring at each other in a more secluded spot with an unhindered view of the sea and the hills. Both explored each other's bodies, hands traveled over surfaces with deliberate slowness, their thoughts honed in on each other. Now and then he would leisurely kiss her fingers with a slow, seductive kiss, and she would chuckle or moan from his warm breath on her skin, anticipating his next touch. His crooked smile the only evidence that he knew what he was doing to her.

Ever so often, Anabella would speculate about the woman, unsure if she should even go there now that Aldrich was relaxed, his mind occupied with only her, but she had to know. Clearing her voice and sitting up—which suddenly broke the soothing contact—she plunged into the unknown after careful consideration.

"Tell me about Pauline. Who was she?"

"She was my wife."

Anabella gasped in surprise. His reply stunned her, and after a brief moment spent in awkward silence, he shifted. He sat up, his attention now on the restless dark liquid that reached far and beyond. When he spoke, it was obvious that he had anticipated this question, because the words had already formed on his tongue.

"We met at varsity. I studied law and she studied medicine—specializing in pediatrics because she loved children. We met by accident in the cafeteria; I knocked her over in my haste to sit at a table, not seeing her behind the books I was carrying. We had a connection from the start and from that moment on we were always together, except during classes, of course. We were both in our fourth year of studies, driven and dedicated toward our chosen fields. Our relationship grew quickly and we decided on a wedding date when we received our degrees. It was to have taken place within three years."

Aldrich paused a moment and inhaling deeply, continued, "Meanwhile, my mom passed away. I received this piece of land handed down by her mother, and I decided to build this house as a wedding gift for Pauline." He moved forward, arms resting on his legs as he glanced back at the house with a pensive look. "Every time I took a break from my studies, I'd come here without her knowing, planning and building this house from the ground up." He looked at his hands, still calloused, but yet softer due to the office work. His thoughts were far away, and the sadness she'd seen earlier was again visible. He made no move to cover it as tears slipped down his rugged face.

"On the 20$^{th}$ of December—the year we finished our studies—we got married in this house. She had complained almost all year about the wedding's location, but I told her that it was sorted, and that she must continue with the preparations as normal." He chuckled at the memory, and Anabella smiled.

She could only imagine how frantic Pauline must have been in not knowing the location.

"She was furious, of course, but I refused to ruin the surprise. A week before the wedding, I brought her here; she was in awe over the house and loved this place from the moment she stepped in the door." He swallowed as the thoughts washed over him. His playful banter had been replaced by melancholy.

Anabella clasped her hands together, leaving him alone—difficult as it was for her not to reach out and console the man she loved. He would talk about it in his own time. When he continued his voice broke.

*He'd really cared for her,* she thought with a fair amount of jealousy, and knowing him, the journey must have been incredibly challenging.

"She was a beautiful bride, radiant in the wedding gown her sister made for her. The thought of spending my life with her overwhelmed me the moment she walked down the stairs." He pinched his eyes and sighed, lost in memories once more. "We stayed for a month and enjoyed each other's company, the house and resort, and relaxed after the hectic years of studies. Exactly a month later, we were back in the city; I had just started at the firm I'm still at, and Pauline would have started on the 1st of February at the local city hospital. That day she'd had a few errands to run and when she crossed the street, a drunk driver crashed into her; every bone in her body broke. She was killed instantly."

Patiently, she waited for him to compose himself, his eyes veiled with sadness.

"It was a traumatic time for both her family and me," he said, meeting her gaze for the first time, his eyes misted with tears. "I was talking to her on the cell phone when the accident happened; I heard bones break as she fell to the ground, sounds that have replayed in my dreams for a long time."

Anabella listened, shocked at the pain he'd had to endure. His shoulders were still solid and straight, showing his strength and endurance on the traumatic road he had traveled. She found herself brushing away the tears that wet her cheeks.

"It was so quick, it was literally seconds, and then a deafening quiet came over the phone. I called out her name, but all I could hear were people running and shouting. Finally, an unfamiliar woman answered the phone and spoke to me. I identified myself, while going out of my mind with worry. I shouted into the phone and after a brief pause the woman said, "Honey, I'm sorry... it's too late, she is gone." I was crushed, literally, and I felt like the world had come to an end. The woman then gave me the address, and like a mad man I rushed to the scene. When I got there, an older woman approached me immediately, stopping my rapid advance toward Pauline who was lying in the middle of the road with only a jacket covering her. She didn't want me to see her body. Later, I learned that she was unrecognizable due to the horrific impact. This lady stood by me for the longest time, and even after Dad arrived, she stayed. That is how I met Mrs. Smit."

Leaning forward to be closer to him, she touched his face for the first time, tender and delicate in her approach, smoothing away the lines on his face.

He kissed the palm of her hand softly and keeping it imprisoned in his, he held it to his lips. "Other than my family, this is the first time I've spoken to anyone about Pauline in three years."

When their eyes met, tears streamed down his face, and without a second thought Anabella scooted over to his chair, bringing his head down to rest over her heart in one quick movement. She felt her top become drenched with his tears, but she didn't mind, he was hurting and her heart was aching for him. Her young heart was overwhelmed with his story as more tears dripped from her face. Stroking the dark hair, she felt him relax against her, his heaviness a comfort that knitted them closer together.

The moonlight filled the earth around them in a soft blanket, the night sky flickering with stars. Nightlife was chirping as the wind picked up speed, the sea adding its rolling sounds; they came together much like a chorus and soft as a lullaby, bathing them in peace. They sat like that for a very long time.

Aldrich's tears eventually stopped. He felt relieved that he'd finally told Bella about his own sorrow. He had loved Pauline, and she would always remain in his heart. Bella was here now, giving him so much more, and he was ready to start a new life with her. He felt at peace, snug in the softness under his cheek, and the calming breaths she inhaled and exhaled beneath his head assured him that life did indeed go on. For a few minutes longer, he continued to rest against her, eyes closed. And then slowly, he moved his head and placed his lips on the swell of her breast.

"I'm the one he's supposed to nestle against," she seethed in disgust as she watched the developing scene before her. "How dare she lay her hands on him!" Her voice rose in the night, but was drowned by the waves pounding onto the sand. The breeze that had picked up was just enough to carry her words away from the couple. "She better not sleep with him, because then I will kill her!" The view she had of the house was especially good. She'd observed them since he'd arrived and kept herself out of sight. It had been touch and go for a few seconds when they'd gone for a walk, passing her hiding place inches from where she hid in the thick bushes. So occupied had they been with each other that they'd hardly noticed. The whole sweet display of her draped over him was nauseating, and she had almost given herself away when she released "Bitch!" on a growl.

She was satisfied that she'd held her tongue, because if she'd lost it, Aldrich would have gotten hurt. She didn't want to hurt him. She loved him. But her anger boiled in her stomach like acid. Cold hatred toward the younger woman nestled itself within her, the hussy that was hell bent on stealing Aldrich away from her.

"Just keep a cool head, it's almost time to go to bed, and then I'll go to her room," she reprimanded herself once again, unclenching her fist. She'd checked the house out when they'd gone for their walk and knew the layout well. She had also established which room the bitch used; her clothes adorned every cupboard in the beautiful room made for her. The bitch would pay she vowed to herself bitterly, because she'd taken her place in the main bedroom. "Who the hell does this bitch think she is!" she fumed when she'd stood in the room, noticing how blatantly she'd made herself comfortable, as if she belonged there. It had taken her some time to calm down, hugging one of Aldrich's shirts she'd found in his room, giving her the peace she needed to complete this mission. His smell still lingered on her clothes and hands, reminding her of the long term goal; she was determined to make this work.

Again she checked the syringe with the colorless fluid, a drug she concocted with ethanol and ammonia, and cooked to the perfect temperature, creating a deadly drug. All thanks to her science nut brother. "Enough to put her to sleep permanently." She giggled with pure pleasure as she placed the syringe back in the small box she'd bought at the pharmacy.

"Soon, my love," she whispered a promise into the night, still focused on the couple.

She watched as they got up from the chairs and walked into the house, sliding the door closed. It was another two hours passed before the lights went out, and the woman stretched to her full length only now allowing herself the luxury to relax, knowing the end was near. An end that would finally bring them together, forever.

"Wonderful," she muttered, her body stiff from lying in an awkward position between the bushes all day. Checking to see that no one was in the vicinity, she strolled cautiously to the house—making sure she stayed in the dark the whole time—and stepped onto the porch in front of Anabella's room. The patio door was slightly open and the curtains danced lazily in the breeze. Pushing the material aside, she leaned in to see if Anabella was in her bed. She almost giggled with glee when she saw her outline, her soft, slow breaths telltale signs that she was fast asleep.

Silently, she sneaked in, the furniture dark silhouettes in the large room, and on tiptoes she crept slowly to the foot of the bed, the thick carpet muffling her footsteps. She studied the object of her frustration and anger, the woman who was giving her endless problems, not the least bit receptive to the hints she'd placed in her room on previous occasions. The things she'd done to get in that house. *Okay, not all was bad,* she snickered, remembering the girl's father. *If only you knew what I did with your daddy, and he with me. It was pure heaven.* She snorted with excitement and immediately slapped a hand over her mouth when the sound came out just a tad too loud, quickly looking in the direction of the door. She waited a few seconds before she looked at Anabella again. Serene calmness filled her being as she watched her breathing. She was curled in a fetus position, her arm hanging over the side. *Perfect,* she thought. *I couldn't have asked for a better opportunity.* Another dose of excitement bubbled through her.

When no movement was detected in the house, she proceeded to the side of the bed and leaned forward just as Anabella rolled, receiving an unexpected punch in the face. With a soft growl, she landed on the floor; angry that she'd been so careless. The thud thundered throughout the quiet room, making her look to the bed anxiously for any signs of movement, but Anabella's continued roll ended with her comfortably on her back, her arm still hanging off the side.

"What the fuck?" she muttered and touched her cheek where the blow had landed. Before she could react in rage, the door opened, and a dark silhouette filled its frame. Aldrich! She stopped the groan that wanted to burst from her lips and rolled away into a dark corner, watching as he approached the bed from the other side and leaned over its occupant. The bed dipped and creaked under his weight. She lifted her head just enough to see him plant a kiss on her forehead. She almost screamed in disgust at his gentle touch, at his betrayal. Surely, he didn't have to act so well? *The bitch is sleeping*, she wanted to yell, aggravated with his tenderness toward her.

Her hand clutched the syringe tightly, and her fingers trembled with her fury as she watched and waited for him to leave. "Just leave, Aldrich," she commanded softly into the darkness, and as if on cue, she watched as he walked away, the door closing behind him.

With no time to waste, she moved into action, and immediately sat on the mattress next to the sleeping form. Taking Anabella's arm in her lap—after making sure the syringe was ready—she pushed the plunger and watched as a small drop ran down the side of the needle. Grinning, she looked at the sleeping woman and pressed the needle against her skin.

"What are you doing?" Aldrich's strong voice filled the room the moment it was flooded by light.

Momentarily blinded, she yelped in surprise, blinking against the onslaught of light and looked over her shoulder toward him. The murderous look in his eyes caused her body to shiver in response.

Aldrich couldn't believe what he was seeing. He'd had a weird feeling when he left the room; an uneasy feeling that crawled down his back, nudging him to turn around. "Chaney! What the hell, woman?" he bellowed, his mind racing with reasons as to why she'd be in Bella's room. It was only when he looked down that he saw the syringe and gasped in shock, his hand clutching the doorknob in utter surprise. He walked, slowly, closer to the deranged female, his eyes a steel-blue as he pinned her down on the spot. He noticed how steady her hand was, the one that held the syringe, its needle pressing down hard on Bella's skin. He had to get her away from Anabella, and quickly.

"I'm getting rid of her, my love," she snickered with delight, her eyes gleaming in the light.

To Aldrich, she looked insane, her youthful face contorted in an ugly grin. He couldn't believe he'd once thought her beautiful. He must have been insane.

Unbeknown to them, Anabella had stirred and was wide awake the moment the light came on. When she tried to move and felt pressure on her arm, she noticed the woman sitting next to her. Her arm was held in a tight grip, and the woman's long fingernails were piercing her skin. She kept her eyes fixed on the woman's hand, the one wielding the syringe too close for comfort and ready to pierce at any given moment.

"Why, Chaney? What did Anabella ever do to you?"

Only then did Anabella look up, right into her father's lover's face.

"You!" Anabella cried out, recognizing the blond instantly.

Chaney grinned smugly as she pulled Anabella's arm. "Yes, me." The syringe ready to do her bidding.

"No, don't!" Aldrich called out, frustration apparent in his voice. "You don't want to do this, Chaney."

"Yes, I do, Aldrich. She's taking you away from me," she whined, glancing at Aldrich before returning her focus to Anabella's arm.

Anabella watched in horror. The woman's fanatic and concentrated stare on her arm gave her the shivers, and the tip of the needle was pressed against her arm. She feared her skin would be pierced at any moment with whatever contents the syringe held. She looked at Aldrich with pleading eyes but he shook his head and gave her a reassuring smile, and she relaxed somewhat.

*Aldrich is here. I'm not alone.* The thought flashed through her mind as she watched in fascinated horror while he spoke to the woman, who was still as determined as ever to get her way. This was the woman who had been so affectionate with her father on that fateful night. She was the one who had whispered those dreadful words in her ear.

Stunned and now wide awake, Anabella glanced between the mad woman and Aldrich. Painstakingly slow, he moved toward the bed, still speaking to her.

"I love her, Chaney," he said with conviction, "and I have asked her to be my wife."

"No, Aldrich, no!" she screamed. "How could you? She's taken you away from me, and you do this... how could you?" Desperation laced her voice, which rose feverously. Her fingers curled firmly around Anabella's wrist, making her wince in pain. She rearranged the syringe in her hand with one fluid movement, as if she was holding a knife, and went for Anabella's eyes. "You tramp!" she seethed as spittle ran from her mouth. "He is mine!" And she lunged forward just as Anabella knocked her wrist away.

Everything that followed from there onward happened quickly, because the moment she lunged for Anabella, Aldrich called out, appearing instantly next to the bed. He grabbed Chaney's wrist—which by now had swung back—inches from Anabella's eyes.

Anabella flinched, staring at the tip of the needle; a single drop released. Instinctively, she rolled her head to the side, and clenched her eyes shut.

With his strong hold tightly on her wrist, Chaney winced and let the syringe fall onto the bed's cover and rolled away from Anabella's body. Aldrich pressed his body against hers and held her in a tight grip as she struggled against him. In one swift move, he hauled the woman away from Anabella.

"Anabella, call Mr. Copeland, now. We need the police here," he spoke to her sharply.

She nodded and on shaky legs carefully moved away from the woman, keeping her focus on both Aldrich and Chaney while he held her unceremoniously against him. She couldn't believe this woman, her mind foggy with realization. Despair threatened to make her slump back into the protection of the bed. Instead, she pushed those thoughts aside and grabbed her cell phone from the side table and made the call, while Aldrich secured Chaney using a length of electric cord, tying her hands behind her back.

She kicked and screamed in rage, but Aldrich ignored her. That was followed by pleading, which had no affect on him, and soon it was followed by another row of fury; this he overlooked with insolence. When he was done, and satisfied that she couldn't get away, he walked to Anabella who was shaking from the fright of it all, and wrapped her in his arms, holding her until help arrived. He murmured soft words of comfort to Anabella who was nestled tightly into his warm body.

She eventually relaxed against him.

All the while, Chaney seethed and hissed, cried and called out to him, but he just walked out with Anabella at his side.

The police arrived an hour later and took their statements, photos of the crime scene, and hauled Chaney into custody. Subdued and with tears streaming down her cheeks, she got into the patrol van. They drove away when the sun began to show its face in the horizon, tinting the sky in hues of golden pinks; a promise of a beautiful day.

Anabella was sitting on a deck chair when Aldrich joined her, holding a warm cup of coffee in his hands.

"Here, sweetheart," he offered, noticing the color had returned to her cheeks.

The trembling had subsided, but still she looked tired, her eyes puffed with black shadows underneath. He placed a kiss on her cheek and she scooted over for him to sit next to her.

"I am so sorry about all of this…" he started as he brushed her arm reassuringly, sending shivers up her spine.

But she looked at him puzzled. "Why? This wasn't your fault, Aldi."

"If I hadn't dated her, none of this would have happened!"

"Aldi, you couldn't have known she'd act like this. But what has me stunned is that she wiggled her way into my house and slept with my father to get to me. Now *that* is sick." She scrunched her face in disgust and took a sip of her coffee, and then pulled another disgusted face.

He smiled, happy to see her back to her old self again. "Yes, it is, and now we know how she got into your house. But, Chaney? I never thought that she would go this far."

"She is obsessed with you, Aldi, and I can't blame her. I'm madly in love with you, myself." She placed a kiss on his stubbled cheek and couldn't help but inhale his scent.

He smiled at her endearing words, taking the cup from her. No amount of words could express how he felt for this young woman and actions were better than words, he'd always believed.

When she offered her lips for a kiss, he moved forward and obliged her with all the pent-up emotion he felt for her. He knew that he could've lost her if he hadn't turned back at that exact moment. And all because of a sick woman who didn't understand the word no.

"You're something else, Anabella Anthony," he finally said after a long silence, enjoying her as much as he could.

"Thank you, Aldi. You are pretty amazing yourself."

His laughter penetrated the morning air and he nuzzled her slender neck with his lips, stroking it slightly as he imparted more soft words of love to her.

A somber look covered her face once again as she said, "I never thought people like that really existed. The fact that she slept with my father doesn't come as a shock since I'm used to women draping themselves over him. But to get to me, surely there had to have been an easier way?"

"You get all sorts, sweetheart, I see them constantly. Yes, it's very mean to do what she did."

"Do they know what was in the syringe?"

"The sergeant said they'll send it to the lab and let us know," he replied. "She didn't want to reveal anything."

"I'm glad you came when you did," she whispered, wiping at wayward tear.

With a crease between his dark brows, he said solemnly, "It was the strangest thing, sweetheart. I woke with this urgency to check on you. When I first came into the room, all was quiet, but she had to have been there because the hair on the back of my neck rose; it felt like little fingers crawling over my scalp, and when I walked out, I couldn't shake the feeling. I walked to my room, but the feeling intensified. That's when I decided to return and found her on top of you. I thought my world was at an end when I saw the syringe in her hand." He shivered slightly, squeezing her tightly to him.

"I'm sorry," she replied, ruefully.

"For?" This time he looked puzzled.

"For scaring you like that."

"Sweetheart, don't you know what you mean to me?"

"You told her," she said softly. "You said you want to marry me."

"Yes, I do, if you'll have me. Today still."

She raised a brow. "Why the hurry?"

"Because, it's the only way I can protect you," he said with conviction.

She looked at him as the biggest and brightest of smiles spread across her face, but then grew silent for a moment. "Yes. I will marry you, Aldi."

"Really?"

"Oh, yes, really." She giggled at his sheepish grin. "You sound like Derek when he is baffled about something."

His grin grew, and she kissed him in an amazing toe-curling kiss; they became lost in their little world.

Mr. Copeland interrupted them by clearing his throat, all the while grinning. He had been quite amazing. Right after she had called him, he'd appeared at the door in a flash and was still there.

"Will you be swimming this morning, Anabella?"

"Yes sir, let me quickly go and change."

"Sure, honey."

With one swift move, she was gone.

"How is she holding up?"

"This shook her to the core, especially knowing her father was used to get to her."

"I don't mean to pry, but what did the girl do?"

"She slept with him," Aldrich said, nonchalantly.

Mr. Copeland gasped in shock and glanced at the door through which she'd disappeared and then looked back at Aldrich, confused but at the same time curious. "What did her mother say?"

"Her mother isn't bothered with it," he simply replied, and their eyes met.

"You mean…"

Aldrich nodded without any comment.

Mr. Copeland again glanced at the door, then back at him. "Now a lot of things make sense."

Aldrich remained silent, trusting Mr. Copeland to keep this tidbit of information to himself.

Mr. Copeland sighed as he shook his head in disbelief. He bid his farewell, then walked back in the direction of the resort. When he reached the pool, she was already hard at work, gliding through the water like a fish. He watched as the water separated before her hands when she propelled herself forward in smooth strokes—the pool a second home to her, the only place of comfort and support where she could be herself and forget about life. With strong, even strokes, she moved in the water, swimming, turning, kicking, and breathing with practiced ease. He was amazed at her slick movements, enjoying the constant pace she managed to keep up. She was relaxed and focused doing what came natural to her.

Mr. Copeland was still watching her when Aldrich joined him. Both men stood admiring her as she completed every lap comfortably; her kicks strong, her body in the correct posture, her breathing rhythmic with every stroke. Last night's ordeal hadn't stopped her from doing what she loved.

"She is looking strong."

"Yes, she is strong." Appreciation was noticeable in Aldrich's voice.

"You like her a great deal, Aldrich?" Mr. Copeland asked carefully, and received his answer by the look on the younger man's face.

"Yes, sir, I do."

"Have you known each other long?"

"We have, for two years now."

"And it's serious?"

"Yes, sir. She'll be the next Mrs. Hagin." Conviction marked his words, because in his mind it was a done deal.

"Then, I'm happy for you."

"Thanks, sir. It's been a long time since Pauline, three years to be exact."

"Is it that long already?"

Aldrich confirmed it with a simple nod of the head; fixated on the pool, not wanting to miss any movement. Mr. Copeland was still talking, but more to himself, for Aldrich didn't hear him so absorbed was he with Anabella. She had made him whole again. He felt alive and part of something bigger than himself. To think he'd almost lost her... the mere thought left him paralyzed for a few seconds, and he had to take a few deep breaths to calm his thoughts.

He still couldn't believe Chaney's delusional arrogance, and that she'd honestly thought he'd been interested in her. She had been willing to kill for him. He shook his head in disbelief. How could she have thought he'd returned her feelings, and that Anabella was simply an obstacle that had to be removed? He remembered her pleading with him, which turned into anger, when he hadn't collaborated her story with the police.

Protectively, he watched the young woman in the pool, hidden in the watery waves as she moved with ease, a woman who had became his life. Every fiber within him was ready to be available whenever she needed him. The past week had been difficult without her, so much so, he'd barely concentrated on work and had been reprimanded by the senior partner when he went to his office one night. His lack of focus had almost cost them a case. He had had no choice but to draw himself out of the slump he was in after that. The demanding case needed his undivided attention, and the client deserved a good defense.

When he'd called Anabella during the week, he heard her longing for him. He'd had to restrain himself from getting in his car and coming to join her, forcing himself to concentrate harder, finishing the court case quickly in order to be here. He was glad he'd come when he did, because if he hadn't, he'd surely have lost her. Aldrich wouldn't have been able to live with it, yet again. It's true what he'd told her; he wanted her close so that he could protect her from any evil, which all but seemed to follow her around these past few months.

"There's a dance tonight, will you be coming?" Mr. Copeland asked with interest, drawing his attention once again to the present. "While her friends were here, she didn't join the dance. I think she missed you too much, but maybe tonight you can bring her?"

"No, not tonight." And he winked conspiratorially to him.

With this, Anabella reached for the side of the pool and hung onto the edge, ending her practice for the day. She barely looked out of breath, her eyes sparkling with the adrenaline that coursed through her veins as she looked at him. She removed the goggles and then waved unabashedly at him. With one smooth motion, she was out of the pool. She sat on the edge and removed the cap from her hair, which tumbled down onto her shoulders.

Aldrich would never get tired of that dark avalanche cascading down her shoulders. He excused himself from his visitor and walked toward her, offering a hand, which she gladly accepted. He lifted her up and into him, laughing as he wrapped his arms around her, drenching himself in the process.

"Come here, gorgeous," he said proudly, "you are an excellent swimmer. Perfection in motion."

She grinned at him as she wrapped her arms around his neck, her smile mesmerizing him once again.

He'd never get tired of watching her smile. "How do you feel?"

"Excellent!" she beamed, not sounding tired at all. "But I am hungry." She laughed at his silly expression and gave him a hug.

He barely noticed the wetness, the heat of the day already warming them. The swim had done her a world of good, he observed, and last night's incident hadn't left its mark on her. She was one tough woman, one who'd had to endure a great deal the last few months, and he knew he'd have to keep a watchful eye on her. She was good at hiding her true feelings. "Then we need to fill your tummy up," he concluded, pulling her away from the pool toward the house.

"Bye, Mr. Copeland," they said in unison, walking away hand in hand.

Back at the house they baked eggs, grilled bacon, and made toast. Anabella was already on her third glass of orange juice, drenching the thirst that normally followed after practice. She'd changed from her swimming costume to a red bikini top and white shorts, leaving nothing to the imagination as she paraded in front of him on bare feet. Long legs graced the kitchen when she darted around, which made Aldrich struggle to keep his focus on what they were doing. Her enticing body distracted him and he smiled knowingly. She was a picture of youthfulness and health. Everything about her captivated him.

"Aldi… what about my parents?"

It took him a moment to understand the question she was asking before he replied with a raised brow. "What about them?" He looked up from the tomato he was about to cut into slices.

"I am under age. We will need their permission."

He tapped against his briefcase, still in the same chair he'd left it on yesterday and smiled arrogantly. "It's covered. I have the permission documents, already signed."

"Really?"

"Yes, really."

"You're perfect," she sighed as she gave him a warm kiss, making him chuckle when he continued with the tomato.

"But, how did you managed to get it?" Anabella wanted to know once they finished with breakfast.

He hesitated to tell her, the appalling event still fresh in his mind.

Thursday at 1pm, Aldrich stopped at the address he received from Roy. Luxurious cars were parked in front of the house. It was situated in an upper, middle-class neighborhood with a well-cared-for garden, the overall image speaking of money and class. Anabella never talked about her parents or their home life, and because she avoided the conversation he'd never asked.

The place looked impressive from the outside. It was large and stretched out over the huge grounds; painted in dark mocha colors with enormous vases in front. The fountain obscured the front door so that you couldn't see it at first. He walked up to massive, wooden doors that presented visitors with two bronze lion heads with rings sticking out of their mouths—which he presumed were the knockers—and taking one in his hand, knocked. A few minutes passed. In fact, Aldrich thought they hadn't heard him and was about to knock again when the door opened.

"Hello," he greeted the casually dressed man, "I'm here to speak to Jason Anthony."

"One moment please, sir," the man said gruffly. His disheveled hair and uneven button-up shirt told Aldrich he'd been disturbed. He disappeared around the corner but returned a few minutes later. Brusquely, he said, "Mr. Anthony will see you now. Follow me, please."

A large, tiled foyer greeted him, gleaming in the sun, and a big bronze chandelier hung from the roof, filling the space decoratively. Directly beneath it, a large, wooden round table sat proudly with a massive flower arrangement dead center. An impressive staircase wrapped in a thick, red carpet led the way upstairs.

From there, they entered the next room; voices filtered through. Aldrich took a few steps inside and stopped. Nothing could have prepared him for the sight before him. A semi-naked, elderly couple stood there, disheveled and unashamedly wrapped around naked bodies. The man, the one who had answered the door, spoke to them loud enough so that he'd be heard. More people were present in the room, but Aldrich chose not to focus on them.

"This is the gentleman who's asked to see you."

The couple dragged themselves from the arms holding held them and curiously looked toward him; both admiring his tall frame with interest, an interest that left him cold, especially evident in the older man's eyes. Aldrich shivered in disgust, averting his eyes to the woman.

Arrogantly, she walked to him, teasing him with a soft smile on her swollen lips, her hips swaying provocatively. He had no idea where to look because of her state of undress. Naked breasts that had clearly seen a knife peeked from the unbuttoned, lacey shirt, making him uncomfortable. Her annoyance was palpable when she didn't receive the attention she was used to. With every step she took, her mouth became a bitter sneer, and the eyes lifeless and unwavering as she stared at him. The closer she got, his surety grew that this had to be Anabella's mother. She was just an older version, arrogantly beautiful but with no traces of the innocence, or sweetness that was part of Anabella. The similarities were too much to be ignored, though, and having to see her in this state was inappropriate.

His future mother-in-law wasn't leaving him with a good impression, and he had to fight the urge to keep his emotions under control. He wanted to lean forward and button her up, but that would be wrong on so many levels. Especially with all eyes now riveted on him, he felt like a caged animal, ready to be devoured in lust.

When Anabella had told him what took place in her house, he couldn't imagine it, but here, right in front of him, eight people were in a sexual position stimulating each other. He had no idea where to look and kept his gaze trained on the woman's eyes now standing right in front of him.

"My name is Sandra. In connection with what are you here for?" Her irritation apparent as she talked in a hushed tone.

He quickly stated his business without offering his hand in a normal greeting. "Hello. My name is Aldrich Hagin, and I'm here to acquire your permission for Anabella's hand in marriage." Disgust dripped from every pore as he watched his sweetheart's mother, her face contorted in an ugly grin.

"Hmph, that high and mighty thing? She is so uptight she can give a man nothing. She is dull and unimaginative."

By this time, shock had replaced anger. Aldrich's blood was boiling. How dare she speak about his Bella in this manner? What kind of mother was she? He mentally reprimanded himself. He knew exactly what kind she was; he'd seen the evidence on Bella. His hand clenched.

His attention was then drawn to the elderly man when he said to the blond with very large breasts, "Wait, Candy, I will be right back." He patted her on the breast, and unashamed of his own nakedness came closer, his attention on Aldrich.

"So you want to get our permission to marry our daughter," he snickered, "that's a laugh."

"Yes, sir." Aldrich forced himself to only say those two words. He had to restrain himself in order to be civil to them. "I've brought the paperwork for you to sign."

"So… did you knock her up?"

"No, sir. I love Anabella."

"Well, well. You heard the wife—she's very uptight. Has never wanted to learn anything from us. How she'll perform in bed, I can only marvel at. The things we'd have taught her..." he trailed off, sighing heavily, as if he was ridding himself of a huge weight. "Only my money was good enough for her." He looked back toward the blond, lust written all over his features. Suddenly bored with the conversation, he finally said, "Oh, well. Where's the paperwork?"

The blond was calling him, curling a lock of blond hair around her finger as she provocatively swayed her body in his direction. "I am cold, lover!"

"I'll be right there, Candy. Gary, keep her busy!" he commanded playfully, and the man who'd opened the door moved forward and crushed his lips to hers, his hands caressing her more than ample breasts while she moaned and pulled at his buttons.

Aldrich swallowed hard, because the result was playing havoc with his own body. He was no saint, he knew that, and watching and hearing everything around him, while containing a stiff posture, was hard on him. Breathing alone was difficult; sexual scents hung heavy in the air. But, years of learning how to maintain control in court allowed him to hand over the paperwork with a steady hand.

"Here it is, sir." He knew he had to get out of there as soon as possible, so handed Mr. Anthony a pen to sign and forced his gaze on the papers, although his hands formed a barrier in front of his crotch due to the visual stimulation, which had caused his body to respond.

Mr. Anthony signed and turned around without a second glance in his direction. His total lack of concern as to the whereabouts of his only daughter troubled Aldrich greatly. She had now been gone from the house for a week, and he hadn't bothered to ask after her. He had shown absolutely no interest whatsoever.

The blond was obviously more appealing, Aldrich and the paperwork already forgotten. The couple's carelessness left him cold, but he could now understand Anabella's refusal to set foot in this place. He stuffed the papers into his jacket pocket, excused himself to the older woman who'd already moved on, and as quickly as his feet could carry him walked out of the house. He opened and closed the door behind him with a deliberate action, shutting out the things he'd seen.

For a while, he sat in the car to calm himself. This was the first time he understood the nightmares and images Anabella had to fight against, and compassion flooded his soul for her. Tears filled his eyes, leaving stains behind as they fell onto his chest. *My Bella, how is it possible that you stayed so pure in this house?* Just thinking about it and the emotions he'd experienced brought more tears, which he blinked away several times.

When he finally calmed down, he switched on the powerful machine and drove to his father's house. Once there, he recounted all he'd seen. The older man was speechless, but the conversation that ensued made him smile again.

"Dad, I want to marry her and take her away from all that. My sweet, innocent Bella can't go back there."

"You're that sure about Anabella?"

"Yes, Dad, I am. This was the final nail in the coffin."

"When do you plan on getting married?"

"Next week, at the beach house. Will you come?"

"I wouldn't miss it for the world!" He grinned.

"Thanks, Dad. I have to go, there are still a few things I need to plan and get in order."

Aldrich's next stop was the jewelry store. He'd seen an emerald ring there on a previous visit, which would be perfect for Bella. It was the same color as her eyes, laced with small diamantes that reminded him of her purity and innocence; the perfect adornment for the perfect woman. Certain that everything would be perfect, he went ahead with the plans for their wedding, keeping it a surprise for her.

She was none the wiser.

Monica had helped him with a few of the smaller details. He expected her to arrive soon since she would be helping the bride-to-be. He was glad that the young woman had played along with his plans, and that she'd managed to keep her mouth from blurting it at all while there for the weekend. He'd had his doubts, but studying Anabella, who was still clueless, he knew it was going to work out. He couldn't help but grin, pleased that the previous night's sordid experience hadn't left its mark. She looked energized and radiant, and he couldn't wait to make her his wife.

He smiled as he listened to her chatter with a friend on her cell phone, her hands all over the place as she described the house.

When their eyes met, she ended the call and walked into his waiting arms. He kissed her with a hunger that overflowed from his body. The constant demand and containment up until this point had allowed his desire to grow, and today all of that would be fulfilled.

Finally, after several seconds, he let her go and patted her on the bottom. "It is time for you to finish getting ready, sweetheart."

"Okay, love, see you later."

"Oh, yes, you most definitely will." He couldn't have been more pleased.

# Chapter Sixteen

When Anabella stepped out of the shower, eyes squeezed shut, she tried to grab the towel which she had left just outside the glass door, but when she couldn't find it she opened them and shrieked in sudden shock.

Monica stood there with a big grin on her face and the dry towel in her hands; a welcoming face after the night she had.

Heart pounding in her chest, she glared at her best friend. "You gave me such fright."

Before Monica could respond, Anabella was in her arms, crying. Her friend wrapped her securely in the towel and held her clumsily—the height difference making it awkward—but in spite of that, she found a way to hold on. Aldrich had phoned her at the guesthouse earlier that morning informing her of the incident. She was furious with the demented person who had tried to ruin her friend's holiday, so she'd rushed to the beach house and made it to the bathroom in record time; she knew Anabella wouldn't mind.

When she explained her reasons to Sam for having to leave so quickly, he just shook his head but offered to go with her. Monica thanked him, but told him it wasn't necessary and that he should just join her later. What was important was that she needed to be with Anabella, alone, especially today of all days.

The ordeal had left Anabella shaken. The mere thought that someone meant her harm, left her vulnerable and feeling small. It was easy to stay positive in front of Aldrich, but deep down she crumbled at the thought of the crazed woman who wanted to take her life; jealousy her motivation. In those splitting seconds, Anabella had really thought her life was over. It was still very fresh in her mind and she still shook. She tried to phone Mrs. Smit, too, but she was unavailable.

When Monica arrived, Aldrich filled her in and answered the questions that tumbled from her mouth in rapid succession. She was bowled over by what had taken place, but was thankful that Aldrich had been there to save her. To think that he had stopped and listened to the promptings of the Lord—if not; the situation could have had devastating results. Monica held on to Anabella and allowed her to cry on her shoulder for the longest time.

When she felt Bella's body start to relax, she relieved her from the deadly grip and urged softly, "Now my friend, we need to get you dressed."

Anabella nodded and lifted her head.

"Today's your wedding day," she continued with a bright smile. It took all of Monica's restraint to hold on to the smile, because her friend was looking forlorn and miserable. "Let's see what we can do to this red face, we need to turn you into a radiant bride." She smiled encouragingly. "This is, after all, a happy day."

Again, Anabella nodded and sniffed. She blew her nose, now calm enough for them to continue.

Monica, however, had to make sure her friend was on the up and up. "You do still want to get married, right?"

"Yes, Moni, with all my heart."

Searching her friend's face she saw Anabella's excitement lingering on the boundaries of her frail emotions. "Okay, then, if you're a hundred percent certain, we've a bride to dress." She winked at her, waiting for an answer.

"I'm certain, okay?" Anabella said, laughter spilling from her lips. "This is really happening, I'm going to be a bride!" Anabella screeched, and they danced around the bathroom.

Anabella's old self had returned with gusto, something Monica was grateful for. She understood Aldrich's reason for this quick wedding and supported his decision. When he'd phoned her on Thursday and asked for her help, she'd been over the moon with excitement. She couldn't have asked for a better man for her friend. He was a rock-solid pillar, supportive of her career, and took a firm stand where she was concerned.

With much banter between the two old friends, Anabella was dressed, her makeup applied expertly to Monica's great delight, but she felt a little melancholy. She couldn't help but wonder if she was worthy of this man after all she'd put him through. He deserved so much more than what she'd given him. Would she be enough for him in the end?

When Monica stepped away from her, she caught the vision reflecting back from the tall mirror. A beautiful young woman stood there, tall and proud, with her head held high, her eyes bright and filled with laughter. Attentively, she touched her face, then let her hands run down her length as she took in the white dress. She couldn't have chosen a dress so beautiful for herself. The delicate lace followed her slender contours, folding gently around her, wrapping her body in its softness; sleeveless, it showed off her long, gracious arms, and her strong shoulders, stopping just above her knees, which complemented her beautiful tanned legs. There were no shoes to be found and she chuckled with appreciation. He knew her very well because from the moment she'd arrived she never wore shoes again, preferring to be barefoot at all times.

Monica brushed her hair until it shone with golden tones that shimmered in the sunlight; it lay soft as silk on her shoulders, completing the breathtaking picture she made. On the dresser sat a multi-pearled bracelet that Monica fastened on to her left arm. Both girls couldn't help but admire the well-crafted piece of jewelry and wondered if it was an heirloom. Aldrich had given it to Monica after she arrived at the beach house with specific instructions to put it on Anabella. He'd looked prideful and sheepish at the same time.

Anabella couldn't have asked for a better wedding day. It was perfect. An already cloudless blue sky was canopying the already hot day, brightening the view with sharp colors of white and blue shimmering in the rays. It was announcing a new day and a new future, for her and the man she loved. As she twirled in the brightly lit room, she smiled as she thought of Aldrich. It seemed that he'd thought of every detail to make this an exceptional day. How could she not love him? This was the perfect place for her to become his wife, to stand with him as Mrs. Anabella Hagin; a place where his dreams were built in every log, every brick, and crafted with so much love. Dreams that were now her dreams, and she knew that Pauline would have approved of Aldrich moving on. Although she had never met Aldrich's former wife, she felt that the heaviness was lifted as a new awareness came to life in the air, filtering through everything. She really felt welcome and at home.

Anabella felt as if she could float with this fresh start in her life and, for the last time, checked herself in the mirror, the sun causing a halo right above her—as if it were blessing her on this day. She had no second thoughts about this marriage, or what it entailed for them; the impact would be positive in her life, and she knew she had the Lord's consent. It just felt right.

At exactly 1pm, Monica opened the bedroom door and waited for her friend to make her grand entrance.

Anabella made her way to the living room, hearing a small number of voices resonating from inside.

Monica had changed into a soft pink sundress, her blond complexion highlighted by the beautiful dress that showed off her petite frame exquisitely. When Sam saw her, he rushed to wrap her in his arms, kissing her soundly on the mouth to the great delight of the guests, which left her blushing as she stared lovingly up at him.

Anabella was met by Mr. and Mrs. Smit, Mr. and Mrs. Richter, Mr. Copeland, Mr. Hagin, two unknown couples, Roy, Derek, and then, of course, Aldrich. He looked beautiful in a tux, and just like her, he was barefoot, his big shoulders straight and broad under the black, cotton cloth, and his white shirt framed his neck allowing her a glimpse of his skin.

Standing to the side, he was talking to an older man she couldn't make out, but the moment he turned and saw her, he beamed with pride. Elated at his approval, she waved at him.

Every one greeted her, but Mr. Hagin took her hand in his and said, "My dear, how beautiful you look."

"Mr. Hagin, it's so good to see you."

"Who is Mr. Hagin?" he asked with a frown, but the glint in his eyes warmed her heart as he continued, "I will only accept, *Dad*, from now on."

"Sorry, sir… I mean, Dad," she corrected playfully, and kissed him on the cheek.

"Much better," he concurred on a wink, hugging her with a welcoming embrace. When he let go, he glimpsed down at her arm and swallowed the lump that had formed in his throat. "Do you know who that belonged to?" he queried, pointing to the bracelet.

"No, Dad, I don't," Anabella replied softly, the word slipping from her lips naturally. She felt at ease with Aldrich's father.

"It was Aldrich's mother's bracelet; she loved it so much that she wore it with everything, every day. I gave it to her when Aldrich was born."

She touched it softly in reverent adoration. It belonged to his mother. She swallowed at the sudden tears, because in that very moment it became priceless. "Thank you," she breathed out, and then kissed him again.

The two unknown couples stood closer, also admiring the bracelet, and her newfound dad introduced them to her.

"Anabella, these are Aldrich's sisters and their husbands; Teresa and Graham—his eldest sister, and Belinda and Johan."

"I'm the middle child," Belinda chimed in, giving her a crooked smile as everyone else in the small group chuckled. She looked just like Aldrich, but much more feminine, of course. Her dark curls were cut in a short bob that framed her face delicately. Heavy jewelry hung from her neck, ears and arms, and lightly tinkled as she moved graciously, her face expertly made up with the latest makeup. Teresa wore her light-brown hair longer with almost no makeup in sight. Both were shorter than she was.

"It's wonderful to meet you both. I've heard so much about you from Aldi."

She received a welcome hug and kiss from each. Belinda told Anabella how beautiful she looked, and what a marvel her brother had become since she had entered his life.

The men greeted her with a firm handshake and complemented her on her swimming achievements.

Happy to see her brothers, she went to greet them excitedly. "I am so glad you could come, I have missed you both so much! When we come here again, you must join us. You'll enjoy the stay here, I promise."

"Thanks, Bella, you look very pretty," they said in unison.

They seemed relaxed for the first time since she remembered, and she was delighted that they had found happiness. Wanda was draped over Roy's arm, looking charming in a light-blue sundress. She congratulated her on this day with a beaming smile of her own.

Derek introduced her to Frank who was about the same height as she was; stocky with dark-brown hair and a tanned skin, one diamond piercing glistened in the light as he greeted her. He had an open face with a wide grin that showed of perfect whites, and she could see why her brother had fallen for the guy. They talked a few more minutes before she joined Aldi, giving him a kiss.

"Did you do all this?" Her hands flailed around, taking in the whole room.

"Yes, I did," he exclaimed with a chuckle and a toothy grin.

She continued to glance over the whole living room, now decorated with white ribbons and flowers in glass vases. She couldn't believe that he had created all of this in such a short amount of time. "You're truly the love of my life. I couldn't have planned, or done it better myself." She sighed blissfully. "I will make up for this for the rest of my life. Thanks for the bracelet, Aldi, it's very precious and I'll treat it in the same manner your mother did."

"Bella, my love," he choked out, hugging her very close to him and placing a chaste kiss on her forehead, his emotions close to spilling over. "Come, let me introduce you to the justice of the peace, Mr. Penning."

The older man stepped closer, extending his hand.

"Please to meet you, sir."

"Can we begin?" Mr. Penning asked after he greeted her.

"Yes, sir, please continue," Aldrich said solemnly.

A sudden hush fell over the small gathering as Mr. Penning took to the center of the room. They stood before him, hands clasped together, a soft smile playing on their lips as they listened with intent.

"Dearly beloved, we're gathered here today to witness these two lovely people becoming one in marriage. Not to be separated, but to complete each other as man and wife, in good times and in bad times. To accept each other's weaknesses and build on their strengths." He then peered at the guests and continued, "They have agreed to walk the road together, and today we are witnesses to their agreement. Their love will always be the bond that will keep them together, no matter what may lay ahead. You, as their family and friends, will remind them of this day, lifting them up so that they shall stay firm in their decision."

"Anabella Francis Anthony, will you take this man to be your husband?"

"Yes, I will," she replied in earnest, admiring her soon to be husband with adoration.

He beamed down at her as Mr. Penning paused, anticipation written over her face.

"Aldrich Thomas Hagin, will you take this woman to be your wife?"

"Yes, I will."

"By the power invested in me by the high court, I now pronounce you husband and wife." He stepped between them, took hold of their hands, turned them to face the guests and declared, "I give you Mr. and Mrs. Aldrich and Anabella Hagin." Smiling at Aldrich, he then announced, "You may kiss your bride."

Anabella was in his arms before the word 'kiss' was out of his mouth. She kissed Aldrich with much affection as tears of joy ran down her cheeks, affirmation sealed as hearts beat as one.

He looked at her proudly, never leaving her side as their family and friends waited for an opportunity to talk to them. It took a while to simmer the small crowd down enough to sign the paperwork, making it all legal. Almost every person had a camera in hand, snapping at the happy occasion from all angles for future reference.

Thereafter, Mr. Copeland invited everyone for cake at his resort.

Mr. and Mrs. Smit took them aside and gave them a wedding gift wrapped in white paper and a golden bow, and shared a few words of wisdom. "You both had victory over traumatic events in your lives. Yet you have chosen to walk this road together, and we see how you compliment each other as a couple. Your lives weren't built on ashes, so from now on look at it as stepping stones to move forward to higher planes. You complete each other, which is sacred to you both; you stand by the other and already protect one another. Your satisfaction and desires will always include the other half. You have become one, thinking and moving as one. No one can come between what you have, unless you allow it. From this day forward, there is no *I* in your sentence, but rather *we* or *us*. You create this marriage from day one, as well as its outcome. You're the sole writers of your lives, make every decision count. But most of all, we will always be with you, standing in the background, and sharing your life. We're proud of both of you, and wish you a wonderful life."

Anabella hugged and kissed them reverently and then turned to Aldrich, holding him close. Words couldn't describe how she felt at that moment, but her cup surely did run over.

More people were present in the hall next to the pool where long tables filled with the most delicate confections Anabella had ever seen were spread out. Even the pool itself was decorated; a red carpet ran all around the rim with floating bouquets of white water lilies on the bright, blue water. At each corner stood huge, iron candelabras with white candles decorated in golden fabrics to emphasize the decorations within the house. She thanked Mr. Copeland profusely but he laughed it off and said it was nothing, that he knew a few women in the region who were more than eager to help him out on such short notice.

More vases filled the hall, and tables and chairs were neatly placed and decorated in the white and gold theme where their guests could sit and enjoy the day with them. Champagne was poured and the celebrations were in full swing. Music filled the air around them and people gathered together, dancing, eating, drinking and chatting while Sam—the main photographer for the event—walked around clicking away on his very expensive camera.

The day was already bathed in dawn when she smelled the fires of a barbeque. Surprised, she queried it with Aldrich who just smiled and said she must enjoy every single second of it. The festivities went on well in to the night.

"Are you enjoying yourself?" Aldrich asked her when she stared dreamily at the ocean during a short break from the people who had been around her constantly.

"Oh, Aldi, this is the best day of my life. I couldn't have done a single thing better myself. Thank you. Thank you for everything."

When their lips met it felt like the world held its breath for them, anticipating the lovers' caresses. Silence fell as they enjoyed each other's company, until one of the children called him.

Reluctantly, he let her go and whispered, "I love you." Then was dragged away.

When Anabella made her way to the dance floor with yet another strange man, her eyes locked with Aldrich's. He called her over to him with a tilt of his head. Excusing herself, she left the man standing and rushed to her husband. After a brief kiss, they disappeared into the dark night, not willing to risk someone else stopping them.

During their walk along the dark path, they would stop and feast on each other's lips, drunk with ecstasy. This was what they had been looking forward to, what had seemed to be a lifetime of waiting.

Anabella dreamed about this day for the last couple of days now, hoping to be united with him at long last. She had never expected it would happen this quickly, always thinking it was still a long way off. If nothing else, Aldrich was very determined in not going any further with the passion they felt growing between them. She gladly followed his lead, knowing he was doing everything to protect her by showing her the correct way and not giving in to their more carnal needs.

When he'd gone over yesterday and proposed casually, she thought her heart would stop, not willing to believe that it could be true. When she saw her friend this morning, she broke down, allowing herself the luxury to crumble in her arms, but also to settle in her mind that this was her wedding day. That it was real and not in the distant future. Now she was Mrs. Aldrich Hagin, loved and accepted by him and his family. She was finally part of a normal family, something she had always wanted.

As she watched him throughout the evening interacting with his family, she couldn't help but feel elated that they were now together, that the things she had suffered were now something of the past. Her parents couldn't touch her now, couldn't force her to do their bidding. She had made a choice, and although it was at times difficult, the reward of that choice had brought her to this place.

Unashamedly, she could give herself to him without any remorse for her past. Her heart was racing with a quick staccato, her body pulsing in anticipation for the long and overdue lovemaking. It was a gentle but deliberate building, an expectation which would now fulfill the yearning born during the months of struggle with her inner demons. Now, finally laid to rest, she could give herself to the one man who had captured her heart.

Aldrich watched her throughout the day, his smile never wavering as he got drunk with the person who was now his wife. She floated through the small group with comfort and ease, a smile always persent on her beautiful face. Throughout the course of the evening, his eyes had lingered on her body, knowing that he would have her. No barriers stood between them. Now, he could take what she wanted to give without holding back. Tonight he would take them both to places where no one else could go with them, a place where he'd know her intimately. He would show her how much he loved her as he explored the wonder that was Anabella. He had been eager to leave the celebration, and when he finally got the opportunity he took it.

Back home, he picked her up in one fluid motion—even with her height she was still easy to carry. She chuckled as she wrapped her arms around his neck, then kissed him while still on the threshold, savoring the moment as they stepped into their house and straight to their bedroom. With the door closed behind them, it became very quiet in the rest of the house.

When their bodies came together as one, Aldrich reveled in the feel of her skin and her touch as she explored his body. He knew that this would be her first time and mindful of this fact, he was gentle and caring. Patiently, he waited for her to relax with him while he worshipped the body he had admired from afar. He acquainted himself with all that was Bella as only a man who loves a woman could. He took them to the highest of a lovers' peak, only to roll back and start anew, each time with more abandon and greater confidence, until she was ready to take him as he wanted. Only then did he give in to his own needs.

For Anabella, this was the fulfillment of all her dreams. The reason she had stayed pure whilst fighting to the bitter end. When she gave herself to him in passionate abandonment, she opened a whole new chapter in her life; one where only Aldrich was welcome as she enjoyed the sweet fruit when he buried himself within her each time. Exquisite torture became new words in her vocabulary as she discovered this man inch by inch, his passion and love washing over her in waves that refused to stop, taking her in with each wave to more exquisite heights, teaching her his likes. She couldn't get enough of him, loving him as much as he loved her. She whispered her everlasting love to him each time their bodies united.

Marvelous. Wondrous. All prevailing love.

The week following the honeymoon Anabella returned with him, having decided that as his wife he wouldn't be alone anymore. At first, Aldrich wanted to stop her, but she didn't want to hear anything about it.

"I'm your wife and there is no way I'll leave your side." Persistent and demanding, she took on her new role as his life partner, and he loved her even more.

"I want to care for you, love you. Besides, there's a pool close by where I can continue with my practices."

"Yes, Bella, my love," he said, not arguing as he wrapped her in his arms and kissed her soundly.

They had had a long talk the Sunday afternoon while still at the beach house, managing to get out of the room to eat the leftover food someone had left in the fridge. He'd laid down the rules in no uncertain terms, and she politely listened to his demands. He wanted her to finish varsity but that she wouldn't be staying at the dorm. On this, he was adamant.

She listened with a playful smile, only to agree to his points in the end; both more than willing to compromise in order to make it work.

"Yes, sir, love," she finally said with a twinkle in her eyes, wrapping herself around him.

"And then afterward, we can discuss children," he whispered softly, with all the hope of the world in his eyes.

"Yes, sir, love," she replied excitedly.

Although the subject had never been raised, she knew he wanted children. Being her senior by eleven years, his desire to have a family was foremost on his mind, and she would do anything to give that to him. Therefore, she could only agree with him.

"Don't 'yes, sir, love' me. This is serious, Bella. I won't hold you back, you have worked hard for it your whole life."

"Yes, sir, love," she repeated, unable to stop teasing him relentlessly with her lips where she could reach his skin. "We will do as you say, sir, love."

"Good," he smirked, his flesh dotted with goose bumps. "Come here, my sweet dessert."

Her giggles were abruptly stopped when he sealed her lips with his.

"Is there any cream?" he asked, coming up for breath.

She could only nod, allowing his lips to roam her body, caressing her with each kiss as he moved them to the kitchen, his hands trailing her skin to find the spots that made her melt in his arms.

The wonder of it all just didn't end.

With renewed vigor, she focused more on her practices and joined the team once again, using her maiden name so as not to draw any unwanted attention through the media.

At the beginning of February, a crowd gathered at the Midmar dam. Excitement filled the air as kids went wild and people walked casually around supporting the different booths with various items for sale. The smell of boerewors—a traditional South African sausage made from coarsely minced beef or lamb, or both, infused with spices—permeated the air as people gathered around the tables where hotdogs were served, seeking the nourishment food would bring them. Competitors stood in small circles warming up, getting ready for the race. Her team was also participating in this event, and every swimmer ended up doing well. They hadn't come for any winnings but more with the intent of training, which gave the spectators something to cheer about. Mr. Clark was very satisfied with their progress.

Classes resumed and they were back in a routine. Both were extremely busy but were adamant in finding time for one another; their honeymoon far from over.

Aldrich still tried to catch up on his work load when Thomas came to see him at his office the day after he resumed work. This was very odd, since Thomas never believed in bothering his children at their respective workplaces, but this was important and he couldn't put it off another day. His father had been very persuasive and insistent. This had made him nervous as he wasn't sure what to expect from him.

The whole thing with Chaney had already cost him time. The previous day his colleagues had confronted Aldrich about her. By now, they knew about her arrest, and that she had been evaluated by a psychologist who found she was unfit to stand trial. She was placed in a psychiatric ward at Groote Schuur Hospital for further observation.

Aldrich and Mr. Dorflinger had an extensive discussion about her, and they appointed a lawyer to her case, one from a well trusted firm in the city. It was imperative to keep this under wraps for as long as possible. The firm didn't want—or need—the unsavory publicity, but they also needed to protect

Anabella's reputation. Both were determined that this wouldn't affect her public profile.

When his father finally arrived at eleven for his appointment, they went to a nearby pub to talk. The wind had picked up considerably since Thomas' arrival, which made it difficult to walk as they clutched their jackets tightly to their bodies. The pub was quiet and they found a table in a private spot where they could talk unhindered.

As Aldrich was on a tight schedule, Thomas got right to the point once their drinks had been placed in front them. Although Thomas struggled with what he was about to share, he knew it was timely and very important, and couldn't delay it anymore than was needed. "Aldrich, I have to share something with you; news you won't like hearing but as Anabella's husband, you need to know."

With this, Aldrich's face cloaked over in a frown.

When Thomas saw the expression, he quickly explained. "I had a long talk with someone over a serious issue. Thereafter, I told him that I had no choice but to tell you and he agreed. I'm convinced that he's genuinely remorseful and wants to do the right thing. He would like to see Anabella as soon as she can fit it in, and the sooner the better," Thomas concluded, all the while watchful of his son's reaction.

"What is it, Dad? You have me worried."

"It is about the attack at her parents' house."

Aldrich shifted in his seat, leaned forward, and gave his father a sharp look. He still had nightmares about that ordeal; finding her in the state she'd been in as Mr. Richter held her in his arms. The words still replayed in his mind when Mr. Richter had stopped him, and when the doctor had wanted to examine her. The fear and the anger all played havoc with him; her broken image still burned into his mind. She hadn't wanted to press charges against the people who'd done that to her, and he had a hard time accepting that fact.

"What about it, Dad?" he asked in a low tone, his voice trembling. He wasn't sure he wanted to hear this and took slow, deep breaths in order to calm himself for what his father was about to say.

"I know this is difficult, Son, but you have to find it in your heart to forgive him."

"Forgive him, Dad? He violently attacked her to satisfy his own beastly lust. There is *no* forgiveness for that." He swallowed at the bile in his mouth. "Who is he?" he seethed.

"Aldrich, this isn't the way. If you don't calm down I'll not tell you. It's hard to face, I know, I had a hard time myself, but we need to get this behind us."

"Never, Dad. Who is he?" he demanded, rising from the chair swiftly as he clenched his hands into fists. The few customers that were inside the pub looked at him wearily, wondering if a bar fight was about to take place.

Thomas followed suit and reached for him as he softly said, "No, Son." He deadpanned him with one inert look. "There will be none of this. Come and sit down." He nodded in the direction of the manager to show him all was well, then silently prayed for patience, and for Aldrich's change of heart.

"Dad, you cannot expect me to forgive him. You were there. You saw the state she was in. They deliberately set her up to be raped, and you want me to forgive this, this..." His hands flailed in the air, and then he stopped. They trembled as he reached for his glass and with one swallow downed its brown, foaming contents.

Thomas looked at his son who was clearly struggling to get his emotions under control. He could see the raw display of pain and anger on his face. He, too, couldn't forget the look on his son's face that fateful night. It looked as if he'd lost something precious. The devastation moved through him and he shook. When he'd arrived, he had had to hold him for a while. Aldrich had suffered greatly when he lost his first wife.

"Dad…" He ran his fingers through his hair.

"Yes, Son, I know. It's difficult."

"Who is he?" This time his voice was strained, soft, and Thomas admired his son's courage.

"Relax, Son, we really need to talk. Can I order you something else?"

He shook his head and straightened himself once again. "Yes, Dad," he said and sat down, his fingers trembling as he laced them together.

"You remember the man we met at the restaurant just before the attack?"

"I do. André Herbst. He insisted on seeing you the following Monday." His eyes grew wide when he saw the expression on his father's face.

"Was it him?" he gasped in horror.

"Yes." He held on to his son's hand while he spoke.

Fire spat from him, but Thomas held him down with a light touch on the arm.

"That Monday, he came to me all right, but he was disorientated and didn't stay long. The next time I saw him, he told me his life story and what a foolish thing he had done to a young girl over the weekend. The way he described it, I knew it was Anabella. He said he was obsessed with her and that all he could think about was that he had to make her his own. He told me how he slept in her room while she was in the States. When I told him I knew the young woman and how she was connected to me, he was shocked, both at the revelation and because I didn't attack him. He loathed himself."

Aldrich grunted but remained quiet. His eyes were settled and unwavering on his father's as he listened carefully to every word uttered, trying to process them as well as he could, his thoughts in disarray. He wanted to shake his father in rebellious agony. He wanted to harm that man who had dared to touch his love. He simmered in anger at the audacity of the man. But instead, he listened, asking for peace and forgiveness within his own heart.

"André is repentant and wants to meet you both. He wants to apologize for his actions that night. He knows no words can ever be enough, but still he wants to see you." Thomas fell silent and watched his son. Again the pain and anger washed over him in succession. This was the most challenging time any child of God faced. Especially when this kind of pain was caused by someone close, but he had to trust that the living word within his son's heart would bear fruit, and that he would accept and grant forgiveness.

Aldrich stared out the window, deep in thought, the restless southern wind was blowing fiercely outside. People were hunched forward as they tried to walk briskly to their destination. One woman clutched a lamp pole with all her might as her sweater blew over her head. Papers were blown all over the street, leaving the place in a mess. *It is so ironic,* Thomas thought, *forgiveness is like this wind—strong, fierce, and at this moment, disastrous. Yet, when it stops and the aftermath is cleared, the promise of a new day will always be there, wrapped in peace.* He prayed for a heart of flesh, not stone, and that the winds of adversity wouldn't destroy what was started in faith. Thomas waited and took the last sip of his coffee. More people entered the establishment in a rush and sat noisily at open chairs, ordering their drinks with shouts above the wind from the bartender but yet, in their little corner, it remained quiet as if they knew that this was a pivotal moment in his son's life.

Aldrich's spine was tense and straight as he leaned against the backrest, the muscle in his jaw working overtime, his mind sifting through his emotions and heart for the peace he so desperately wanted. He understood that forgiveness was a pinnacle stone in his Christian faith. He tried to rationalize his own thoughts with what the scriptures said, but scripture upon scripture reminded him of the love of Christ and the message that went along with it. He tried to reason with God about this, but all that remained like a mantra was "My grace is sufficient for thee." He couldn't ignore the promptings knowing the healing that those words brought. He felt the icicles around his heart break as his faith overturned his emotions and he relaxed. He turned and gazed at his father with surrender. "I will speak to Bella and hear what she says."

"Fair enough, Son, but this has to be done soon for all parties to continue with their lives."

"Understood."

"I will wait for your call."

They decided it was time to leave since Aldrich had so much work to do. He hurriedly said goodbye to Thomas at his truck, which was parked directly in front of the offices.

For a long time, Aldrich stood at his office window and looked at the storm outside. He knew what had to be done, but Anabella would have a hard time with this; her faith was still new and fragile. The Word not matured enough for her to grasp the full meaning of forgiveness. What would she say?

She was still experiencing nightmares about that night, not as frequent as before, but it was still there. He knew how she felt about her parents and until now, hadn't spoken to either of them, nor about them. He never pushed her, but that didn't mean she didn't suffer or didn't remember. How could he blame her?

At the end of May she would leave for Germany, a whole month during which she'd participate in more competitions. However, she was focused and more determined on her sport and studies. To bring this under the spotlight could unnerve her and open the wounds she so desperately tried to forget. But he knew this was necessary.

"What did they say?" André asked exasperated. He wasn't a nervous person, had never had to wait on anyone, but these things had been making him jumpy for some time now, and he wanted it behind him—sooner rather than later.

"Aldrich will talk to her and let us know. This was not easy for him."

"Yes, yes. I understand," he reasoned, sighing into the phone. "You will let me know?"

"Yes, the moment they contact me, but be patient, André. This was not easy for both of them."

"Yes, of course. I just feel jumpy that's all." He sighed again and taking a deep breath, proceeded. "I really am sorry for all the hurt."

"I know, André, but you need to understand she is battling with this equally. What you all wanted to do to her, first with her parents' deceit, her father not protecting her, and then of course, you. She still battles with nightmares about that and the after-effects of the lifestyle she grew up in, so it's a lot of stuff to work through."

"Yes." He grew silent as flashbacks of that night tortured him once again. The things they'd done in that house, knowing that the children were there. He was part of all that and couldn't blame her. He'd dished out his fair share, both to her and her brothers. Now to play all innocent was too much to take in, even for him. "Okay, please let me know," he agreed, running his hand through his hair.

"Of course, André. Have a good evening."

He grinned. "I will be seeing Annie again." This woman had become like a light in his dark world. He had told Thomas about her.

"The pretty blond?"

"Yes, she is pretty. She is nothing like all the others I've had. And I've had plenty."

"Please, don't remind me. Enjoy your evening."

"I will, thank you."

The two men had formed a friendship over the last few weeks and André was content with this. He found the man's friendship remarkable. They shared many interests in the business field and socially, and loved to talk about the old times. As he'd had no children he was often lonely and loved to tell stories about his life and experiences, appreciating the fact that Thomas listened.

He told him about his dreams for the future, as well as his plans regarding his business. In this short time, he bared more to him than he had to any other person before. He became more content, more relaxed about his life. There was no need to prove himself to Thomas because he had his own successes and never felt like he was being judged when he revealed something of his past.

When Thomas told him about the marriage between his son and Anabella, he was stunned at first and had a difficult time dealing with what he'd done to her. He shuddered at the mere thought. Thomas had also suggested that he correct this wrong and resolve it with them. It was difficult to swallow at first, this forgiveness thing. He'd never had to worry about other people's feelings before, but since he had met Christ, going to church and reading the Bible it was important to do. Especially if he was to continue seeing Annie.

He smiled. Now this was a woman he'd love to get to know better. She reminded him of his grandmother; a strong independent woman who started with a business when his grandfather passed away and was left with four small children. She never married again, her love for him continuing until her own death only a few years ago. But she'd built a business along with various other smaller businesses, which turned into a big name—something he was proud of. The business André inherited. He didn't want it to die down with him, because he owed it to her memory to continue what she started.

She had done such an amazing job that when he took over the reigns there was not much for him to do as everything ran smoothly, and he'd had a lot of time on his hands. It led him into indulging in a lifestyle which had at first seduced him, like a drug, until the night reality sank in.

Annie was like that and even though he'd only had one date with her, he knew he wanted to continue with their 'friendship'. He determined she was of the same stock; very witty and as capable as his grams, yet quite adamant in wanting to keep him away. He smiled. She was keeping him at arm's length, but he wanted to narrow that space. Whatever this was, he wanted to explore it completely.

He had already implemented big changes in his life, to be the man a woman would consider as a partner, or husband. Only months ago, these weren't the thoughts he would have contemplated. His friends called him often, including Sandra and Jason, but he wanted nothing to do with them. They'd both left a bitter pill in his mouth. He couldn't understand what he'd seen in them in the first place. In many ways, that fateful night did do some good in that it brought him back from an insane spiral in which he played with people's lives, including his own. But no more.

At 8pm, he stopped at Annie's town house and knocked on her door. Seconds later the door opened and he gasped, allowing a grin to spread over his face. She took his breath away in the simple white sundress she wore. Her smoky eyes were inviting, at the same time hiding something beautiful inside. He wanted to know what that something was. He voiced his thought, and she blushed while granting him entrance into her house. It had been a week since he'd last seen her, and he could swear she was more beautiful than before. He planned to take her out for a light meal and a stroll on the beach, but with the wind still howling he knew it would be unpleasant. He decided to enjoy her company, having her all to himself for the evening.

He did everything he could to keep her smiling, to see the dimples playing over her face, to listen to her soft laugh; it filled the air with electricity. He couldn't help but wonder on more than one occasion how she would feel in his arms. She was vibrant and passionate about her life, and he took notice of every small detail about her. But mostly, his body was confused. With any other woman, he would have had them in bed by now and more than likely forgotten about them the moment he stepped out the door. With Annie, however, it was a different matter.

He actually wanted more than just her body. The thing was that to date a woman like Annie was a new experience—one he actually cherished. He couldn't believe what he'd missed all these years, and he had to admit he was wading in unknown territory. His hands were sweaty and his heart pounded, but yet his whole body shook with excitement.

At the restaurant he led her on to the dance floor, just to enjoy the feel of her in his arms. He'd deliberately chosen this place hoping that she'd love it as well. She was a great dancer as they glided over the floor, swaying to the soft romantic music playing. What played, though, he had no idea. He didn't want this night to end. At one point she stumbled, but that only gave him an excuse to intensify his hold on her.

Feeling the life pulsing through him, she looked up and smiled, the dimple enticing. He lowered his head and kissed her softly. At first he felt her tense, but when he moved his lips to capture hers, she relaxed into him. He sighed in relief, practically standing still in the middle of the dancing couples.

"I really like you, Annie Blignaut," he mused a while later.

She looked up at him puzzled, before she pushed him away and left his arms without a word.

He saw her emotions change from contentment to bewilderment, and he knew it was foolish, but that one kiss convinced him he'd do anything to have her. Later, when he dropped her off at home, she invited him in for coffee. They sat and drank in silence, listening to a DVD of Dana Winner. When he put his empty cup down, ready to leave, she stopped him and said softly, "I had a great night tonight."

He smiled, appreciating the fact, but he felt uneasy since she looked away, avoiding his eyes.

"But this can't work, André. I'm on the rebound after a bad and painful divorce. I'm not looking for and don't want a relationship at this moment."

Dread filled him, but he sat quietly and listened to her, watched as painful emotions washed over her beautiful face. This was the first time she'd spoken about herself. He really didn't want to lose her friendship.

"My marriage fell apart after I found my husband in the arms of a co-worker and friend. That led to more discoveries of his unfaithfulness and betrayal." She became quiet, almost distant, but continued obviously shaken. "You see, he infected me with a sexual disease and I'm still under observation, my medical bills are extremely high, and I don't want to saddle any man with my problems."

André gasped softly as he looked at her, a band of protectiveness clutching at his heart. He wanted to be with her, he wanted to remove all obstacles from her. He hated this man.

"Right now, I don't trust any man with my heart. It's just too painful," she continued softly as a tear ran down her face.

He knelt before her and took her cold hands in his in comfort. "Don't push me away, please. I want to be your friend. I want to be here for you."

She placed her head on his shoulder and sighed heavily.

André rubbed her back softly, allowing this moment to bring them closer, feeling her sobs.

"I don't want to burden you, André, you deserve better than me."

"No, never," he protested, "it's actually the reverse. I need you more than you will ever know. I need your strength and faith to continue on the path I have begun." He sat back on his haunches and lifted her face to look at her directly. "You see, Annie, I was like your husband," he admitted. He didn't think tonight would be the appropriate time for a heart to heart, but he knew he couldn't lose her. Not when he'd just found her. He felt her cringe in pain, but he gripped her hands when she wanted to pull away. "Please, let me explain before you judge me." Silently he waited for her permission and when she agreed, he told her a little about his life, including what led to his change. He could feel her body react in shock and she became anxious, pulling her hands out of his, but he sat in front of her, willing her to understand—to give him a chance.

"I can't do this, André, not again."

"I would never expect that from you. All I ask is to be given a chance to show you how much I've changed. I have asked to speak to the young lady in question, as well as her husband, and when they agree to see me, I want you to come with me. Please, Annie."

For a long time she watched him, then averted her eyes momentarily to look at her hands before meeting them head on again.

"Okay, André, but as friends, nothing else."

"Thank you. You don't know how much that means to me. Just don't leave me, please." Funny how it seemed he was begging, he detested people who pleaded for something; had always thought it a sign of weakness. But now that he found himself on the opposite side, he was the one pleading because he needed this. He needed her and if she was willing to give him friendship, he would take it any way he could to prove to her that he had indeed changed. He smiled and whispered, "Thank you, Annie." He wanted to kiss her, but she placed her hand on his chest and pushed him away. Reluctantly, he let go and got to his feet, knowing it was time to leave.

"Good night, Annie," he bid, and left.

# Chapter Seventeen

A week passed from the time his father had talked to him as Aldrich watched his wife hunched over an assignment, which was due the next day. The right words continued to escape him every time he wanted to talk to her about forgiveness. Whenever the subject was mentioned, she would become silent. It bothered him that she couldn't grasp the necessity of it.

Mrs. Smit advised him that it would be best to get this over with quickly, as it would help Anabella put it behind her. She struggled with her parents' betrayal and the perpetrator's actions, but in order to get the closure she craved, she had to forgive. He knew this from bitter experience. He hated the man who'd killed his wife, ranted about it for a very long time until he found the closure he needed. Unforgiveness was like a parasite that would grow and squeeze the life out of you, until there was nothing left. Now, to expect her to meet the man who was part of the problem was difficult to do, especially as he knew how she felt about the situation.

Anabella concentrated profoundly on the laptop, her fingers rattling non-stop over the keyboard. Open books were strewn over the desk; all about sport injuries and the impact it has on an athlete's body. Although in the best physical form, she was tired, weariness lined her mouth and eyes, though she wouldn't admit she was dead on her feet.

Again, he thought it best to take her to the beach house for the weekend, just to have a break from her hectic schedule. From the time they married, not a day went by that she wasn't busy, scurrying around to keep up with the hectic pace. He had no doubts about her love for him as she reminded him often about that very fact, but at night when he wanted to cuddle she would already be fast asleep. He sighed. He couldn't blame her, her schedule left her with no downtime, and her strong will and determination in giving everything to both was commendable, but he felt left out.

"How about we go to the beach house this weekend, sweetheart?"

She looked up, beaming him a smile. "That sounds wonderful but I can't. I have that function to attend. Maybe next time?" she replied, once again concentrating on her laptop.

"It's only Saturday morning, we can leave right after that," he insisted and walked over to her, stopping her hands by holding them together.

This time she glanced up, frowned momentarily, and then he was blessed with another smile. "That sounds wonderful." She sat back and sighed, her shoulders slumping as she relaxed for a few seconds.

"It does. You leave all your books at home and spend some time with your husband, how does *that* sound?"

Wrinkling her forehead and pouting her mouth, she giggled. "Is my husband lonely?"

Aldrich grinned sheepishly. "Yes, I am. I feel left out," he complained, crouching before her so that they were at eye level.

She leaned in to kiss him and said, "That really would be wonderful, because I miss my husband, too."

When their lips touched, he groaned appreciatively and asked, "How long before you're done?"

"Give me an hour tops, and you will have my undivided attention."

"Promise?"

"Promise." She leaned forward and kissed him—a kiss filled with sweet promise—and when she let go, he whimpered but said nothing more. Instead he rose and walked to his desk to continue with the case he was working on.

"You want me to meet with the man who attacked me?" she seethed. Stunned shock was evident on her face as she rose from the chair where they were sitting on the patio and walked around in agitation. The breathtaking view now forgotten as he finally steered the conversation toward his father's request.

They arrived just after one at the beach house, and enjoyed the afternoon playing on the beach and making love. By then, they were both relaxed so he shuffled her outside—with much protestation—and made them a late supper, which they ate in contented silence.

On their way to the beach house, she'd talked about forgiveness and what Mrs. Smit told her about it; how it would influence your life if you didn't find closure and that in principle she agreed with the concept. Until now, that was. Trembling with rage, she continued to pace.

Aldrich watched, his own hands clenched tightly, holding his breath in anticipation. Her face was flushed, her eyes cold. He had never seen her like this before. He had prayed about this for the last few days, knowing that this was important to her. And if he was honest, he knew she'd be angry, but this rage was so uncommon for her he could only watch and wait, giving her the time she needed to work this out on her own terms.

However, he had something to add. "Dad said he wanted to speak to us both, Bella, that he has apparently changed." He gulped, not sure he believed it himself. "He wants to set things right."

"Never, you hear me!" she shouted and ran into the house.

Moments later, he heard the bedroom door shut with a loud bang and sighed. He knew this would happen. There was no way that she would get past this without any help. She had accepted God's forgiveness for her own life and was growing strong in her faith but yet, at this juncture, she couldn't forgive. The damage that these people had done to her was catastrophic and she still refused to talk to her parents.

He walked to their bedroom and opened the door. She was sitting on the bed, her hands covering her eyes as she rocked back and forth. He could hear the pain in each sob and his heart ached for his beloved. When he took her in his arms she leaned into him, her body shaking. "I am sorry, Bella. I am so sorry for what they did to you but, sweetheart, as long as you hold on to the anger and bitterness, the longer and stronger the chain that keeps you bound will be. You want to get rid of that, don't you?" He waited awhile for her reaction, rubbing her back in slow rhythmic strokes. When she lifted her tear stained eyes he swallowed.

"Yes," she replied quietly, "with all my heart I want to be rid of this but, Aldi, it hurts."

"I know, sweetheart, I know. That day is imprinted in my mind. I wanted to kill that man and your parents for what they did to you." He brushed her hair from her face, cupped it and looked at her with all the love he possessed.

"But I had to let go of that hatred and it wasn't easy, I'll admit, but just as we have received the redemption power of the Cross, he received it as well. God applies the same rule to everyone, and he expects the same from us. We can't confess we love Him if we cannot forgive a brother in Christ."

She cried once again, and in a hushed voice he whispered endearing words to her, kissing her while his hands brushed against her to keep her relaxed.

When she lifted her face again she was more at peace and she nodded in agreement. "Okay, I will meet him."

"Thank you, sweetheart. I will call Dad tomorrow and he will set it up, okay?"

"Okay." She brushed a wayward tear away. "I love you, Aldi. I cannot do this without you."

"I will be there, me and paps."

"Thank you." She leaned in and lifted her lips. He accepted them with all the devotion he felt for her.

"You know what I'm in the mood for?" he finally said.

"No, but I can take an educated guess." She chuckled.

He laughed softly, asking, "Am I that predictable?"

"Yes, you are, Aldi. Come, let me satisfy that sweet tooth."

"Followed by more dessert?" he concluded, wiggling his eyebrows.

She laughed. "Always, Aldi." Her face was bathed in a soft shade of pink, and he chuckled.

She was still beautiful to watch and now that he had her body as well, it was just that much more wonderful. She was everything he had ever wanted in a woman. Passionate, sweet, headstrong, never a quitter and sexy —which still reminded him of his favorite dessert. And he could never get enough of that.

Anabella had been quiet ever since they'd arrived at Thomas Hagin's house a week after they got back. Thomas was relieved when Aldrich phoned and informed him to go ahead with the meeting. He knew his daughter-in-law was struggling tremendously with this and for her to agree to it meant it had taken a lot of courage, which he admired greatly.

Silently, she sat in the chair, her hands clutched together, her face pale and her emerald eyes wide. Both men watched and admired her bravery at the same time. Aldrich could see her mind was racing. She'd been reluctant to go that morning, making excuses, but in the end she'd gone. From the time they had returned, she had peppered him with questions—sometimes difficult questions—but the Lord always came through with an answer.

Anabella couldn't believe what she was about to do; face the man who had wanted to buy her and rape her, all to get his own way. A man she couldn't stand from the moment she'd seen him. Memories rushed back of the time she met him, chastising herself for being so dimwitted that she hadn't recognized him on that fateful night. That she had walked into that trap and barely escaped was part of her reluctance to forgive. Ever since Aldrich had spoken to her, she'd spent time with the Bible trying to find reasons not to go through with this insane thing. She argued her best case before the Father, but He kept on reminding her that it was His grace that would lift her up, that He would never leave her or forsake her.

Then this morning, she read again: "I know the plans I have for you," declared the Lord, "plans to prosper you and bring you no harm, plans to give you hope and a future." She knew by now that her future was laid out perfectly before her, and that this hurdle had to be passed over so that she'd continue with her life. For the last time, she cried about this, feeling cleansed when she uttered the words of forgiveness in the silence of the study. The weight that rolled away from her was visible on her posture. Her heart felt lighter, unhindered by any restraints; it had simply vanished.

She steeled herself the moment the doorbell announced his arrival. To face this man was one of the hardest things she had had to do, although she still wanted to run and hide. She had faced many things in her young life, but this was by far the toughest. Yet, she felt a peace settle within her that she couldn't describe, a peace that enveloped her with grace and she could feel herself relax into the comfortable chair.

She watched as the man in question walked into the living area, a blond close at his heel, and she wanted to huff in disgust but remembered her manners. *This isn't about him, but me,* she thought. *I need to do this for myself.* She watched the older man greet Aldrich, then introduce his friend as Annie Blignaut.

Thomas greeted them with a warm smile and asked them all to have a seat. Just then their eyes met and she swallowed.

The man definitely had changed, there was something different about him, and the blond wasn't clinging to him. She merely walked over to Anabella and shook her hand, then sat down in the chair next to her with a gracious smile, whereafter she turned her attention back to the man.

He was still standing there, looking uneasy. He'd lost weight Anabella noticed, the neat, short trimmed style showing even more gray. His eyes were filled with remorse and guilt as he walked in her direction, and then knelt before her.

Anabella wanted to run at his proximity, but a firm hand on her shoulder helped her to stay put and when she looked up, Aldrich was next to her with a reassuring smile on his face. She smiled in return, but couldn't keep the tremble from her lips. The corner of her mouth twitched nervously.

André held out his hands and waited for her to place hers within them, and out of the corner of her eyes she saw Thomas moving closer. Aldrich's hand was still on her shoulder, which gave her the strength to proceed and finally she met his steel-gray eyes. Now they were softer, pretty even, like a clear alabaster radiating trust and care.

She placed her hands in his.

"Anabella," he started, his voice so low and soft she had to strain to hear. "I'm so pleased that you were willing to meet me under such circumstances."

They both swallowed in remembrance. "I wish I could turn back the clock and remove the memory completely from your mind, but it would be impossible. Sorry will never cover, or excuse, what I wanted to do to you." He swallowed, his Adam's apple bobbing.

Anabella blinked a tear away.

"What I did to you," he corrected. "I was obsessed with you and wanted you all for myself. I was blind to anything else. I had no consideration for you as a woman, or person. I wanted you and it didn't matter how. But after that night, I have done much introspection. I met Thomas and Annie who helped me to see the error of my ways and I wanted to rectify it as best I can."

He looked at Aldrich and then at Anabella. "I implore of you both. Please forgive me for my part in the attack. For thinking less of you and mistreating you the way I did. There's no excuse for that, but nevertheless I need your forgiveness as mush as Aldrich's. I want to start over, if you will let me, Anabella. You are a lovely young woman I almost destroyed with my selfishness. Please, if it is in your heart, could you find a way to forgive me?" He grew silent, the pressure his hands caused her during his confession was painful.

She made to move her hands, and immediately he let go, blushing. Anabella watched the man, looking past all the gray to see the kindness in the eyes and the person buried inside, and all she could see was genuine remorse. She could see the lines of age etched on his face. They looked tired and sad, as if he'd struggled with something for a very long time.

"I have lost all contact with my former life. I have turned my back on that lifestyle and in the process met true friends." He looked at Annie and Thomas and smiled sheepishly. "I hope that I can count you as one, Anabella. I want to be a part of your life as a friend. I still admire you greatly, you and Aldrich." He looked up at Aldrich before he met her eyes again.

Anabella remembered the night as if it had happened yesterday, the night that had changed her in so many ways. She looked at the people gathered around her—all expectant—especially André, whose eyes were watery; pleading with her to forgive him. Her animosity toward him dwindled before her. As she studied him closely, she sensed the genuine feelings of remorse radiating from him. What touched her more was the fact that he had now turned his back on that life and walked away. That had to have been very difficult. It had consumed him, and she would know, she had been there. But what she saw here, now, was a different man from the man she met that first time at the stairs, the one groping at her. They had both come a long way since then.

"Please, Anabella, say something," he finally pleaded, after minutes had passed.

"You don't see my parents anymore?" she finally queried, clearing her throat.

"No, Anabella, I don't. I have changed my ways and am turning over a new leaf. Please, Anabella, I implore you." He squeezed her hands, and she could feel Aldrich's hand pressing down at the same time.

He gently whispered, "Let go of the chain, Bella."

She met his eyes and gave him a lopsided grin, before meeting Andre's again. "I forgive you, André," she said softly, squeezing his hands.

"Oh, honey, those are the most beautiful words I have ever heard." Tears ran down his face and his shoulders shook with pent-up emotion. "Do you mean that?"

"Yes, I do." He hugged her with the greatest affection. "You have made me the happiest man. I don't deserve this." He turned to everyone present. "None of this. And now I have a lot to make up for, but this gives me hope to continue."

"That is right, my friend," Thomas concurred, "you have come a long way."

"Yes, thanks to all of you." He sat back on his haunches for a few seconds just to allow the greatness of it all to sink in, then got up with a huge grin on his face.

"You did good, Bella. I'm so proud of you," Aldrich said softly. "How do you feel?"

She looked at him, and then smiled. "Wonderful, Aldi, as if a weight has fallen away."

"I am so happy for you, sweetheart."

# Epilogue

Eight years passed by very quickly.

Aldrich was sitting in the waiting room of the maternity ward, a proud but very tired smile on his lips. His father had left to check on the kids he adored, who were currently with Monica and Sam; they'd offered to babysit the bunch. Her friend's wedding had taken place three years ago, and Monica was now expecting their first child.

He rested his head against the wall, thinking about Anabella and how much they still loved one another after all these years. She had truly made him the happiest man. Their twin girls had just been born, making it a total of five kids. With a lopsided grin he thought how busy they had been over the last few years. His collogues ridiculed him for his efforts but he couldn't help himself, so he just shrugged them off and smiled.

They still had contact with André, given that he and his father were good friends. The man was now a dedicated husband.

After six months of marriage, they received word that Anabella's parents were involved in a horrific crash. A heavy vehicle had jacked-knifed, rolled into them, and burst into flames. There were no bodies to identify. When she received the news, she wiped away one tear, and that was the last time she ever showed any emotion where they were concerned.

Anabella and her brothers inherited quite a substantial amount of money, which was divided equally between them. The house was sold and when they wanted to give her her due portion, she refused to have any part of it.

Roy was madly in love with Wanda and finally asked the big question. They got married a week after the funeral. He had a brilliant mind and worked as a stockbroker; he was doing well as a businessman. He was also a wonderful husband and father, and their second child was expected within the next month.

Derek was not so lucky. He and Frank separated within a year, but then he met Tony—a software designer. Together they started a business creating websites, which he admitted Tony was brilliant at. Their relationship also died down, although the business continued. It led him to meet another businessman, Ralph Haden—an Englishman—who traveled between London and South Africa regularly. For now, it was going smoothly, but only time would tell if it would last. Although they had spoken to Derek a few times about the Word and what God had to say, he was convinced that this was the life he wanted to live. They showed him respect and love, accepting him for whom he was. Plus, the kids adored him.

With her part of the inheritance, Anabella bought them a beautiful house, two houses away from his dad's house, and renovated it to her liking. Anabella started the Sports Institute with the rest of her inheritance. Her coach, Mr. Clark, became a partner. The two of them were a good team, developing, managing and coaching talented newcomers to swimming.

They kept his apartment, or love nest as they called it; their place in which they could hide from their hectic life and where they spent time with each other, enjoying his favorite dessert often.

Anabella returned with four gold medals from the Olympics. It was a joyous occasion and was celebrated thoroughly. When her obligations toward her sport were completed, she retired.

At first, Aldrich wanted to stop her from doing this because she'd worked hard to accomplish her goals and to just walk away made him feel like she was cheating herself out of greater things. She could have continued for at least another ten years, but she had been adamant in her decision. Eleven months later, the twins, Thomas and Richard, were born; they were named after his father, and of course, Mr. Richter, whose name was Richard. Three years later, Sarah was born, named after his mother—a sweet gesture from his loving wife. Now the new born twins, Monica and Danielle, were named after her best friend and Mrs. Richter.

The kids kept them busy and at times he wondered where they would find the time for themselves, but they managed. They always did. He smiled crookedly. Anabella had become a first-rate mum, handling the bunch much like a team, showing them all the love she could muster. She still had a gorgeous shape, her body well taken care of and still as fit as always.

He became her partner shortly after the birth of the first twins, and for the last five years was practicing on his own, helping with contracts for the institute and taking on cases for the loyal clients who had chosen to stay with him when he'd left.

As often as they could, they would visit the beach house, commiserating with Mr. Copeland at the resort, now an honorary and loving uncle to their family.

Their kids loved the beach. Thomas was showing that he would follow in his mother's footsteps.

Richard had an inquisitive mind, with a righteous attitude, and showed a keen interest in his work. Sarah loved sports, all sports, but which one she would choose was still to be seen, after all, she was only four.

With the newest additions added to their life it had just become more exciting, but his Bella had also warned him that this would be the last pregnancy, which he was grateful for. Not that he would ever say anything to her about it. In the end, what she wanted to do with her life would always be her choice. Not his. He was just happy—and so very thankful—that she had tagged him along.

# AUTHOR'S HISTORY

Lynelle Clark is a native of South Africa.

Born again in 1992, she's had a love for the Word since then. "I have learned about God's faithfulness, and His love and provision through life's trials and tribulations."

In 2010, she started writing her first story.

# THANK YOU FOR READING MY BOOKS

Please take a few moments of your time to leave a review.

I would love to hear from you.

Email me on: lynelleclark@gmail.com

OR

Connect with me on Facebook:
http://www.facebook.com/profile.php?id=10000353 2834628

For further information, please visit my website and blog:
http://lynelleclarkaspiredwriter.blogspot.co m/